Praise for
Hot Time in the Old Town

"Going into that August, Roosevelt had angered most New Yorkers by ordering strict enforcement of the city's Sunday tavern-closing ordinance. But by month's end, Roosevelt ranked as a hero of sorts.... This slender volume makes for interesting reading—especially if you read it in the summer heat."   —*St. Louis Post-Dispatch*

"Edward Kohn's use of detail in telling this story will make you sweat and gasp for air. You will feel the desperation of the people of New York as the stale air and sweltering temperatures visit misery on America's largest city.... Kohn has merged good story-telling with American political history. *Hot Time in the Old Town* is an enlightening tale."   —*Roanoke Times*

"A book about an intense heat wave that gripped New York City in 1896, which [Kohn] says is one of the worst natural disasters in American history. It killed roughly 1,300 people, far more than the Great Chicago Fire of 1871. [Roosevelt is] an interesting figure.... He was born as a privileged New Yorker ... [but] had long been interested in the difficulties of urban life and efforts at reform."
              —"Fresh Air," NPR

"Long before Americans could retreat into air conditioning to escape the worst of the summer, a 10-day heat wave claimed the lives of about 1,300 New Yorkers.... The year was 1896, when poor laborers living in crowded tenements had few options for relief from the heat. In *Hot Time in the Old Town: The Great Heat Wave of 1896 and the Making of Theodore Roosevelt*, Kohn recounts how Roosevelt, then New York City police commissioner, came to the aid of the working masses."   —*US News and World Report* (online)

"It isn't easy to blow the dust off of more than a century of history and make it relevant but historian Edward P. Kohn has managed to do just that. . . . [He] recreates this event with such graphic detail the people and their story seem to literally leap from the printed page. . . . It is this humanization and Kohn's first rate research that give this highly readable book its literary legs." —*Florida Weekly*

"Kohn details how New Yorkers faced hellish conditions over 10 brutally hot days in early August. Over that time, 1,300 people died in Manhattan alone, making it the worst urban heat-related disaster in US history. . . . Only on the last day of the crisis did the city finally take action, directing the police to deliver free ice to those in need. The distribution was at the urging of police commissioner—and future president—Theodore Roosevelt." —*New York Post*

"Kohn raises two novel arguments: that the heat wave was responsible for destroying William Jennings Bryan's political career, and that it was responsible for bolstering that of Theodore Roosevelt's." —*Roll Call*

"The scorcher of 1896 had seemingly vanished into the mist of history until Edward Kohn, in his recently published *Hot Time in the Old Town*, rescues the events of those brutal mid-summer days from oblivion. . . . [A] well-told tale." —*Floral Park Dispatch*

"[Kohn] succeeds in bringing this little-known tragedy to light." —*Publishers Weekly*

"Although the 1896 heat wave remains a minor footnote in New York history, Kohn creates a solid narrative that makes for absorbing reading. He also points out that notwithstanding huge progress made to improve responses to heat crises, these occurrences continue to claim many lives to this day. Students of historical meteorology and shows like *When Weather Changed History* will enjoy this, as will anyone interested in off-beat American history." —*Library Journal*

"By capturing the intersection of a forgotten but devastating American catastrophe, the quick rise and sudden fall of one of America's most meteoric political figures, and a snapshot of the embryonic Rough Rider in action, Kohn presents a fascinating triptych of American history — and a timely rejoinder to New Yorkers who think they had it bad this past summer." — *City Journal*

"Reading about the heat-wave suffering is depressing, but such a disaster can hardly be ignored in any study of this country's history. The book's author is to be commended for so skillfully mixing tragedy and politics." — *The Oklahoman*

"[A] fascinating and well-researched tale about the impact of the needs of the local and disfranchised poor on national, even world, events. Kohn reminds historians that sometimes the best part of studying the past is listening for the narrative and resurrecting the stories of the obscure, the powerless, and the forgotten." — *Bilkent News* (Bilkent University, Ankara, Turkey)

"*Hot Time in the Old Town* is an enlightening account of the brutal 1896 scorcher that pushed the heat index in New York City above 120 for over a week, killing at least 1,300 people and driving countless others to bizarre acts of madness and despair. Along the way, Kohn makes a strong case that the most prominent casualty may well have been the presidential campaign of William Jennings Bryan, whose disastrous visit to the city during the height of the crisis helped win the White House for William McKinley. That same heat wave, Kohn reveals, also did wonders for the political career of the city's dynamic young police commissioner, Teddy Roosevelt. History at its best." — EDWIN G. BURROWS, co-author of the Pulitzer Prize-winning *Gotham: A History of New York City to 1898*

"Of the writing of books about Theodore Roosevelt there seems to be no end. But Edward P. Kohn's book is one that does not recycle old facts in new form. Here is a window on the world of Roosevelt that is entirely new. His activities during a fierce heat wave in New York City in 1896 that killed hundreds of people and horses are depicted in chilling episodes. City government was slow to act, but department heads like Roosevelt, who was police commissioner, took initiatives and showed the kind of leadership that led to future fame. With a wide lens Kohn scans this horrific happening during a critical campaign for president. His portraits of Roosevelt and his contemporaries are skillful and memorable."

—AIDA D. DONALD, author of *Lion in the White House: A Life of Theodore Roosevelt*

"Kohn's well-written and dramatic story of New York's 1896 killer heat wave exposes vast human suffering and city government's bumbling response, but it also gives us a fresh snapshot look at Police Commissioner Theodore Roosevelt and presidential candidate William Jennings Bryan responding to the moment of crisis during hot times. An entertaining slice of New York history!"

—KATHLEEN DALTON, author of *Theodore Roosevelt: A Strenuous Life*

HOT TIME
IN THE
OLD TOWN

The
GREAT HEAT WAVE *of*
1896 *and the* MAKING
of THEODORE ROOSEVELT

EDWARD P. KOHN

BASIC BOOKS
A Member of the Perseus Books Group
New York

For
my family

Copyright © 2010 by Edward P. Kohn

Hardcover first published in 2010 by Basic Books,
A Member of the Perseus Books Group
Paperback first published in 2011 by Basic Books

Books published by Basic Books are available at special discounts for bulk purchases in the United States by corporations, institutions, and other organizations. For more information, please contact the Special Markets Department at the Perseus Books Group, 2300 Chestnut Street, Suite 200, Philadelphia, PA 19103, or call (800) 810-4145, ext. 5000, or e-mail special.markets@perseusbooks.com.

Designed by Pauline Brown

The Library of Congress has catalogued the hardcover as follows:

Kohn, Edward P. (Edward Parliament), 1968–
    Hot time in the old town : the great heat wave of 1896 and the making of Theodore Roosevelt / Edward P. Kohn.
        p. cm.
    Includes bibliographical references and index.
    ISBN 978-0-465-01336-4 (alk. paper)
    1. New York (N.Y.)—History—1865–1898. 2. Heat waves (Meteorology)—New York (State)—New York—History—19th century. 3. Heat waves (Meteorology)—Social aspects—New York (State)—New York—History—19th century. 4. Mortality—New York (State)—New York—History—19th century. 5. New York (N.Y.)—Environmental conditions. 6. New York (N.Y.)—Social conditions—19th century. 7. Roosevelt, Theodore, 1858–1919. 8. Bryan, William Jennings, 1860–1925. 9. New York (N.Y.)—Biography. I. Title.
    F128.47.K76 2010
    974.7'104—dc22
                                                                        2010006274

Paperback: ISBN 978-0-465-02428-5
E-book: ISBN 978-0-465-02258-8

10 9 8 7 6 5 4 3 2 1

CONTENTS

PROLOGUE:
THE HEATED TERM

O N AUGUST 15, 1896, while preparing to depart for a three-week vacation out West, Theodore Roosevelt wrote to his sister Anna: "We've had two excitements in New York the past week; the heated term, and Bryan's big meeting. The heated term was the worst and most fatal we have ever known. The death-rate trebled until it approached the ratio of a cholera epidemic; the horses died by the hundreds, so that it was impossible to remove their carcasses, and they added a genuine flavor of pestilence, and we had to distribute hundred of tons of ice from the station-houses to the people of the poorer precincts." Roosevelt, then thirty-seven and president of New York's Board of Police Commissioners, was describing one of the most extraordinary weeks in the city's history.

The "heated term" was an unprecedented heat wave that hit New York over ten days in August 1896. Temperatures in the 90s were accompanied by high humidity. For the duration, thermometers never dropped below 70 degrees, even at night, and over the course of a week and a half the heat wave wore New Yorkers down. The eventual death toll numbered nearly 1,300.

Yet the 1896 New York heat wave remains one of the forgotten natural disasters in American history. It is in the nature of heat waves to kill slowly, with no physical manifestation, no property damage, and no single catastrophic event that marks them as a disaster. For that reason the heat wave is only infrequently remembered, even though it claimed more victims than the 1863 New York City draft riots or the 1871 Great Chicago Fire.

Our collective failure to remember this disaster may also have something to do with the identities of the victims. While the very young and very old were the most vulnerable, the heat wave took a terrible toll on the working poor, the death lists containing the names of hundreds of surprisingly young men who were literally worked to death.

The living conditions of New York's poor were dire. By August 1896 the entire country had been suffering through a severe economic depression for three years. Millions were out of work. New York, experiencing a wave of massive immigration, seemed particularly hard hit. The tenements of the Lower East Side teemed with recent arrivals who could scarcely afford food or medical care. The combination of poor living conditions, poor working conditions, poor diet, and poor medical care, with temperatures inside the brick tenements easily reaching 120 degrees, killed hundreds of New Yorkers.

Roosevelt compared the heat wave to a cholera epidemic for good reason. Although the heat wave was not an epidemic by any medical definition, the slow unfolding of the tragedy resembled the periodic outbreaks of cholera that had plagued New York throughout the century, more than it did such spectacular disasters as the

Great Fire of 1835 or the Blizzard of 1888. Like cholera, the heat in August 1896 struck quietly and undramatically.

New Yorkers remembered 1832's cholera epidemic as the worst they had ever experienced. That summer the disease had swept through the city. Those who had the means to leave town did so as quickly as possible, leaving New York almost half-empty. For the poor souls that remained—quite literally, the poorest of the inhabitants—some neighborhoods took on the cast of Bruegel's *Triumph of Death*. Pedestrians risked being trampled by the hearses that plied the streets day and night. The air was hazy from the burning of the sick's bedding and clothing. Dead bodies lay in the street untouched by the living, who were scared to approach them, while rats feasted on those buried in shallow graves. Turned away from private hospitals, over 2,000 sick New Yorkers swarmed into Bellevue. Attendants stacked bodies in the morgue, while patients lay dying in hallways. In the end over 3,500 died.

It would take concerted preparations to defeat cholera. Epidemics recurred in the 1840s, '50s, and '60s. Finally in 1892, with a new epidemic sweeping across Europe, New York officials prepared to combat the epidemic on the basis of the latest advances in microbiology. Indeed, the city prepared as if for war, readying a special corps of doctors, hospital ships in the rivers for quarantine patients, and an army of workers to scrub and disinfect 39,000 tenements.

In the end, New York won the war. Although the epidemic of 1892 killed 2,500 Russians each day, only 9 New Yorkers died, and the dread disease would never menace the city again. Defeating cholera illustrated what steps a determined nineteenth-century city must take to prevent a catastrophe from killing its citizenry. In 1896, however, New York City made no concerted effort to combat the heat wave as it had cholera only a few years before. The results were tragic.

Yet it is difficult to entirely blame government officials for failing to respond to the crisis. The especially insidious and subtle nature of heat waves made it difficult to combat them. Furthermore, decades before the New Deal or Great Society reforms, there was simply no social safety net for the poor. During the depression of the 1890s government officials had once again eschewed any responsibility for the poor, the hungry, or the unemployed. "It is not the province of the government to support the people," New York governor Roswell P. Flower sniffed. President Grover Cleveland proclaimed that "while the people should support their Government its functions do not include the support of the people." Clearly "the people" were on their own.

No surprise, then, that the mayor of New York did not even bother to call an emergency meeting of department heads until more than a week into the heat wave, when it was almost over. Only a handful of city officials addressed the crisis. The commissioner of Public Works changed his men's work hours to the coolest parts of the day and arranged for the streets to be hosed down—or "flushed"—to cool them off and wash away the filth and garbage. Theodore Roosevelt recommended that the city purchase and give away free ice to the city's poor. This simple and relatively cheap measure may have saved many lives, and it marked Roosevelt's continuing education as an urban reformer. Despite these small efforts, the heat wave illustrated the way New York failed to care for its neediest citizens during a great disaster.

THE SAME WEEK of the heat wave witnessed the start of the 1896 presidential campaign. While Republican nominee William McKinley stayed at home in Canton, Ohio, conducting his campaign from his front porch, his adviser Mark Hanna came to town to open the Republican National Headquarters. Hanna took time to consult with Republican Party leaders about campaign matters, including raising money and arranging campaign speakers. One Republican ready to take the stump for the party nominee was Theodore Roosevelt.

William McKinley was a former Ohio governor and congressman who had chaired the powerful House Ways and Means Committee. In 1890 he had made himself a household name after introducing a bill that raised tariffs to historically high levels. Both the McKinley Tariff and the bill's namesake remained the favorite of American business interests. This remained especially true after the Panic of 1893, an economic meltdown caused by overbuilding and a contraction of credit. In February of that year the Philadelphia and Reading Railroad had been the first major American business to fall, sending shockwaves throughout the economic system. Credit froze, and by year's end hundreds of banks and nearly 16,000 more businesses followed. With the current economic crisis occurring on the watch of Democratic president Grover Cleveland, men like John D. Rockefeller of Standard Oil, Andrew Carnegie of Carnegie Steel, and J. P. Morgan of the "House of Morgan" financial empire looked to the Republican candidate to maintain stability and foster steady growth. This became even more imperative as many Democrats called for the United States to leave the gold standard and back the American dollar with both gold and silver. Seeming to signify inflation and a weakened dollar, "bimetallism" haunted the dreams of American businessmen.

Not all Republicans shared such an intense interest in protecting American business. As part of the progressive wing of the Republican Party, Roosevelt had always been more interested in government and urban reform than trade and the money supply. The words "tariff" and "bimetallism" might have been the burning national issues of the various presidential campaigns, but Roosevelt had never been particularly keen on economic issues. Instead, Roosevelt had made his career attacking corruption in New York and had also spent six years as civil service commissioner in Washington, DC, trying to ensure that the government filled its offices based on merit and not political affiliation.

Despite his high ideals, Roosevelt had had a tough going in New York. He always had something of the crusader about him, but by August 1896 one of his crusades had brought him little but scorn in the city of his birth. Attempting to enforce the highly unpopular Sunday Excise Law, mandating that saloons close on the Sabbath, Roosevelt had alienated such important Republican constituencies as New York's German population, who had switched their votes to New York Democrats in the last election. City and state Republicans blamed Roosevelt and had even tried to legislate the job of president of the Board of Police Commissioners out of existence. In the face of such opposition from his own party, it was fairly clear to Roosevelt that his New York political career was over. By the start of the 1896 campaign, in spite of his differences with McKinley, he was one of many Republicans pinning their hopes on a Republican victory and a new posting in Washington.

As top Republicans descended on New York to plot campaign strategy, the Democratic nominee, William Jennings Bryan of Nebraska, also prepared to visit New York. Fresh from his triumphal "Cross of Gold" speech the month before at the Democratic National Convention, Bryan planned to kick off his campaign in what he called "the enemy's country." Bryan's candidacy reflected the split in the Democratic Party over the money supply—the gold standard versus bimetallism. Yet the debate over monetary policy simply reflected the larger question of who exactly held power in the United States. Farmers wanted a looser money supply so that credit might be attained more easily, while the resulting inflation would mean higher prices for their crops. For these farmers, American business's hostility to bimetallism reflected agriculture's marginalization at the hands of the "Money Power." After all, it was reasoned, banks, railroads, corporations, and even political parties kept their headquarters east of the Mississippi and north of the Mason-Dixon line. Banks set interest rates, railroad companies set freight rates, and the government adopted a laissez-faire attitude that favored these commercial interests at the expense of the American farmer. The playing field had to be leveled, and backing the American dollar with both gold and silver was one answer. Many had their doubts. Republicans almost uniformly rejected bimetallism. In American cities, laborers feared inflation would dilute their paychecks. Urban Democrats, such as New York's Tammany Hall political machine, therefore backed the gold standard and viewed Bryan's candidacy with skepticism if not utter distaste.

Bryan's trip to New York was supposed to change that. He planned to officially accept his nomination at a huge meeting in Madison Square Garden. He would avoid the drama and biblical imagery of his "Cross of Gold" speech in favor of a careful, reasoned defense of bimetallism. By presenting himself as a sane and cautious statesman, as opposed to the fire-breathing revolutionary that news accounts had painted him to be, Bryan hoped to win the workingman's vote and convince skeptical gold Democrats in the urban northeast. Only in this way could Bryan maintain the momentum of his campaign after the Chicago convention.

On Friday, August 8, Bryan and his wife boarded the train in Lincoln, Nebraska, as the heat wave settled over the Plains and Midwest. Across the country, temperatures in New York crept upward, toward the 90s, and as the train sped across the country toward its final destination, it was as if Bryan was bringing the heat with him.

INTRODUCTION:
FIGHTING FOR AIR

B Y AUGUST 1, all of New York was talking about the disaster.
"HALF A HUNDRED DEAD," screamed the front-page headline
in the *New York Times*. "HOSPITALS ARE FILLED," read another. "PITIFUL SCENES IN THE MORGUE." At the latest count, forty-
seven people had died, and of the seventy or so injured, many were
expected to perish, victims of one of the most common, yet horrific,
tragedies of late-nineteenth-century urban America: colliding trains.

The story was familiar. Two evenings before at 6:45 P.M., the West
Jersey and Seashore excursion train had left Atlantic City, driven by
engineer John Greiner with fireman Morris Newell stoking the engine. Only minutes later Greiner saw the Reading express train on a
perpendicular track flying toward the same crossing he was approaching. Since his train had the white flag, which meant the Reading train had the "stop" signal, Greiner assumed he had a clear track
ahead of him. But as the Reading train continued to thunder toward

the crossing, Greiner shouted to his fireman, "My God, Morris, he's not going to stop!" With a collision imminent, Greiner ran to the engine's steps and prepared to jump. For a moment he stood on the steps and watched the ground rush by. Then, with a change of heart, he returned to his duties in the cab.

A second later the crash came. The Reading train struck Greiner's excursion train in the middle of the second of its six coaches, killing over forty people instantly. The engine of the Reading express was smashed to pieces, and its engineer, Edward Farr, was killed on the spot. While most of the excursion train's cars derailed, the engine continued untroubled along its track for several hundred feet, after it was severed from the rest of the train. Greiner jumped from his cab and ran back to the rest of the train. "When I got back to the scene of the accident," he recounted, "the sight which met my eyes was appalling. Dead bodies were strewn about everywhere, and the cries of the dying and injured filled the air. It was a heartrending spectacle."

Survivors later described to journalists the horror inside the train. Charles Seeds was sitting with his wife in the fourth car of Greiner's train when the front part of his car "was smashed to kindling wood." Seeds called to his wife to follow him, and jumped out the car's window. He hurt his leg when he hit the ground, and as he looked around, he could not see his wife anywhere. When he jumped back up into the window, smoke filling the car blinded him. Through the gloom inside, Seeds saw a glittering object. He reached out and picked up his wife's gold pocket watch, its chain broken by a piece of heavy timber that had just grazed her. Now finding his wife alive nearby, Seeds grabbed her by the hair and pulled her through the window to safety.

In the late-nineteenth century police did not use "Do Not Cross" tape, and within hours, thousands of spectators surrounded the wrecks. People continued to flock to the site for days. In Atlantic City, the usual greeting of "Are you going to the boardwalk?" gave way to "Are you going to the wreck today?" And as one newspaper affirmed, "Everyone went." The dead were wrapped at the scene in blankets and sacks, then placed in another train car for return to the station, to be stored temporarily in the baggage room. Visiting the site, though popular, was traumatic. Benjamin Maull, a veteran of the Civil War, said seeing the wreck affected him more than any scene of carnage he had witnessed during his four years of service.

Less than two days later, speculation was rife among newspapers that Farr, the driver of the Reading train that ran the signal, had a friend in his cab at the time of the accident. "That raises the suspicion that he may have been more occupied in conversation than in watching signals," the editors of the *New York Tribune* noted.

The paper also sought to comment on the tragedy of the accident's many victims. Men who died on the battlefield, the paper believed, earned a measure of glory in the process. "Tornadoes and earthquakes and fire and flood kill thousands, but man bows submissive to the resistless elements. There is even something grand in being a victim of Nature. But to meet death from the blind fury of a Frankenstein, to suffer and be crushed by the misbehavior of one's own creations, to go out for pleasure trusting in the perfection of civilization and have that civilization turn and rend one, is to fall without any compensation." Industrial and technological developments such as trains—the "perfection of civilization"—had conquered the vast distances of the nation, but at a price. In the modern era people faced new and horrible agents of death.

IN URBAN AND INDUSTRIAL centers like New York by the end of the nineteenth century, human disasters appeared to have largely replaced natural disasters. Few New Yorkers could remember the massive death tolls that had accompanied the cholera epidemics in the 1830s, '40s, and '50s. The Great Fire of 1835, which had destroyed over six hundred buildings, was a distant memory. More recently, the Blizzard of 1888 had killed hundreds of people all along the eastern seaboard, from Maryland to Maine. But no one in New York expected another two-foot snowfall in March anytime soon, while the last cholera epidemic of 1892 appeared to prove that that disease had been defeated for all time.

Modern, scientific, industrial people had evidently conquered the natural disaster. Science and germ theory had certainly ended cholera epidemics, and by the summer of 1896 the city's Board of Health and Department of Sanitation were together making great progress stamping out dysentery and other infectious diseases. Science had even seemed to overcome weather itself. True, in May a great tornado had twisted its way through St. Louis and East St. Louis. Yet in the end it caused mainly property damage, and only about 250 people died. New York's own man in the U.S. Weather Bureau, William "Prophet" Dunn, noted that the St. Louis tornado had been "predicted" by E. B. Garriott of the Chicago Bureau, allowing precautions to be taken and countless lives to be saved. The St. Louis "disaster" was so mild, in fact, that it could not even delay the Republican National Convention to be held there the very next month.

Human-made disasters like the New Jersey rail accident now seemed the norm. Recent events had demonstrated iron and steel's greater capacity to kill and maim on a massive scale than mere water or wind, fire or ice. Indeed, most Americans marked their lives by the still recent Civil War. If anything, that human-made disaster put nature to shame. What hurricane could have killed 600,000 with such efficiency and cold-bloodedness? What fire could have found fuel for four long years?

Even on a smaller and more local scale new inventions seemed to turn on their creators with frightening regularity. In 1871 the boiler on the Staten Island Ferry exploded, killing 125. In 1876 a fire begun by a kerosene lamp tore through the stage scenery of the Brooklyn Theatre, killing 276. Trains crashed. Ships sank. Dams broke. The above-ground horse-drawn railway trolleys that plied New York streets would regularly clip an unfortunate pedestrian, taking a toe or an entire foot. And as America industrialized, the dangers to the industrial worker increased: Smelters exploded, chains broke, sparks flew, pulleys snapped, and blades slipped.

The American industrial worker also faced economic dangers. The Panic of 1893 had been caused by railroad overbuilding and the collapse of huge firms such as the Philadelphia and Reading Railroad and the National Cordage Company, also known as the Twine Trust. Over the next several years the country experienced a crushing depression. By the time the heat wave struck in August 1896, 70,000 New Yorkers were out of work, and another 20,000 were homeless.

In the eyes of many New Yorkers the unemployment problem was exacerbated by the arrival of thousands of immigrants. Starting around 1890, millions of citizens of southeastern European countries—Italians, Hungarians, Russian Jews—left their homes and made their way to the United States. Two-thirds of the new arrivals would pass through Ellis Island, the new immigrant reception center established off the southern tip of Manhattan in 1892. By 1897 about 1.5 million immigrants had been screened at the center. While many of the new arrivals moved on to other cities, or even returned home, thousands settled in New York.

This was the beginning of one of the largest demographic shifts in world history. Between 1890 and 1900 Greater New York added about 1 million persons to its population. By 1900 over a third of New Yorkers—nearly 1.3 million—were foreign-born, and 84 percent of the city's white heads of families were either of foreign birth or the children of immigrants.

The new arrivals and the city's poor packed into the ill-maintained tenements of lower Manhattan. There, ten people might share a single interior room without access to light or fresh air. The toilet often consisted of little more than a single latrine out back used by as many as two hundred people. To climb a dark staircase one risked stepping on playing children or becoming the victim of faceless attackers. In 1890 Jacob Riis had documented the plight of the tenement dwellers in his *How the Other Half Lives*, taking haunting photos that lit the darkest corners of the Bowery with the new technology of flash photography. Homeless children and exhausted laborers renting a place on the floor for a nickel stared back at the camera.

The conditions on the Lower East Side became unbearable during the summer. To avoid the stifling tenement air, the inhabitants stayed outdoors on doorsteps and roofs, even sleeping there at night, hoping to catch the faintest breeze. In summers, families would keep ice stocked not only to prevent food from spoiling but also to bring down overheated body temperatures. The economic crisis of 1896 had made matters worse, as laboring families were so impoverished they could not afford to purchase ice.

Work in the home compounded the squalor. Tenement rooms doubled as places of work for cigar makers and other pieceworkers, including children. When in the 1880s a bill had come before the New York State Assembly forbidding the manufacture of cigars in tenements, labor leader Samuel Gompers had taken a young assemblyman named Theodore Roosevelt on a tour of the Lower East Side. Roosevelt had not believed the horror stories about the tenements, and Gompers meant to educate the wealthy brownstone Republican. Accompanied by Gompers, Roosevelt came into contact with the city's poor for the first time, and years later he remembered:

> There were one, two, or three room apartments, and the work went on day and night in the eating, living, and sleeping rooms— sometimes in one room. I have always remembered one room in which two families were living. On my inquiry as to who the third adult male was I was told that he was a boarder with one of the families. There were several children, three men, and two women in this room. The tobacco was stowed about everywhere, alongside the foul bedding, and in a corner where there were scraps of food. The men, women, and children in this room worked by day and far on into the evening, and they slept and ate there.

Tenement dwellers daily faced a precarious economic situation. New York's Lower East Side was dominated by the expanding needle trade, one of the fastest-growing sectors of New York manufacturing. The vast majority of the contractors had their shops below Fourteenth Street, within easy walking distance of the tenements. In 1890, before the slump, 10,000 garment firms had employed around 236,000 workers. In early 1896 the tailors of New York went on strike for more pay against the wealthier contractors who filled orders for the large clothing companies. In good times a tailor might have made $12 or $15 a week, but during the depression he was often lucky to receive only half a week's work. Now 20,000 tailors, all members of the Brotherhood of Tailors union, were out of work. This meant that about 100,000 residents of the tenements clustered around the intersection of Hester and Essex Streets were without means of support. A reporter walking along Hester Street at night found "at least half of the population of that street seeking sleep on the fire escapes, the stairways or the doorsteps. In most cases, fighting for air, they had carried their blankets and mattresses from their dens, but often I found men and women scantily clothed sleeping, or trying in vain to sleep, upon bare wood or iron, glad of the fresh air—fresh only by comparison with the evil atmosphere of their living rooms."

The strike had left the tailors in a desperate situation. Local grocers and merchants stopped extending credit to the strikers. Thousands were forced to sustain themselves with "bad fruit, questionable meat, and stale bread," one New York paper noted. Bad air and bad food combined to make many sick, though they were unable to afford a doctor. Esther Greenhaum lived in a tenement on Essex Street and had fallen very ill. Her husband, a striking tailor, failed to return home, apparently ashamed he could not provide for his wife. Not wanting to ask her neighbors for help, Esther suffered in her room quietly until she cried out in pain. Hearing this, a neighbor summoned a doctor, who asked if Esther could pay his fee. "Yes," the neighbor woman lied, "she will pay," knowing that this was the only way to lure the doctor to the tenement. When Esther could not pay, the doctor became enraged. The neighbor cut him off, saying, "God will pay. No one else can."

***

IT WAS THE AGE of reform. While the suffering of the urban poor in New York had led to the rise of labor radicalism and various efforts at city reform, in the West and South farmers also sought relief from the tyranny of eastern business interests. Farmers relied on credit, but bankers from eastern cities like New York controlled the money supply. They also relied on the railroads to bring their crops to market, but the railroads collaborated to set rates, giving large discounts to big customers like Rockefeller's Standard Oil, while squeezing the individual customer with higher rates. Manufacturing interests kept tariffs high to protect American industry from cheaper imports, but this raised the prices of everyday necessities. Banks, railroads, big business, and political leaders made their headquarters in the big cities of the East, while there appeared to be nobody willing to be the voice of the farmer. The North-South division of the Civil War had given way to new American divisions, that between city and country, farmer and banker, East and West.

In 1892, 1,300 delegates from various labor and farmers' groups met in Omaha, Nebraska, to form the People's Party. The Populists, as they would come to be called, adopted a platform that included many of the remedies agrarian and labor advocates had been discussing for years: government ownership of railroads, redistribution of wealth through a graduated income tax, the eight-hour day, and direct election of U.S. senators. Many of these ideas would remain the cornerstone of the so-called Progressive Era, the age of reform that lasted through the First World War and culminated in women's suffrage and Prohibition.

Central to the Populist platform was reform of the money supply. By 1896 the United States had been on the gold standard for almost a quarter of a century. Every paper dollar circulating in the country was backed by an equal value of gold. For business leaders, this placed the American dollar, and thus the whole American economy, on a sound foundation. Gold-backed currency kept inflation down and reassured European lenders of the dollar's stability. For farmers, however, the gold standard kept their crop prices low and placed a stranglehold on credit, the lifeblood of the farming sector.

The solution for many was not to go off a metal-based currency altogether, but rather to expand the backing of the dollar with both gold *and* silver. Bimetallists believed this would increase the supply of money, allowing easier credit and modest inflation that would result in higher prices for their products.

Since 1890, when he ran for Congress for the first time, William Jennings Bryan had emerged as one of the leading advocates of bimetallism. Born in 1860, Bryan had been raised on the prairie soil of Salem, Illinois. Deeply influenced by his father, who was both a Baptist preacher and a local judge and politician, Bryan studied law with an eye toward politics. Yet even as an aspiring lawyer, Bryan always had something of the preacher about him. In college he won awards for his skills as an orator, and his initial ambition had been to enter the clergy. Settling in Lincoln, Nebraska, Bryan became involved in the Democratic Party, whose state leaders were delighted to let the young orator speak on behalf of the party. In 1888 Bryan had campaigned for Democratic nominee President Grover Cleveland. In 1890, at age thirty, Bryan became only the second Democratic congressman elected in Nebraska.

In light of the economic crises of the 1890s, the issue of the money supply soon became pressing. In 1892 Grover Cleveland returned to the presidency largely on the issue of tariff reform, but the economic crisis of the following year brought to the fore the money supply question. Calling a special session of Congress, Cleveland called for the repeal of the Sherman Silver Purchase Act of 1890. This act, backed by farming and mining interests, required the government to purchase massive quantities of silver every month. Special Treasury notes were issued for the silver purchase, notes that could be redeemed for either silver or gold. The plan backfired when investors turned in the Treasury notes for gold, thus depleting the nation's gold supplies. Anti-silver forces blamed the Sherman Act for the 1893 crash and called for its repeal before the country's gold supply dwindled even further. In addressing Congress over the repeal, Cleveland pointed out that in the three years since the Sherman Act, gold bullion reserves had decreased by more than $132 million, while silver reserves increased by more than $147 million. Repealing the act would send a strong message about the soundness of the American dollar and, Cleveland hoped, revive the economy.

Speaking against repeal of the Sherman Act, Bryan addressed the House of Representatives in his typical preaching style, with biblical references and vivid imagery:

> [The president] won the confidence of the toilers of this country because he taught that "public office is a public trust," and because he convinced them of his courage and his sincerity. But are they willing to say, in the language of Job, "Though He slay me, yet will I trust Him?" Whence comes this irresistible demand for unconditional repeal? Are not the representatives here as near to the people and as apt to know their wishes? Whence comes the demand? Not from the workshops and farms, not from the workingmen of this country, who create its wealth in time of peace and protect its flag in time of war, but from the middle-men, from what are termed the "business interests," and largely from that class which can force Congress to let it issue money at a pecuniary profit to itself if silver is abandoned. The president has been deceived. He can no more judge the wishes of the great mass of our people by the expressions of these men than he can measure the ocean's silent depths by the foam upon its waves.

In the end the "Boy Orator" was unsuccessful, and the Sherman law was repealed. Cleveland had scored a victory but split his party in the process. Moreover, "free silver" had become the burning issue of the day, and Bryan one of its leading voices.

IN 1894 BRYAN lost a bid for the Senate, and by 1895 he had become the political editor for the Omaha *World-Herald*. Bryan used his job as a forum for his ideas and maintained his place as a leader of the silver forces. Like the rest of the country, Bryan looked ahead to the political showdown of 1896. With Cleveland stepping down after two nonconsecutive terms, Republicans, Democrats, and even Populists would be vying for power, while within the Democratic Party, silver advocates sought to place a bimetallism plank in the party's platform.

In July 1896, when the Democrats gathered in Chicago for their convention, Bryan brought his wife along, just in case he won the presidential nomination. Far from being a dark horse, Bryan was recognized as one of the leading contenders for the nomination, with the *Chicago Tribune* predicting he would be the nominee. July 9 of the weeklong convention was the day set aside for the platform debate on the money issue. As this was not only an important issue nationwide but also the most important issue splitting the Democrats since 1893, the speeches this day were widely anticipated and closely watched.

Bryan, having already established a reputation for oratory, was given a place of honor in the debate and allowed to give the last speech. Democrats in Chicago dozed through the series of poor speeches that preceded Bryan's and waited for the fireworks. He did not disappoint, giving one of the greatest speeches in American history, replying to the Democratic gold delegates and their defense of American business interests.

You come to us and tell us that the great cities are in favor of the gold standard; we reply that the great cities rest upon our broad and fertile prairies. Burn down your cities and leave our farms, and your cities will spring up again as if by magic; but destroy our farms and the grass will grow in the streets of every city in this country. . . .

Having behind us the producing masses of this nation and the world, supported by the commercial interests, the laboring interests, and the toilers everywhere, we will answer their demand for a gold standard by saying to them: You shall not press down upon the brow of labor this crown of thorns, you shall not crucify mankind upon a cross of gold!

With these final words of the speech, Bryan spread his arms wide, like Christ on the cross.

The delegates went wild. The convention responded to the speech with a roar "like one great burst of artillery," as one newspaperman described it. The next day Bryan was named the Democratic nominee. The silver Democrats had prevailed.

The telegraph wires to Chicago hummed with congratulatory telegrams. "Thank God we are to have a President who knows that the western boundary of our country is beyond the Mississippi," wrote former Colorado governor Alva Adams. "Every member of the Nebraskas [sic] wild west exhibition including Indians and representatives of all foreign nations send congratulation to the boy orator of the Platte and the young Giant of the west," wrote William "Buffalo Bill" Cody.

Joy seemed widespread throughout the West. Nebraska congressman J. H. Broady tried to capture the scene in Bryan's hometown:

"All Lincoln rejoicing whistles blowing bells ringing and bonfires burning in pride of your genius which rises with the mantle of Jefferson in a blaze of oratory unsurpassed in all the ages and moves towards the chair once occupied by him, for whom this city is named."

Two weeks later in St. Louis, the People's Party also nominated Bryan for president, yet, peculiarly, with an alternate vice presidential nominee. The Populists held no love for the Democrats and stood for a different vice president as a means of maintaining their party's independence. The question of vice presidents reflected the Populist dilemma. The Democratic nominee was Arthur Sewall, who hailed from an old New England family that had made its fortune in shipbuilding. Like other American tycoons, Sewall had diversified into banking and railroads and thus seemed exactly the sort of person the Populists held responsible for America's ills. Nominating him for elected office would have been like nominating Morgan or Vanderbilt.

Instead, the Populists chose Tom Watson, a Georgia congressman and one of the founders of the People's Party. Having a different nominee for vice president allowed the Populists a strange sort of independence. It also raised the question of whether Bryan would even accept the nomination, which he deliberated over for several days. The Democratic governor of Texas urged Bryan to accept the nomination and to "discuss *nothing* but the money question." Sewall even wrote to him, observing that Bryan's indecision seemed to be based mainly on not wanting to insult his Democratic running mate by also accepting Watson as his Populist running mate. "I desire that you will do just what you believe is best for the success of the head of the ticket," Sewall said. "The principles we are fighting for are so paramount to any personal relations that the latter should not have any weight or influence whatever with your action."

Bryan accepted: He would need those Populist votes come November. But this strange coalition between the Democrats and Populists came at a cost. By allying himself with the more radical People's Party, Bryan played into the hands of his Republican opponents, as they cried "Anarchy!" and quickly dubbed Bryan the "Popocrat" candidate.

Bryan could now only hope that the Populists would allow themselves to be absorbed by the Democrats. Indeed, by early August "fusion" was the word of the day. Would the Populists simply fold themselves into the Democratic Party? The answer seemed to be a resounding no. The *New York Times* reported that the Populist National Committee had opened its campaign headquarters in Washington, DC. The spokesman for the Populists stated that they would campaign completely independent of the Democrats, "just the same as if Bryan was not the nominee of the Chicago convention."

In New York, Democrat political leaders were still feeling the aftershocks of Bryan's nomination. Residents of the country's financial center, New York Democrats cared little for the silver issue, and Bryan had been nominated against their wishes. "Only two papers in New York supporting your candidacy," the editor of the then-Democratic *New York Mercury* wrote to Bryan at the end of July.

Both Republican and Democrat leaders in the city were used to getting their way in national politics because of the importance of New York in national elections. Over the past four presidential elections, New York City alone had provided the crucial margin of victory. Now the city's Democrats, and the leaders of the Tammany Hall political machine, were faced with the unsavory task of backing a candidate who represented southern and western agrarian interests and offered little to attract New York voters. In 1896 Tammany Hall was a force to be reckoned with. Since 1788, it had produced leading American politicians like Aaron Burr and Martin Van Buren. By mobilizing the massive immigrant base of the city, and seeing to the needs of these newly arrived New Yorkers, Tammany and its minions were able to control much of the politics of the city, from the mayor's office to the fire department. In the mid-nineteenth century, boss William Tweed had adopted the tiger as the insignia of his volunteer fire brigade, and Tammany quickly adopted it as its symbol. With the importance of New York in national politics, support by the Tammany Tiger could make or break a candidacy. After his nomination Bryan had waited expectantly for news from Tammany. On July 31, exactly three weeks after his Chicago nomination, Bryan finally received a telegram from New York informing him that "Tammany endorsed ticket executive session this p.m." On the surface this seemed like good news, but a close observer of politics would have noted that the news from New York indicated nothing about New York Democrats endorsing the Democratic platform with its silver plank.

Aside from the New Jersey train disaster, this was the top story of the day. "Tiger Takes the Ticket," the *Times* declared. "Swallowed by the Tiger," echoed the *Tribune*. Yet everyone also noted that New York Democrats had taken the rather absurd step of endorsing Bryan, the convention's nominee, but not free silver, its platform. "The resolution that turned Tammany over to the 'Pops' ticket absolutely ignored the platform," the staunchly Republican *Times* smirked. "The Tiger even could not stomach that. He swallowed the ticket without much of a grimace, but even his stout stomach could not take the platform as well."

The party was in a state of crisis. Faced with a nominee whose policies they could not abide, New York Democrats were already quietly defecting to support McKinley. Bryan's campaign had to take action to salvage the support of his own party.

In a bold move to take the fight to the gold-standard capital of the country and reverse Democratic defections, the Bryan campaign decided to come east and officially accept the Democratic nomination at a huge rally in Madison Square Garden. The gravity of the situation facing Bryan necessitated such a move, even before Bryan knew of Tammany's decision to support his candidacy. Bryan didn't wait for news from Tammany: Two days *before* Bryan received its endorsement, he received word from New York that the auditorium had been booked.

The dates of Bryan's trip to New York were now set. Accompanied by Mary, he would leave Lincoln, Nebraska, on Friday, August 7, and arrive in New York Tuesday evening, August 11. The following day, Bryan would address thousands at Madison Square Garden, thus kicking off his national campaign in a daring move that might make or break it only three months before the November election.

***

OUT ON LONG ISLAND, Theodore Roosevelt was also looking ahead to November. Saturday, August 1, was a warm, bright day, the sunlight almost blinding off Oyster Bay, beside which stood the Roosevelt family home, Sagamore Hill.

It was a large house, built near where Roosevelt had summered with his family as a child and initially designed for his first wife, Alice. With so many bedrooms, Theodore and Alice were apparently expecting to have a large family. Then in February 1884, soon after giving birth to a baby girl, Alice Hathaway Roosevelt died of Bright's disease, an inflammation of the kidneys that had gone undiagnosed during her pregnancy. The same night Roosevelt's mother, Mittie, died of typhoid fever, which had first appeared to be merely a bad cold. The devastated Roosevelt destroyed his diary entries relating to his wife, left his newborn baby in the care of his sister, and fled west to the Badlands.

Over Christmas 1886, Roosevelt married his childhood friend Edith Carow, and by August 1896, almost ten years after their marriage, Edith and Theodore had filled those bedrooms with four children in addition to Alice Lee, now twelve years old. These were Theodore Junior, who would turn nine the following month; Kermit, age six; Ethel, only two weeks away from her fifth birthday; and two-year-old Archie.

It was perhaps with his growing family in mind that Roosevelt hosted a special guest that weekend. Maria Longworth Storer was a wealthy Washington matron active in her support for the Catholic Church. Her husband, Bellamy Storer, was a former congressman from Ohio and son of a former congressman. (He was also uncle to Nicholas Longworth, another Ohio congressman, and Alice Lee Roosevelt's future husband.) The Storers were longtime supporters of fellow Ohioan William McKinley. When the economic crash of 1893 had wiped out all of McKinley's investments, thus threatening his promising political career, the Storers had bailed him out with a $10,000 loan. The Republican presidential nominee was literally in their debt, and Bellamy Storer had his eye on a cabinet post or ambassadorship. Roosevelt was hoping to leverage his friendship with the Storers into a new job in Washington.

Roosevelt had decided to row Mrs. Storer across Oyster Bay before asking her for her support. Perhaps he wanted privacy, not wanting his family to see him as a suppliant. On the other hand, it may have been a shrewd psychological ploy, asking his guest for a favor when she was absolutely at his mercy in the middle of Oyster Bay. It was also typical Roosevelt, always needing an outlet for his seemingly boundless energy.

Whatever the reason, Roosevelt helped his guest into the rowboat and began pulling on the oars, while Mrs. Storer tried to shield herself from the sun. She liked Theodore. Though he was thirty-seven at the time, the "attraction" of Roosevelt, she would later write, "lay in the fact that he was like a child; with a child's spontaneous outbursts of affection, of fun, and of anger; and with the brilliant brain and fancy of a child."

Part of Roosevelt's success was his ability to play on people's image of him, whether as a cowboy, Rough Rider, reformer, or diplomat. Now rowing the matronly Mrs. Storer across Oyster Bay, he lamented to her that the future of his children depended on his getting a post in a new McKinley administration, without which, he cried, "I shall be the melancholy spectacle . . . of an idle father, writing books that do not sell!" Mrs. Storer assured Roosevelt that something could be secured for him, while Roosevelt promised to support Bellamy Storer in his quest for his own Washington post.

The conversation that warm August afternoon must have come as a great relief for Roosevelt. His current position in New York City had become sadly untenable, despite his long history there. He had been born in Manhattan to a wealthy New York family. From old Knickerbocker Dutch stock, his grandfather Cornelius Van Schaack Roosevelt was one of the richest New Yorkers of his day. His father, Theodore Roosevelt Sr., was one of the founders of the American Museum of Natural History and the Metropolitan Museum of Art, two great New York landmarks. Theodore Roosevelt Jr. had started his career in New York, first elected to the New York Assembly from his Manhattan brownstone district in 1881. While in Albany he had served on the Cities Committee, dedicated mostly to legislation regarding New York itself, and in 1884 had chaired an investigating committee looking into the graft and corruption in city departments. He had also championed the Roosevelt Bill, signed by then-governor Grover Cleveland in 1884, taking power from the appointed Board of Aldermen and investing it instead in the elected mayor. Roosevelt ran unsuccessfully for mayor of New York in 1886, sacrificing himself at the polls that year to unite a divided Republican Party.

In 1894, after spending six years in Washington as civil service commissioner, Roosevelt had been approached about again running for mayor. He turned the offer down, apparently because Edith did not think they could afford the campaign. Much to Roosevelt's chagrin, that year a reform Republican very much like him won the election. Roosevelt wrote to his sister Anna with some regret: "I made a mistake in not trying my luck in the mayoralty race. The prize was very great; the expense would have been trivial; and the chances of success were good. I would have run better than Strong . . . But it is hard to decide when one has the interests of a wife and children to consider first; and now it is over, and it is best not to talk of it; above all, no outsider should know that I think my decision was a mistake."

After Republican William Strong became mayor, he offered Roosevelt a place on the city's Street Cleaning Commission. In other words, the ambitious Roosevelt would have been responsible for hauling away the city's garbage. He turned the position down, though he still hoped to play a part in Strong's reform government. Roosevelt wrote a letter to his old friend Jacob Riis, perhaps hoping Riis would soothe any ill feelings held by Strong: "As I told you, I am afraid the Mayor may have taken it a little amiss that I would not accept the position of Street Cleaning Commissioner. I would like to have done so very much, because I want to help him out in any way, and I should have been delighted to smash up the corrupt contractors and to have tried to put the street cleaning commissioner's force absolutely out of the domain of politics; but with the actual work of cleaning the streets, dumping the garbage, etc., I wasn't familiar." It was a diplomatic excuse from someone who simply did not want to be New York's chief garbage man.

The mayor's race of that year may also have shown Roosevelt the need to get back to New York and pay his dues locally before the important 1896 election. If he could campaign again for a successful Republican nominee as he had in 1888, he might expect a large reward, like the appointed position he discussed with Maria Storer. From his vantage in Washington in 1894, Roosevelt could see that the Republicans had a very good chance of success in 1896. After all, with Cleveland leaving office, Republicans did not have to battle a Democratic incumbent. There were also the facts of the present economic crisis and the split over bimetallism within the Democratic Party. Roosevelt watched their effects on the historic 1894 midterm congressional elections. In the House of Representatives, Republicans gained 117 seats, while the Democrats lost 113 seats, the largest transfer of power between parties in American history. In twenty-four states in 1894, no Democrats were elected to national office. The year 1896, then, was shaping up to be a Republican year.

Roosevelt had his doubts when Strong eventually offered him the position of one of four police commissioners for New York City. Would such a position be a step back for Roosevelt's career? As he often did, Roosevelt asked for advice from his close friend and political ally Henry Cabot Lodge of Massachusetts. Roosevelt wrote, "The average New Yorker of course wishes me to take it very much. I don't feel much like it myself, but of course realize that it is a different kind of position from that of Street Cleaning Commissioner, and one I could perhaps be identified with." So unsure of his future at such an important crossroads in his career, Roosevelt exclaimed, "It is very puzzling!" Lodge pressed his friend to take the job.

Roosevelt accepted the position, apparently with the understanding that he would be named head of the commission of four. Since the position was called "president," Roosevelt enjoyed two years of being addressed in person and in the press as "President Roosevelt." Following his appointment Roosevelt wrote to Anna of his excitement: "I think it a good thing to be definitely identified with my city once more. I would like to do my share in governing the city after our great victory; and so far as may be I would like once more to have my voice in political matters. It was a rather close decision; but on the whole I felt I ought to go, though it is 'taking chances.'"

Excited as Roosevelt was for his new job in New York City, Lodge expressed concern that Roosevelt must still keep an eye on *national* party politics. Lodge knew Roosevelt perhaps better than anyone else. He knew of Roosevelt's streak of moral righteousness and had seen it in action, up close. In attacking corruption and graft, Lodge coaxed Roosevelt, *Just don't burn your political bridges.* The 1896 election was still of paramount importance for anyone interested in ascending to a higher position. "You need not have the slightest fear about my losing my interest in National Politics," Roosevelt reassured Lodge. "In a couple of years or less I shall have finished the work here for which I am specially fitted, and in which I take a special interest. After that there will remain only the ordinary problems of decent administration of the Department, which will be already in good running order. I shall then be quite ready to take up a new job."

THE NEW YORK CITY Police Department was the linchpin of corruption citywide. The chief of police admitted to being worth $350,000, although Roosevelt would later speculate he had amassed a fortune of well over $1 million. The money trickled down from there.

Gambling houses and brothels paid the police to ensure against raids. Saloons paid thousands of dollars to obtain a liquor license. Even local green grocers paid perhaps a dollar a day for the ability to stack their produce on the sidewalk. Just before Roosevelt took his position, an investigation had reported on the widespread corruption in the force. The Lexow Commission had concluded that the only remedy for such a rotten organization was to indict the entire police force. Upon taking office Roosevelt was able to force the resignation of the police chief as well as other corrupt officers. Accompanied by Jacob Riis, Roosevelt began to take midnight walks through the city, making sure that officers were on duty when and where they were supposed to be, instead of asleep, in taverns, or in brothels, "partly concealed by petticoats," as one paper colorfully put it.

Roosevelt's main and most difficult struggle would be to enforce the Sunday Excise Law that forbade the selling of liquor on Sunday. This was a state law that reflected the rural, upstate temperance vote and had long been flatly ignored in the city. Roosevelt himself was not a drinker, but even he believed the Sunday anti-liquor law to be a bad law. Nevertheless all laws needed to be enforced. Saloons were also the most public and profitable of the city's illegal ventures, with ties both to the police force and to political corruption. Many saloon keepers were political bosses in the Democratic Tammany political organization, and saloons often doubled as unofficial Tammany headquarters. As a result, Roosevelt was not simply undertaking a moralist crusade against the evil drink but appearing to work in the interest of the Republican Party.

When Roosevelt took office in early 1895, there were between 12,000 and 15,000 saloons in New York City. By the end of June,

Roosevelt had succeeded in closing 97 percent of the saloons on Sundays in accordance with the law, stopping the normal flow of 3 million glasses of beer. Roosevelt referred to the Sunday closing fight as a "war," while the *Times* called it a "crusade."

Whatever the label, it made Roosevelt the most unpopular man in New York. He was attacked by Tammany Democrats, of course, but also by German-Americans, who usually voted Republican and enjoyed a traditional drink of beer on Sundays. Some unknown drinker even sent Roosevelt a letter "bomb" that a postal clerk opened to find it packed only with sawdust.

When a U.S. senator from New York, Tammany Democrat David Hill, attacked Roosevelt for wasting police resources enforcing the Sunday law at the expense of fighting crime, Roosevelt responded in a speech to German-Americans, the second largest ethnic group in the city after the Irish. The law, Roosevelt said, was never meant to be honestly enforced:

> It was meant to be used to blackmail and browbeat the saloon keepers who were not the slaves of Tammany Hall; while the big Tammany Hall bosses who owned saloons were allowed to violate the law with impunity and to corrupt the police force at will. With a law such as this enforced only against the poor or the honest man, and violated with impunity by every rich scoundrel and every corrupt politician, the machine did indeed seem to have its yoke on the neck of the people. But we threw off that yoke.

Republican senator from Massachusetts George Hoar wrote his congratulations to Roosevelt, saying, "Your speech is the best speech that has been made on this continent for thirty years. I am glad to know that there is a man behind it worthy of the speech."

Roosevelt's anti-saloon crusade, however, had proven widely un-popular with the mass of New York voters. Republican leaders blamed Roosevelt for the poor showing among city Republicans during the 1895 Assembly elections, and party leaders had not even allowed him to campaign for Republican candidates. Roosevelt de-spaired that his efforts at reform had destroyed any future career in the city. As always, Lodge encouraged the younger Roosevelt to maintain a broader view. "You are making a great place and reputa-tion for yourself which will lead surely to even better things," Lodge wrote. "Remember too that apart from the great principle of enforc-ing all laws there is a very large and powerful body of Republicans in the State who will stand by you and behind you because you are enforcing that particular law. This may be a narrow view but it is of the greatest political importance." Lodge hinted that Roosevelt's path may soon lead to a seat next to his in the Senate.

Despite Lodge's encouraging words, 1896 had been a tough year. In January Roosevelt had fought to keep his job, in danger of being legislated out of existence by an Assembly bill engineered by Repub-lican leaders. The following month Roosevelt began a dispute with a fellow commissioner, Democrat Andrew D. Parker, which would color the rest of his time in New York.

On the face of it, a bipartisan police commission seemed like a good idea. Yet an equal number of Democrats and Republicans in-vited deadlock. Moreover, it simply made the commission a new po-litical battleground in the city. While like-minded reformers might applaud Roosevelt's efforts, Parker had plenty of allies among Dem-ocrats and those who desired to continue having the police force re-flect political influence. Time and again Parker, in alliance with the new chief of police, threw up obstacles in the path of Roosevelt's conduct of the commission—holding up officer promotions and not attending commission meetings. In April Roosevelt testified in Albany in favor of a bill to break the commission's deadlock. He and Parker squared off in their testimony, as Parker accused Roosevelt of playing politics with the police promotions. During Parker's testimony Roosevelt stalked about the room, unable to contain his rage. The bill died in committee, a defeat for Roosevelt. In May, when the city comptroller lectured Roosevelt about using taxpayers' money to pay off informants, Roosevelt challenged him to a duel with pistols. In June, unable to remove Parker without a trial, Mayor Strong had decided to bring him up on charges to prove "neglected duty." Using "evidence" supplied by Roosevelt, the mayor accused Parker of missing numerous meetings and falling behind on paperwork. It was a dull and dreary affair, possibly the low point of Roosevelt's New York career. While testimony ended in July, the matter was never fully resolved, and Parker would eventually enjoy the pleasure of outlasting Roosevelt on the board. Little wonder that Roosevelt tired of New York and found new hope in McKinley's nomination.

Even as Roosevelt sought to decrease the political influence of the police force, he actively sought that influence on his own behalf. In this endeavor Roosevelt had a number of important allies. Lodge was in the Senate, and the Storers had McKinley's ear—the outlook seemed bright indeed. Yet Roosevelt also had to take into account the new kingmaker of the Republican Party, Marcus Alonzo Hanna. Hanna was an Ohio millionaire active in Republican politics who had worked for the past two years to secure McKinley's nomination for the presidency. His reward for spending $100,000 of his own money in that endeavor was to be named chairman of the Republican National Committee. For Roosevelt to advance politically after a McKinley victory, he would need Hanna's support.

On July 28 Hanna was in New York to establish his headquarters at the Waldorf-Astoria, and Roosevelt was there to meet him. Roosevelt placed himself at Hanna's disposal, ready to work for McKinley's election to the presidency—and his own move from New York to Washington. He had a second talk with Hanna the next day, finding him "a good natured, well meaning, rough man, shrewd and hard-headed, but neither very farsighted nor very broad-minded," as he wrote to Lodge, "and as he has a resolute, imperious mind, he will have to be handled with some care."

Roosevelt was not just interested in advancement. He viewed Bryan's nomination with alarm. To his sister, Roosevelt wrote, "I saw Mark Hanna. I can't help thinking we shall win in November; but we have to combat a genuine and dangerous fanaticism. At bottom the Bryanite feeling is due to the discontent of the mass of men who live hard, and blindly revolt against their conditions; a revolt which is often aimed foolishly at those who are better off, merely because they *are* better off; it is the blind man leading the one-eyed." Roosevelt did not use the word "revolt" lightly, and he vowed to take part in the fight against that dangerous revolutionary, William Jennings Bryan.

Roosevelt and Bryan were more alike than either man would have admitted. While Roosevelt has been compared to his distant cousin Franklin Roosevelt and his fellow progressive Woodrow Wilson, he also shared characteristics with Bryan. Born less than eighteen months apart and with political careers seemingly shadowing each other, Bryan and Roosevelt shared much of the same political and moral world.

Yet their differences are so striking that it is tempting to see the two men as mirror opposites. Certainly they were fierce ideological opponents. With his call for free silver and his railing against eastern, urban interests, Bryan represented the country's agrarian backbone. Roosevelt's message, on the other hand, was born of his urban background, with an emphasis on good government, civil service reform, and the need for a level playing field in politics, business, and the law.

Their political views derived from their upbringings. Roosevelt was born in Manhattan to a wealthy family and entered politics at a young age, making his way from the state assembly to Washington as civil service commissioner before returning to New York. He would gain fame in the Spanish-American War and be elected New York governor before being placed on the Republican ticket in 1900. Bryan, on the other hand, came from a modest family background in rural Illinois. First practicing law, he became involved in the Nebraska Democratic Party before being elected to Congress. This was the only political office he held before becoming his party's nominee in 1896. Bryan was deeply influenced by his Christian fundamentalism, which often made him seem more preacher than politician. While raised a Presbyterian and a churchgoer, Roosevelt did not ascribe to religion as closely as Bryan.

Yet there was always something of the preacher in Roosevelt, too. While Bryan may have made his career with the words "Thou shall not crucify mankind upon a cross of gold!" Roosevelt would rally his Progressive Party followers in 1912 by saying, "We stand at Armageddon, and we battle for the Lord!"

Both men had similar ideas about American superiority, Anglo-Saxon superiority, and the duties of citizenship. They were infused with a sense of self-righteousness, a sureness in their cause no matter what the consequences. Roosevelt had already shown this characteristic on a number of occasions by 1896, although his most notorious example would come when he split the Republican Party in 1912, handing the election to Democrat Woodrow Wilson.

By 1896 Bryan had helped split the Democrats with his stand for free silver against the position of Democratic president Grover Cleveland. This was not the last time he would embarrass a sitting Democratic president. In 1915, with the United States still neutral in the war in Europe, Bryan held the important position of secretary of state to Woodrow Wilson. After the sinking of the British passenger liner *Lusitania* killed 128 Americans, Wilson demanded that Germany pay reparations and disavow U-boat attacks on passenger ships. Bryan resigned in protest, fearing Wilson would trigger war. A secretary of state undermining his president's foreign policy in a time of war was unheard of. Newspapers referred to Bryan's "unspeakable treachery" and noted that "men have been shot and beheaded, even hanged, drawn and quartered for treason less heinous." To such savage criticism, the fundamentalist Bryan might have replied, "Blessed are the peacemakers, for they shall be called the children of God."

Both Roosevelt and Bryan enjoyed hunting, yet neither were very good shots. Both men had made an effort to build up their bodies, which they relied on during cross-country political campaigns. Perhaps most importantly, though, both lived their entire lives in absolute awe of their fathers. After his father's death, Bryan recalled that after being enjoined to follow his father's shining example, he "could not help weeping . . . for I felt so unworthy to take my father's place." Roosevelt dedicated several pages of his *Autobiography* in describing the elder Roosevelt in glowing terms: "My father, Theodore Roosevelt, was the best man I ever knew." Both Roosevelt and Bryan suffered through the deaths of their fathers when they were in college, Bryan at age twenty and Roosevelt at age nineteen.

For both men, their grief for their fathers seemed to solidify the foundations on which they would build their public lives. A driving desire to live up to their fathers' examples helped shape two of the most important figures of late-nineteenth-century America.

In the campaigns of 1896 and 1900, Bryan and Roosevelt often shadowed each other across the country. Indeed, with his western ranching experience and heroism in Cuba, Roosevelt served Republicans well by countering Bryan's popularity in the West. And both men served as colonels at the head of regiments during the Spanish-American War, although Bryan never embarked for Cuba. For Bryan and Roosevelt, service in the military during wartime was an important duty of both the man and the citizen.

These common romantic ideas of the Victorian era hint at the basis of many of their similarities. Reverence of one's father and of masculinity, faith in both Anglo-Saxon and American superiority, belief in the duties of citizenship and the necessity of fulfilling this duty on the battlefield all made up the creed of America's civic religion of the time. Despite their differences, and despite their sincere concern for the poor, Roosevelt and Bryan absorbed the beliefs of America's white, Protestant elite.

AUGUST WAS SHAPING UP to be an eventful month for New York. In less than two weeks Bryan was coming to town to accept the Democratic nomination at Madison Square Garden. McKinley's headquarters had just opened at the Waldorf, with Hanna leading the Republican troops. Roosevelt's fate was deeply entwined with that of all three men. As president of the board of police commissioners Roosevelt would be responsible for security at Bryan's speech at Madison Square Garden. Meanwhile, Roosevelt would continually meet with Hanna to discuss the campaign and his possible role in it, in service to a McKinley victory.

Atlantic City hospitals remained full as officials identified the dead and injured from the New Jersey train crash. President Cleveland vowed that America would stay neutral in the new Cuban uprising against Spanish rule in the island. And St. Louis was suffering through a killer heat wave. In the past two weeks twenty-two babies had died as a result of the heat. For a week the maximum temperature recorded was 99 degrees. Newspapers reported many people dying every day, with the death rate "increasing at an alarming rate." Little did New Yorkers realize what was in store for them: a heat wave whose death rate would dwarf the New Jersey railroad disaster.

I.
CHOLERA INFANTIUM

DURING THE SUMMER of 1896 Theodore Roosevelt fled Manhattan and his troublesome work as police commissioner as often as he could. As in his youth, the Roosevelt family summered on Long Island, offering him a needed reprieve from his public dispute with fellow commissioner Andrew Parker. The time at Sagamore Hill acted as a balm. Leaving on Sundays to return to his duties in the city must have caused him intense pain. He always remembered life there in the most idyllic of terms: the snow-covered woods during winters, the "blossom-spray of spring," and the deep, leafy shades of summer, when he and Edith would spend entire days rowing out on Long Island Sound, sometimes accompanied by one of their boys and sometimes lunching on one of the small uninhabited islands. Perhaps these very images flashed through his mind during the train ride back to the city, giving him strength for the work ahead.

AFTER THE JULY Chicago convention, William and Mary Bryan had checked out of their hotel room and prepared to return to Nebraska. Adding up his expenses for the week, Bryan noted that he and Mary had spent less than one hundred dollars, "a sum probably as small as anyone spent in securing a Presidential nomination," he would later write.

Thrift was of great importance to Bryan's political persona. Bryan was sitting with his friend, journalist Willis Abbot, when a message arrived from a railroad company offering the Bryans use of a private Pullman car for their return trip to Nebraska. "Mr. Bryan," Abbot said, "you should not accept this offer. You are the great commoner, the people's candidate, and it would not do to accept favors from the great railroad corporations." Bryan agreed with his friend, and the journalist helped popularize Bryan's title as "The Great Commoner."

Wherever the Democratic nominee went, crowds formed, and local officials convened great outdoor meetings. Bryan and his wife ventured to Salem, Illinois, then St. Louis and Kansas City, before heading back to Lincoln, Nebraska. Dark clouds and the threat of rain could not deter a huge crowd from welcoming home Lincoln's favorite son, the man whose name now echoed across the country, from newspaper headlines to private letters. The crowd roared its approval and escorted him to the capitol building, where he spoke to the adoring hometown crowd. "I desire to express tonight our grateful appreciation of all the kindness that you have shown us," Bryan proclaimed in his booming voice, "and to give you the assurance that if, by the suffrages of my countrymen, I am called to occupy, for a short space of time, the most honorable place in the gift of the people, I shall return to you. This shall be my home, and when earthly honors have passed away I shall mingle my ashes with the dust of our beloved State." Although a touching sentiment, this promise would not be fulfilled. Upon his death in 1925 he was buried in Arlington National Cemetery.

Bryan's trip west from Chicago—the cheering throngs, the speeches, the newspapermen hanging on his every word—must have made an impression on the candidate. It certainly did on his wife. "Our very house had altered its appearance," Mary recalled of their return to Lincoln. "Streamers of bunting festooned it from porch to eaves; small boys sat in rows along the roof; the crowd which filled the front yard overflowed into the house; flowers and smilax decorated the crowded rooms. It was a symbolic atmosphere. The public had invaded our lives." Yet it was an adoring public, a public that shared the Bryans' rural origins and small-town values.

Bryan knew he had already won over the men and women of America's prairies. The real battle would take place not among western farmers but among the bankers and industrialists of America's cities. This was why Bryan wanted to give his opening campaign speech in New York, "believing," he said, "that it would arouse the enthusiasm of our supporters to attack the enemy first in the stronghold of the gold sentiment."

In late July, Bryan came to another controversial decision, one that would haunt him the remainder of his life. Bryan, the "Boy Orator," author of the "Cross of Gold" speech, and one of America's greatest public speakers, decided he would read his Madison Square Garden speech from a prepared text. In doing so, he would be following closely in the footsteps of one of his heroes, Abraham Lincoln.

Just as the Civil War remained the great watershed by which late-nineteenth-century Americans measured the life of their nation, Abraham Lincoln remained the great American figure by which most Northerners measured their politicians and, indeed, their own lives.

"When an ordinary man dreamed of the future of his son," an historian wrote half a century ago, "he thought of Lincoln as embodying everything he wanted his own boy to be." Lincoln influenced both William Jennings Bryan and Theodore Roosevelt in profound ways. A civilian commissioner during the Civil War, Roosevelt's father returned home to tell stories of taking rides through wartime Washington, DC, with Abraham and Mary Todd Lincoln. Not surprisingly, as an aspiring Republican politician Theodore Roosevelt often sought to cast himself as a latter-day Lincoln.

For William Jennings Bryan, born in Illinois, growing up about one hundred miles due south of Springfield and eventually destined to make his career in a town named for the sixteenth president, Lincoln's legacy was everywhere. Like most young midwestern men, Bryan studied Lincoln and, after reading his biography, wrote, "He was ambitious and is the most humble statesman we have ever had. He had an eloquence which seemed born of inspiration. He spoke the truth and with it won the hearts of his hearers. . . . He is a good character study." Humility and inspired eloquence were the very characteristics that made Bryan a national figure, a persona possibly modeled on his understanding of his idol.

Lincoln's example may have played a part in Bryan's decision to go to New York and give a career-changing speech. In early 1860, Lincoln had been little known outside of Illinois, having served only one term as congressman and losing his 1858 bid for a seat in the Senate. The ambitious Lincoln had an eye on the Republican nomination for 1860, so when a telegram came inviting him to come east and speak in New York, he jumped at the chance. On the evening of February 27, 1860, Lincoln spoke to about 1,500 New Yorkers at Cooper Union. He reached out to Southerners with a moderate hand and concluded by urging that same moderation on fellow Republicans.

The speech was a resounding success that led to his nomination—and to the presidency.

Bryan's goals for his Madison Square Garden speech were similar to Lincoln's. Bryan hoped to quiet fears that he was a socialist or anarchist. As only a two-term congressman who had lost his own Senate bid in 1894, Bryan sought to present himself as a true national figure, and not just some rural populist. Perhaps most of all, the Garden speech would test whether, like Lincoln, Bryan's own appeal could "extend from the podium to the page." Bryan decided to eschew his customary extemporaneous delivery and read his speech from a page—after all, at Cooper Union Lincoln had read from a manuscript.

BY EARLY AUGUST obstacles to Bryan's visit to New York were mounting. He faced significant defections from the party, most recently former Democratic congressman William Bourke Cockran. Originally elected in 1886, Cockran was a longtime Tammany man and in 1884 had even crossed swords with a young Roosevelt. Early that year Roosevelt had chaired the City Investigating Committee of the New York State Assembly, charged with looking into corruption in the city departments run by Tammany appointees. Cockran served as counsel to Sheriff Alexander Davidson, who ran the Ludlow Street jail like his personal fiefdom. During Roosevelt's questioning of the sheriff, Cockran came to his client's defense with pointed remarks directed at Roosevelt. Two years later, during the 1886 mayoral campaign, Cockran, by then a top aide to the new Tammany boss Richard Croker, helped convince Abram Hewitt to run as the candidate representing a united Democratic Party. Hewitt, with Cockran's help, crushed Roosevelt at the polls.

As he toured Europe in the summer of 1896, Cockran had followed closely the news coming out of Chicago, as Bryan won his party's nomination and the Democrats adopted the silver platform. By the time of his return to America on August 2, Cockran had been mulling over the consequences of the nomination for more than three weeks but stayed silent on the subject except to various fellow travelers. Now he was ready to talk.

Stepping off the American liner *Paris*, Cockran had immediately been set on by a reporter for the New York *Sun*. In his interview Cockran condemned Bryan and the silver platform in the strongest language possible.

Q. What is your opinion of the present political situation?

A. I regard it as the gravest in the history of the country, exceeding in importance the crisis of 1860. The secession movement was but an attempt to divide this country between two Governments, each of them designed to protect property within the limits of its jurisdiction. The movement launched at Chicago is an attempt to paralyze industry by using all the powers of Government to take property from the hands of those who created it and place it in the hands of those who covet it. This is a question of morals as well as of politics. No political convention can issue a valid license to commit offenses against morality, and I decline to follow Mr. Bryan in a crusade against honesty and the rights of labor.

Q. Do you mean to say that you will actively oppose the Democratic Party, or abstain from active support of it?

A. In a contest for the existence of civilization no man can remain neutral. Whoever does not support the forces of order aids the forces of disorder. If I can do anything to thwart a movement the success of which I would regard as an irreparable calamity not only to the country but to civilized society everywhere, I shall certainly do it.

Q. What do you think of Tammany's action in indorsing the ticket?

A. I simply cannot understand it. . . .

Cockran would become one of the most powerful voices among Bryan's opponents. Less than a week after Bryan would give his Madison Square Garden speech, Cockran would rebut Bryan at another Garden rally that Roosevelt would admiringly call "a phenomenon." Clearly Bryan would have his work cut out for him, winning over skeptical Tammany and hostile New Yorkers.

NEWS OF THE MOST recent defection from the Democrats must have brought a smile to Mark Hanna's face. With only three months to go until the election, Hanna appeared on the verge of achieving his long-time goal of placing William McKinley in the White House. Hanna was so identified with McKinley that after the latter's June nomination, many pundits joked that it was really Hanna who had been named Republican candidate for president. Hanna was perhaps all of the things McKinley was not: brilliant, canny, and hyperaware of the dynamics of power. Cartoons often depicted a diminutive McKinley tied to, or in the pocket of, a giant-sized Hanna.

McKinley, on the other hand, had been rising steadily through the Republican ranks both in his native Ohio and on the national stage. He impressed people with his honesty, loyalty, and forthrightness. A Civil War veteran, McKinley had driven a wagon full of hot food and coffee into the thick of the fighting to bring relief to the troops at Antietam. Not only would this simple and courageous act result in a battlefield memorial commemorating the deed, but at the time it brought McKinley to the notice of his regimental commander, future president Rutherford B. Hayes. Serving with distinction throughout the war, McKinley left the army with the rank of brevet major, a title that would follow McKinley even into the presidency. Just as Roosevelt was often referred to as "Colonel," an acknowledgment of his service in the Spanish-American War, a visitor to President McKinley's office might announce, "I am here to see the Major."

After the war McKinley studied law and joined a practice in Canton, Ohio. He soon began campaigning for Republican candidates, including his old commander, Hayes. McKinley was elected to Congress for the first time in 1876 and secured himself a place on the Ways and Means Committee. From this position McKinley would become one of the leading advocates of the protective tariff, which, until the silver question superseded it, was the burning political question of the day.

Hanna and McKinley had known each other for many years, and their paths frequently crossed both in Ohio political circles and also as Ohio delegates to the Republican national conventions in 1884 and 1888. But it was at the 1888 convention that Hanna began systematically to champion McKinley's career. "For all these years I have been Major McKinley's personal friend and admirer," Hanna told a reporter. "Becoming convinced of the great and good qualities of his nature, of his devotion to principle and of his patriotic motives and feelings, and believing that I had some interest in helping to shape the affairs of my country, I contributed my best efforts to the organization which finally resulted in his nomination."

Hanna was born in Ohio in 1837 to a Virginia Quaker and a Vermont Presbyterian. "So Scotch and Irish, the staid, determined Quaker and the rigid blood of the Puritan crossed in the child," the *Tribune* observed after Hanna's arrival in New York in August 1896. "The result is somehow apparent in the quiet, sturdy insistence of the man who is today wielding a President-making power." Hanna worked as a clerk in his father's wholesale grocery and provision business, taking the firm over after his father's death in 1861. A few years later Hanna married Augusta Rhodes, daughter of an Ohio coal and iron tycoon, whose various interests Hanna reorganized as M. A. Hanna and Co. Having also inherited from his father a lake schooner used in the grocery business, Hanna began improving the shipbuilding side of the firm until he became the largest steel shipbuilder on the Great Lakes as head of the firm Globe Iron Works Company. By 1896 the Ohio millionaire had diversified into oil, banking, city railways, and a controlling interest in the *Cleveland Herald*.

With Hanna's backing, McKinley's star began to rise. Even with all of his own noble characteristics, McKinley certainly benefited from Hanna's support of American business interests. In 1889 Hanna had traveled to Washington to back McKinley in a failed bid to become Speaker of the House. Though this position would have meant much power over subsequent national legislation, the consolation prize that year of the Ways and Means Committee chairmanship served both men's interests quite well. As chairman of the committee McKinley introduced the bill that would become the 1890 McKinley Tariff.

This was only the beginning of McKinley's meteoric rise. Two years later McKinley became Ohio governor and, perhaps more importantly, permanent chairman of the national party convention, which was being held in Minneapolis that year. Although the Republican nominee, President Benjamin Harrison, lost to Grover Cleveland in 1892, McKinley emerged from the convention extremely popular and the party favorite for 1896.

Traditionally, potential presidential nominees did not attend the national conventions. Instead candidates for the nomination let their supporters speak for them in the convention halls and hotel corridors, while they stayed at home awaiting the news. Unlike Bryan, McKinley followed tradition and did not attend the convention in St. Louis that June. Hanna and other Ohio power brokers pressed the flesh and made deals in dimly lit rooms filled with blue cigar smoke. On June 18, the day of the convention vote, McKinley sat in his library in his Canton home, surrounded by a few associates and newspapermen. Out in the parlor a group of ladies attended to his wife. Upstairs in the hallway telegraph machines delivered the latest news from the convention hall, while Mrs. McKinley's cousin Sam Saxton relayed messages from the telephone. When the men in the library heard over the wire that the Ohio delegation had nominated McKinley, they anxiously awaited news of the crowd's reaction.

Fifteen minutes passed, then half an hour. Had the convention simply listened politely to McKinley's nomination before moving on to another candidate? Perhaps the telephone was not working. McKinley lifted the receiver himself to find that someone had left the convention hall phone's circuit open, and he heard for himself the ongoing pandemonium. A full half hour after his name had been put forward for the Republican candidacy for president, the hall still resounded with cheers. For these men of the late nineteenth century, including Civil War veterans, it was an eerie experience, listening to events unfold six hundred miles away. According to one of the men in the library with McKinley that day, it sounded "like a storm at sea with wild, fitful shrieks of wind." McKinley easily won the nomination, and Mark Hanna received the congratulations of the delegates.

Hanna's backing of McKinley had always represented his faith in the need for a sound American financial system based on the gold standard and a high tariff wall surrounding the United States. Now the

McKinley campaign would face a worthy opponent in Bryan and have the opportunity to defeat the Populist forces of chaos and anarchy that so many business interests felt a Bryan presidency would herald.

The late nineteenth century had already witnessed the power of anarchy: the Chicago Haymarket bombing that killed eight policemen in 1886; the Homestead steel strike of 1892, which left sixteen dead and steel magnate Henry Frick wounded by an assassin; and the Pullman strike of 1894, which had left thirty-four dead. For men like Mark Hanna, Andrew Carnegie, and J. P. Morgan, what lay behind the violence was not inequity in the workplace or frustration at the impoverishment of the worker. No, the forces of socialism, communism, and anarchism seemed to threaten the very Republic itself. A McKinley presidency would strike these forces a deathblow.

***

MONDAY, AUGUST 3, was not unusually hot for the time of year. This made Officer Wiebers's suffering all the more peculiar. Assigned to keep order during cases brought before the judge at Jefferson Market Court, Wiebers perspired all through the day, barely making it to the end of the proceedings. True, Wiebers was a large man, tall and fairly stout, and tended to suffer during warm days. But the temperature inside the court was not at all exceptionally high. Still, by the end of the day Wiebers was close to collapse and had to be helped out of the courtroom.

Wiebers's fellow court officers commented on his condition as they helped their nearly overcome comrade out of the chamber. Fetching some cold water, one of the other officers poured it over Wiebers's head in an effort to revive the prostrated policeman. Opening his uniform to make his breathing easier, Wiebers's fellow officers saw the cause of his suffering: He was wearing a heavy flannel shirt over an undershirt of homespun wool, nearly a quarter of an inch thick. The clothing was "suitable for an arctic campaign," one man noted.

Once Wiebers was revived, the other court officers teased him. "Did you think it was Christmas?" "Has your best girl given you the cold shoulder?" "Are you training to be a jockey? You only need to sweat off about 200 pounds."

Wiebers asked his partner, Mahoney, to send the other men away, and confided to his friend that all his summer underwear had been stolen from the clothesline in back of his home on West Twelfth Street. The thieves had even taken Wiebers's much-prized sets of silk underwear sent to him by his cousin, an officer in the German army. Not having the money to replace the underwear, Wiebers had decided to try to make it to his next paycheck at the end of the month wearing his woolen winter underwear.

The other officers offered him their advice on how to recover the underwear. The recommendations ranged from the use of bloodhounds to trapping the thief by setting out even more underwear. "And mind you, sew them to the line," Officer McGuckin advised. But they all stopped to listen as the most senior man present, Officer Carr, cleared his throat and prepared to speak. "I think," he said slowly and with great deliberation, "that there can be no doubt that some dishonest persons took those things."

Exasperated, Wiebers told the men, "I want the clothes, and if you fellows can't help me, shut up." With that he stood up and stormed out of the room. "It is a fact," the court reporter from the *Times* observed, "and a rather curious fact, that no one suggested reporting the matter to the police."

AFTER MORE THAN A year of trying to make the New York City police a serious crime-fighting organization, Theodore Roosevelt could not have been happy to read such a comical account of his men. Roosevelt had a good relationship with the newspapers, having befriended journalists like Jacob Riis and Lincoln Steffens. And early on, the press had given Roosevelt rave reviews as he made his midnight inspections around the city.

But now even the press had turned against Roosevelt and his police. The fight to close saloons on Sunday, the resulting Republican losses at the polls, and the shabby dispute with Parker on the police commission had soured the fourth estate on "the biggest man in New York," as one Chicago paper had called him. Roosevelt was dangerously close to leaving the New York police department a laughingstock.

Always aware of the power of the press and public opinion, Roosevelt had made a great effort to explain his actions and motivations. When at the beginning of his Sunday Excise crusade the New York *Sun* had questioned why Roosevelt would act against public sentiment, Roosevelt had replied with a statement that began, "I do not deal with public sentiment. I deal with the law." Roosevelt also pointed out that lax enforcement resulted in a system in which saloon keepers bribed policemen or hid behind political influence. For Roosevelt the problem was having a law "which is not strictly enforced, which certain people are allowed to violate with impunity for corrupt reasons, while other offenders who lack their political influence are mercilessly harassed. All our resources will be strained to prevent any such discrimination and to secure the equal punishment of all offenders."

Equal enforcement of the law, and equal treatment of all citizens by the government, was a hallmark of Roosevelt's thought. It underlay many of his beliefs about good government, the evils of the spoils system, the need for an American civil service based solely on merit, and police promotions based on meritorious service rather than political influence.

Years later in 1903, after becoming president, Roosevelt gave a speech at the New York State Fair in Syracuse that described what became known as the "Square Deal." "We must treat each man on his worth and merits as a man," Roosevelt told the crowd. "We must see that each is given a square deal, because he is entitled to no more and should receive no less. Finally we must keep ever in mind that a republic such as ours can exist only by virtue of the orderly liberty which comes through equal domination of the law over all men alike, and through its administration in such resolute and fearless fashion as shall teach all that no man is above it all and no man below it." "Orderly liberty which comes through equal domination of the law" might have been Roosevelt's motto for his time on the police commission and his crusade against Sunday liquor selling.

Despite such good intentions and confidence in his crusade, Roosevelt's actions had brought him only scorn. He now had little hope of career advancement in the city. Roosevelt had no choice but to make another trip on August 3 to visit one of the busiest men in New York, Mark Hanna. Roosevelt himself was only just back in the city after his weekend at Sagamore Hill. And Hanna's suite at the Waldorf was hardly in the neighborhood of Roosevelt's office on Mulberry Street in Lower Manhattan. Like many other Republicans and hopeful office seekers that day, Roosevelt made a special trip to pay tribute to the newest Republican kingmaker. While Roosevelt may not have liked money's influence in American politics, Roosevelt understood the politics of power and working within the political apparatus. If this meant being a supplicant to a man like Mark Hanna, then so be it. And by the summer of 1896, Roosevelt and Hanna may not have been too far part in their ambitions. If nothing else, Roosevelt and Hanna shared an intense desire to secure McKinley's election and Bryan's defeat.

BRYAN'S NOMINATION AND HIS triumphant Midwestern tour en route back to Nebraska had sent a chill through Republican ranks at the end of July. Before the Democrats' Chicago convention and the "Cross of Gold" speech, Republicans readied to wage war over the issue of the tariff. McKinley's nomination was meant to affirm Republican support of the national tariff, the single most important issue in recent elections. For most Republicans and their allies in American business, the tariff issue seemed to be even more important in 1896, the third year of a depression. Bryan's nomination had suddenly changed the rhetoric of the campaign. A fight over the gold standard was not the fight Hanna had been spoiling for, to say the least. With lame duck Democrat Grover Cleveland in the White House and his Democrats split by the silver issue, the Republican nomination had seemingly all but given the crown to McKinley. Mark Hanna even left for a summer vacation, certain that the real work would not begin until later that summer.

But Bryan's nomination, although not a complete surprise, had immediately shifted the very language of the national contest. McKinley was no gold Republican and had even supported the backing of the dollar with silver earlier in his career. Instead, he was solely the author of the McKinley Tariff, and this was his only campaign theme. Bryan's nomination now made silver, not the tariff, the burning issue of the campaign. McKinley was not Bryan's natural foil. Indeed the Republican Party would have been hard pressed to find a pure "gold Republican" to counter either a silver Democrat or a

Populist. In Bryan, McKinley faced both, and his candidacy now appeared, the *Nation* observed, as illogical "as a Methodist preacher would be in an election for Pope of Rome."

McKinley was no longer a sure thing. Whole swaths of the country that Republicans had counted on seemed in doubt. After Bryan's nomination, Republicans had to scramble to catch up. Hanna cut short his vacation and worked tirelessly to establish headquarters in Chicago and New York.

Now Hanna did his most important work of the campaign: raising money from the great New York financiers. The amount he raised was unprecedented. Rockefeller's Standard Oil and Morgan's banking firm each gave the Republicans a contribution of $250,000. This $500,000 was larger than the entire Democratic Party's campaign war chest for 1896. In the end corporate America would provide the bulk of the $3.5 million that Hanna would send out from the Republican National Committee, twice as much as the party raised for the 1892 election.

Money was not the only difference between the Bryan and McKinley campaigns. Bryan's Madison Square Garden speech scheduled for the following week would touch off an unprecedented speaking campaign by a presidential candidate. By election day the nominee would travel some 18,000 miles, giving six hundred speeches in twenty-seven states to an estimated 5 million people.

McKinley, himself no great orator, stayed at home. Clearly he could not match the younger Bryan in energy or speaking skill, and trying would only damage his dignity. Except for a week's vacation in August and three days given to nonpolitical speaking engagements scheduled before the nomination, from the day of his June nomination until the November election McKinley never left his home in Canton. Instead, the mountain came to McKinley.

McKinley's visitors to Canton reflected a cross section of every American commercial, working, ethnic, and religious group. Hungarian-Americans came from Cleveland. Western railroad men made the two-thousand-mile pilgrimage. Hardware men, commercial travelers, and farmers' associations crowded onto the McKinley front lawn. Laborers from Carnegie's furnaces in Pittsburgh donned their best Sunday suits to make the trip. Where Confederate veterans of the Civil War had stood one day, black Republicans stood the next. On some Saturdays the trains arrived from morning until night, bringing as many as 30,000 people to Canton. McKinley spoke to them all.

Despite the seeming spontaneity of the various groups' excursions to Canton, and the unaffected nature of McKinley's reception, in reality the front-porch campaign was rigorously planned. In addition to raising money and arranging speakers, Hanna and the Republican National Committee spent a great deal of time and effort arranging these visits to McKinley. The railroads that supported the McKinley campaign with thousands of dollars of contributions also subsidized the trips to Canton with fares so low it was "cheaper than staying at home," as one Cleveland paper noted.

Once the delegations stepped off the train at the Canton railroad station, a well-oiled reception machinery kicked in. Committees of greeters met the visitors, who were escorted to the McKinley home by uniformed squads of the mounted Canton troop. Bands played music as the parade passed through a town bedecked with American flags and red, white, and blue bunting. Townspeople cheered from the sidewalks. It was as if all of Canton had been transformed into some kind of political amusement park, a Republican Disneyland for 1896.

When the faithful finally reached their destination, the candidate came out of his house, mounted a chair, and addressed the crowd on his front lawn. Just as Hanna and other supporters had once been drawn to McKinley by his warmth and sincerity, now the mass of dusty and tired travelers forgot for a moment their weariness as they basked in the presence of the Republican presidential candidate. The addresses of the delegations and McKinley's response seemed extemporaneous and from the heart, but in fact, just as everything else, they had been well planned. Spokesmen for the various groups were required to send advance copies of their remarks to be approved and even edited by McKinley. In turn, McKinley's replies were carefully crafted, both to take account of the individual interests of the delegations and to speak to the larger nation beyond Canton. After all, newspapermen were now permanent fixtures around the McKinley home. A speech of welcome crafted specifically for, say, the St. Louis Methodists for McKinley, would be taken down and printed in hundreds of papers the following day.

As McKinley spoke from the porch, his elderly mother and his invalid wife often sat alongside. The front-porch campaign, then, had the added feature of framing McKinley not just as a politician but as a devoted family man. This sat particularly well with the women who visited Canton that summer and early fall. Although still without suffrage nationally, women had become a moral force in politics through groups like the Women's Christian Temperance Union and the General Federation of Women's Clubs. And the National American Woman Suffrage Association had had some success at the state level by the 1896 election: Wyoming entered the Union with women's suffrage in the state constitution in 1890, and Utah followed in 1896. The issue, however, would not find a prominent place in the 1896 campaign.

Camped around the McKinley front porch, the newspapermen kept their ears pricked for the magic words "silver" and "gold." By

August 3, though, they had been largely disappointed, as had many of the sound-money advocates around the country. When asked about the silver question, McKinley would quickly change the subject to the tariff. This made Hanna's New York fund-raising efforts more difficult, as the big financiers waited for McKinley to come out strongly in favor of the gold standard.

About a week before, when McKinley had made a rare trip off his front porch and out of Canton to address supporters in Pennsylvania, the candidate had made a passing reference to the issue. "Our currency today is good," McKinley stated. "All of it is good as gold, and it is the unfaltering determination of the Republican Party to so keep and maintain it forever." It was only a small mention of that magic word, but this, McKinley's first public use of the word "gold" after his nomination, reverberated throughout the country and cheered the sound-money advocates. According to the *Nation* McKinley had uttered the word "in a somewhat furtive way . . . hastening to take a good pull at the tariff to steady his nerves."

Yet a passing reference to gold was not enough. What people were really waiting for was McKinley's official letter of acceptance of the nomination. This carefully crafted political statement by presidential nominees would eventually evolve into the acceptance speech at the national conventions, with Franklin Roosevelt delivering the first acceptance speech in 1932. McKinley's letter would state the candidate's official position on the money issue.

They would have to wait awhile yet. On August 3 the papers reported that McKinley was still working on his letter and that it would not be delivered for perhaps another three or four weeks. Meanwhile, Republican planners looked to kick off the official campaign with a mass meeting in Ohio on August 15, three days after Bryan's speech at Madison Square Garden.

Even McKinley's hometown was not safe from Bryan's charismatic presence. It was expected that on his way to New York, Bryan would stop in Canton. The Democrats were making preparations for a grand reception at the railroad station to make a strong political statement of Bryan's support even on McKinley's home ground.

MEANWHILE, THE SILVER FORCES were finally staking out their territory in New York. William St. John, playing the role of treasurer for both the National Democratic and the National Silver Committees, opened his headquarters in the Bartholdi Hotel at Broadway and Twenty-Third Street on August 3.

St. John was a rare breed, a New Yorker and former banker who advocated bimetallism as the way for the number of dollars in circulation to keep pace with America's growing population. St. John had chaired the National Silver Party's convention in St. Louis at the end of July, and the delegates had consciously thrown in their lot with the Democrats by nominating Bryan and Sewall. Now occupying several large and luxurious rooms on the hotel's second floor, St. John and his assistants readied for Bryan's visit to New York.

Democrats across the country, however, continued to defect, and a third-party movement was growing, with sound-money Democrats expected in September to meet at an independent convention in Indianapolis. Many New York Democrats echoed William Bourke Cockran in questioning Tammany's hasty endorsement of Bryan. Former mayor Abram Hewitt, who defeated Roosevelt for the office in 1886, called Tammany's action "stupid, an extremely foolish thing." Former New York governor Roswell P. Flower also called the endorsement stupid and foolish. When a reporter pressed him, asking if he also thought it was premature, the ex-governor brusquely replied, "I think 'foolish' and 'stupid' about cover the case." Only weeks after his nomination, Bryan's campaign was in serious trouble. His trip to New York would make or break his chances for election.

***

ALTHOUGH NO ONE REALIZED it at the time, the heat wave began on Tuesday, August 4.

Heat waves are not like other disasters. Heat kills slowly, over days. It does not leave marks on the victim's body. Nor does it destroy buildings or leave any physical evidence of its destructive force. There is no single moment when a heat wave strikes, no specific time allowing survivors to recall the moment when it began.

Heat waves produce few dramatic photos or visual images like rubble and flames. Victims of heat can remain unaware that they are being slowly killed, suffocating alone in a closed, airless space. An assassin strikes quickly and flees, but heat lingers, remaining in the same room with its victim for days.

The city itself becomes an accomplice to heat's murderous effects. Anyone who has ever lived in a city during extreme heat knows that cities bake their inhabitants in ways unknown to rural areas. In later years this would become known as the "urban heat island effect."

In a 1967 article called "The Climate of Cities," William Lowry noted the several factors that combine to elevate temperatures in cities. The concrete, brick, and stone of the buildings and the asphalt of the city's streets can conduct heat three times faster than soil. Unlike the hills and trees of the countryside, urban walls, roofs, and streets act like a maze of reflectors, bouncing the heat back and forth between absorbing surfaces. Cities contain a variety of human-made heat sources, such as factories and furnaces. And ironically, the sanitary conditions provided by modern sewer systems can intensify a city's heat. By draining water away, the heat energy that would have been used to evaporate the standing water instead heats the air. Finally, and particularly true for the late nineteenth century, city air contains high concentrations of particulate matter, such as dirt, ash, and soot, that act together to stop the outflow of heat. Cities are perhaps the ultimate greenhouses.

During heat waves, humidity is one of heat's deadliest accomplices. When a person's blood is heated above 98.6 degrees Fahrenheit, a body can dissipate the heat in various ways, such as varying the rate of blood circulation, panting, and especially sweating. Sweating cools the body through evaporation, but high humidity retards evaporation, leaving the body unable to cool itself.

As body heat begins to rise, heat-related illnesses and disorders develop. A body's temperature can rise to 106 degrees in ten or fifteen minutes, but it only takes a rise above 103 degrees to cause hyperthermia, more commonly known as heat stroke. Red, hot, and dry skin, a rapid pulse, throbbing headache, dizziness, nausea, confusion, and unconsciousness are all warning signs. If the body's temperature is not immediately lowered, namely by placing the victim in a cool bath or shower, permanent disability or death can occur. Even survivors of heatstroke can suffer serious permanent damage, such as loss of independent function and organ failure.

The temperature a body feels when the effects of heat and humidity are combined would later be called the heat index. An 85-degree air temperature with 85 percent humidity will feel like 100 degrees. Small increases in either temperature or humidity will have dramatic effects on the heat index. Only a 5-degree temperature increase will produce a heat index of 118. A 90-degree air temperature with 90 percent humidity will feel like 122 degrees. A temperature of 94 degrees with 90 percent humidity feels like over 140 degrees. After only two days of exposure to temperatures like this, the body's defenses start to break down, and heat prostration strikes.

This is what began to occur on Tuesday, as several people in Manhattan and Brooklyn were admitted to hospitals. Although the month began fairly mild, with the official high temperature on Saturday the first of August reaching only 71, temperatures now rose to the high 80s, accompanied by 90 percent humidity.

Based on the official temperatures recorded by the United States Weather Bureau that day, the high temperature for New York City was 87 degrees. With 90 percent humidity this created a heat index of nearly 110 degrees. Yet as would be noted by New Yorkers virtually every day of the heat wave, the official temperatures for the city were recorded high above street level, where a thermometer was free of much of the urban heat island effect and able to catch at least some small amount of breeze. Down on the street, thermometers regularly recorded temperatures ten degrees higher than the official record indicated, while temperatures inside the brick tenements of the Lower East Side easily reached 120 degrees. This would be the general condition for the next ten days.

The elderly are at great risk during heat waves, and they were the first victims in this case. Sixty-five-year-old Annie Kelly fell victim to the heat on the street not far from her home on West Twentieth Street and was taken to New York Hospital. Fifty-nine-year-old Patrick Murray was overcome on the Upper East Side and was taken to Flower Hospital at Sixty-Third Street. Lersen Present, sixty-three, suffered heat stroke downtown on East Broadway.

In addition to the elderly, New York's many laborers risked serious injury by working and sweating all day in the sun. Even the healthiest could easily fall victim if undertaking strenuous labor during the heat wave. This was evidenced by an Italian worker named Rolis, who suffered heat stroke and was hospitalized. He was only twenty-two years old.

During the heat wave, heat prostrations became public knowledge when they occurred on the streets or were reported to the police. In addition, the New York coroner and the hospitals often provided information concerning victims of the heat. The extensive newspaper accounts of the heat wave and the lists of victims led previous writers to assert that perhaps 400 New Yorkers died during the heat wave, a number reached by adding up the total number of deaths as reported in the papers. Yet as the vast difference in number of deaths between the same periods in 1895 and 1896 indicates (see Appendix A), this total fails to account for about 1,000 extra deaths, including deaths that occurred in the days immediately *after* the heat wave.

In later years doctors and social scientists would go to great lengths to define exactly what constituted a "heat-related death." They concluded that indicators of heat stroke leading to death went beyond simple physiological symptoms, such as dehydration, body temperature, and organ failure. Instead, officials and medical experts would consider both physiological *and* environmental factors in a heat-related death. An elderly man found dead in his chair without a mark on his body may or may not have been a victim of heat. But if he was found in a room with a temperature of 110 degrees during a heat wave, it can be safely concluded that heat was a contributing factor to his death. And if a young man who worked all day stoking a furnace in the basement of a factory fell ill inside his stifling, airless tenement, in this case, too, heat must have been a contributing factor.

A modern observer of the 1896 heat wave can do the same thing. Even though New York doctors or coroners failed to note "heat" as a cause of death in perhaps 1,000 cases, it is only logical to assume that the ten-day heat wave contributed in some way to these deaths among the very old and very young, the poor and sick, and laborers who could simply not afford to stop working.

According to the death certificates filed in Manhattan on August 4, the first victim of the heat wave may have been fifteen-month-old Hyman Goldman. Hyman had arrived from Russia with his family only nine months before. For three weeks the baby had been suffering from what doctors frequently referred to in the nineteenth century as "cholera infantium"—a common diarrhea suffered by children during summer months that often proved fatal. Already weakened by this affliction, Hyman had little reserve strength when the heat settled on his family's tenement apartment at 55 Broome Street. According to the doctor the direct cause of his death was "Exhaustion."

Over the next ten days doctors in Manhattan alone would fill out over 2,200 death certificates—almost double the number during the same period in 1895—using various euphemisms for describing victims of the heat. Many infant deaths were listed as caused by "Summer diarrhea" or "Convulsions," while adults died from "Asthemia," "Exhaustion," "Thermic fever," "Heatstroke," "Sunstroke," and "Insolation." Little Irma O'Brien, only four months and eighteen days old, died later on August 4 from "Tubercular meningitis," while the doctor listed as the indirect cause of death "Heat."

Thursday, August 6, found the president of the Health Department, Charles Wilson, collecting statistics concerning the total death rate for New York in July, including the death rate from "diarrheal diseases." Wilson evidently liked what he saw, as he put his results in a letter to Mayor Strong highlighting the drop in the death rate as a result of better sanitary conditions in the city. In an accompanying table, Wilson placed the total deaths and death rate for July for the years 1892 to 1896, along with the deaths and death rate just from diarrheal diseases. From 1892 to 1896, total deaths in July had dropped from 5,463 and a death rate of 38.37 per 1,000 to 4,238 and a death rate of 26.29. Deaths from diarrheal disease during July had dropped from 1,635 in 1892 down to 973 in 1896—during an economic depression and even as the population of the city was booming. As such diseases were most common in children—that ubiquitous "cholera infantium" on summertime death certificates—Wilson's results illustrated how much better the children of the city were faring.

With the temperature climbing, Wilson's euphoria was sadly out of touch with the disaster about to befall the city. "The remarkable decrease in the death-rate for July and in the death-rate from diarrheal diseases for the same period indicate improved sanitary conditions in this city," Wilson proudly proclaimed. Wilson penned his remarks in a month that would witness hundreds of "excess" infant deaths from just the sort of diseases against which the Health Department president claimed such progress. Wilson would not send such a letter to the mayor again.

**

IN LINCOLN, far from the heat, Bryan took a break from receiving callers at his home on Tuesday to work on his Madison Square Garden acceptance speech.

Already expectations ran high. The *Chicago Tribune* expected the speech to be, according to its headline, "the Oratorical Effort of His Life." With Bryan and his wife due to board the train to New York in only three days, time was running short. The train was scheduled to stop in every town along the route, with a longer overnight stop in Chicago the coming weekend. Once aboard the train, he would have little time for thoughtful reflection.

While his acceptance of the Democratic nomination in New York would mark the official beginning of the campaign, in fact the minute his foot left the Lincoln train station platform, the candidate would be in full campaign mode, giving a dozen speeches a day that would then speed across the telegraph wires and appear in newspapers the next morning. And with a heat wave already settling over the Plains and Midwest, causing deaths from St. Louis to Chicago, the trip east was destined to be hot, dusty, and exhausting. It was best to sit quietly in the cool of his home and prepare for the tough journey ahead—and the tougher audience awaiting him in New York.

Although barely a town compared to Manhattan in 1896, Lincoln was one of the fastest-growing cities west of the Mississippi. Home to both the state capital and the state university, it was an important railroad center and metropolitan hub of an agricultural hinterland. More than just a sleepy prairie town with farmers in dusty overalls taking their produce to market, Lincoln had an industrial and commercial flavor as well, provided by banks, newspapers, factories, and paper mills. Bryan's own occupation reflected this, although his law practice of Talbot and Bryan did not keep pace with the increasingly affluent city. In fact Bryan's legal career seemed merely a platform from which to launch his political career.

In preparation for running for office, Bryan had joined every community and fraternal organization in Lincoln, from the Odd Fellows to the Masons, and from the bar association to the chamber of commerce. He was an Elk and a Moose, a Sunday School teacher at the Presbyterian Church, and a lecturer on moral themes at the YMCA. Through these organizations Bryan became a well-known figure among Lincoln's political and economic elite, and in them he found like-minded compatriots in what would become his crusade against the moneyed interests of the East. Such groups reinforced Bryan's ideals of fairness, universal brotherhood, and devotion to the common people.

It was perhaps through these organizations, and the Round Table discussion club founded by Bryan, that the young lawyer with political aspirations began to champion "free silver." With an eye to winning the Democratic nomination for Congress in 1890, Bryan railed against the McKinley Tariff and echoed farmers' concerns against falling land and crop prices. Faced with fixed payments for mortgages and railroad rates, the Nebraskan farmer had seen the price of his corn drop from 63 cents a bushel in 1881 to 26 cents in 1890. Wheat fell from $1.19 in 1881 to 49 cents. And the farmer's land, on which he owed debt based on the land's value at the time of purchase, had reverted to pre-1870 prices. In some cases land had fallen from as much as $30 an acre during a recent land boom to less than $5 an acre.

Economic cycles, bad weather, and the changing character of America from an agrarian to an industrial and urban country all held little interest for Bryan. When looking for someone to blame for the plight of his Nebraska constituents, the foe always resided in the big eastern cities. This was a fine strategy for a local or state politician from west of the Mississippi. Yet it seemed doomed to failure as a national campaign theme in the United States of 1896.

Bryan's ideas appeared out of step with his contemporaries. America was now a country that lauded its industrial, not agricultural, output as a measuring stick against the great European powers. Entire states now defined themselves by their manufacturing industries, from Massachusetts paper mills to New Jersey chemicals and Pennsylvania steel. America's largest city—the nation's commercial capital—had provided the margin of victory in the last several presidential contests. And that city now prepared to defeat Bryan on two fronts: Both hostile gold Democrats and the heat threatened to make New York a living hell.

Many New York Democrats, rather than preparing for their nominee's visit, prepared instead for the Sound-Money Democratic Convention due to meet in Indianapolis in September. They worked, as one member of the Sound-Money Democrats' executive committee told the papers on August 4, "to hold the party true to its traditions and defeat the un-Democratic ticket nominated in Chicago upon a platform that is anything but Democratic."

IF THE SOUND-MONEY Democrats represented a small but threatening front in the fight against Bryan, a far more serious threat on August 4 came from a single Republican. Mark Hanna was the political dynamo that would defeat Bryan not by matching the Great Commoner's charisma or oratory, but by building a fund-raising and campaigning apparatus the likes of which the country had never seen. In Canton McKinley continued to receive visitors, including Reuben Herman of Baltimore, who told the Major about the revolt of Sound-Money Democrats in Maryland. Perhaps more importantly, McKinley received some of the advance sheets of the "campaign text book," the book that would serve as the manual for all Republican writers and speakers for the next two and a half months until the November election. With profiles on the various candidates, the manual also contained sections on platform issues such as the gold standard, the tariff, foreign policy, taxation, labor, and the civil service. At four hundred pages, the manual reflected the sophisticated campaigning technique of "staying on message," begun only eight years before, in the 1888 election. The textbook clearly spelled out for potential candidates the party's position on all topics. A stump speaker like Roosevelt may have had no trouble discussing civil service or foreign policy, but he would need to take a close look at the money supply section before going forth to speak for McKinley.

On August 4 Hanna met with representatives of the city's black Republicans who impressed on the Republican campaign chief the strength of their numbers in the city. According to the *Times*, "Reference was made to other times when they had been promised large rewards for their support, which they claimed had not been forthcoming after election. They wanted a business understanding at the outset."

Addressing the needs of black Republicans was a standard promise among city politicians, and even a young Roosevelt had campaigned for the black Republican vote in his failed bid for mayor in 1886. Disenfranchised in the South after Reconstruction ended in 1877, the 60,000 blacks in New York in 1896 usually voted Republican, the party of Lincoln. What the black men demanded from Hanna that day was a headquarters "where all the colored men of the city might rally" and money to maintain the headquarters. Hanna appeared to favor the suggestion; in the age-old move of deft politicians, he established a committee for further study.

If black Republicans represented the least powerful branch of the party in New York City in 1896, perhaps the Union League Club represented the most powerful. Founded in 1863 to show support for the Union cause in a city with sharply divided loyalties, after the war the club turned its attention to civic projects, such as founding the Metropolitan Museum of Art and cleaning up New York city government. Theodore Roosevelt Sr. had been a prominent founding member of the club that had later supported Theodore Roosevelt Jr. for mayor in 1886. On August 4, Hanna had dinner at the club and received the greetings of men who were top contributors to the Republican Party. Yet by simply entering the club's building, Hanna walked a fine line between the forces of political reform it represented and the state Republican machine run by "boss" Thomas Platt. It was a line Roosevelt himself would walk during much of his political career in New York, attempting to remain as independent as possible while necessarily dependent on the support of the Republican machine run by Platt.

Hanna had already been approached by anti-Platt men over the possibility of running the campaign through a county committee rather than a state committee controlled by Platt. Indeed they had approached Roosevelt over the very same issue earlier in the year, with *New York Tribune* journalist John E. Milholland and New York merchant Cornelius Bliss asking the police commissioner for his support. In spite of his fondness for reform, Roosevelt doubtlessly made the right choice in staying loyal to the Republican machine. At the club that night, Hanna himself made it clear to Milholland and Bliss that he would give them "no show in the management of the campaign in any other capacity than as good Republicans. As a faction they will not be recognized, for, as the case was put here by one of Mr. Hanna's friends, 'He will use the regulars for his fighting, and will not trust to the militia.'" With his future uncertain and desiring a new post in Washington, Roosevelt made sure he was one of Hanna's "regulars."

Hanna also struck a blow against Platt concerning the handling of the millions of dollars in campaign money. He had maintained Cornelius Bliss as Republican National Committee treasurer, a position Bliss had held since 1892. The millions of dollars that Hanna would raise for the 1896 campaign, then, would flow through Bliss's hands. Opposing Platt and the machine's dominance of any state campaign that fall, Bliss was able to take a measure of revenge through his position as committee treasurer. Hanna and Bliss decided to hand over to the Republican state campaign only a very small amount of the national committee's funds, as most Republicans remained convinced that the main fight with Bryan would be in the West. In other words, Platt's machine that fall would not be fueled by any McKinley campaign funds.

McKinley was not the man Platt wanted running for president. In 1895 at the Republican state convention, Platt had helped engineer a unanimous endorsement of New York governor Levi Morton for the Republican presidential nomination. Morton was known as a sound-money advocate even more than the tariff-championing McKinley, so his chances the following year seemed good. Even Roosevelt had written to Lodge the previous June saying, "This State shows very strong symptoms of going in good earnest for Morton," and noting he had heard "there is an immense amount of talk about Morton in the West."

Nevertheless, Morton was a creature of Platt, and as the Republican National Convention drew near in 1896, a revolt against Platt's coronation of Morton began to grow. At Platt's urging, Morton had signed the controversial Raines Liquor Bill and the Greater New York Consolidation Act, both of which were seen as conferring more power on the state political machine run by Boss Platt. When Morton then publicly expressed his opposition to the creation of a Greater New York, Platt was forced to reassert his control over his man in Albany. The chastised governor suddenly had a change of heart, and such open subservience to the Republican boss caused his support in New York to dwindle.

With the governor's image tarnished by his association with the Republican machine, anti-Platt men organized clubs to promote William McKinley's candidacy as an alternative to Morton. With only three months until the Republican convention, Platt tried to maintain control over choosing the state's delegates in an attempt to counter the enthusiasm for McKinley and prove to the country that New York firmly supported Morton. Platt called a snap convention to meet in New York City, but his scheme backfired. Someone introduced a resolution supporting McKinley, and amid the frantic cheering a McKinley banner was unfurled from the top gallery, partially covering Morton's banner. Platt's men were unable either to take down the McKinley banner or to stop the wild demonstration in favor of McKinley. Although the resolution supporting the Major was defeated, it was a severe blow to the governor's candidacy and heartened McKinley supporters across the nation.

The national convention itself held even more embarrassments for Platt. Six contested McKinley delegates from New York City were admitted against Platt's wishes. Platt had claimed that sixty-eight of the seventy-two New York delegates were for Morton, but actually seventeen of those seventy-two backed McKinley on the first ballot. Aside from the remaining fifty-five New York votes, Morton received only three other votes, one from Alabama and two from Florida. Although Platt tried to save face and have Morton named as vice presidential nominee, McKinley's overwhelming nomination on the first ballot gave the boss no leverage. In the vote for the vice presidential nominee, Morton received only one vote—and that single vote came from Maine, not even his home state. Platt returned from the St. Louis convention humiliated and largely shut out of the great national campaign about to take place.

***

A FTER THE VIOLENCE AMONG the striking tailors on Sunday, August 2, Theodore Roosevelt toured the precinct houses of the area. Newspapers singled out his Sunday saloon-closing crusade as the reason for the violence. Had the police not been preoccupied rousting Sunday drinkers, a larger police presence among New York's laboring class might have kept the peace. Roosevelt, however, saw the Sunday closing law as in labor's best interest.

Years before, Roosevelt had urged labor to make "war on the saloons that yearly swallow so incredibly large a proportion" of workers' wages. Yet New York labor largely resented Roosevelt's crusade against the saloons. The previous summer the *Commercial Advertiser* had noted that at a meeting of the Central Labor Union, the attitude was, "The workingman wants his beer on Sunday, and what are we here for if not to benefit the workingman?" The American Federation of Labor may have believed that if saloons were "not permitted to adjoin the mansions of the wealthy neither shall they be permitted to intrude upon the wage earners' precincts." But trade unionists in New York did not agree and focused much of their resentment on Roosevelt personally. Labor leaders noted that while there had been over 8,000 arrests annually for excise violations under Roosevelt, there were only 104 arrests for violations of the factory law in 1895 and only 21 arrests for violation of the law in 1896. Roosevelt might say he was acting in labor's best interest, but the slight enforcement of a law prohibiting minors from working more than *sixty* hours a week, and stopping children under *thirteen* from working in factories, seemed to show otherwise.

Now, on Tuesday, Commissioner Roosevelt tried to take control of the situation on the Lower East Side, issuing orders to precinct captains on handling the strikers. He directed the captains to order their men "not to use harsh measures with the strikers unless actual violence was done and above all not to use firearms."

Roosevelt had a certain sympathy for the strikers, particularly because of the great poverty and historically bad working conditions of the tailors. Roosevelt frequently noted that he supported the workers' right to organize but expected the law to be upheld. This included dealing firmly with any violence among the strikers. As police commissioner Roosevelt had witnessed strikes among New York metal workers, bookbinders, cab drivers, and street cleaners. He was very sensitive to the perception among New York's political and business leaders that one of Roosevelt's main tasks as police commissioner was to prevent riots among strikers. On almost every occasion afforded to him, whether speaking to the public or directly to the police, Roosevelt underscored his determination to see rioters "put down quick" and "keep in order the turbulent portion of the population." Addressing newly promoted police captains at police headquarters that July, Roosevelt urged the police to do their duty "like soldiers on the field of battle," since "sooner or later in this city there will be turmoil and riot."

This same day 2,000 vestmakers joined the tailors' strike, complaining that they worked fourteen hours a day for a weekly wage sometimes as low as $5. Now they demanded a fifty-nine-hour workweek—about ten hours a day not including Sunday—and a slight increase in their wages.

While they certainly deserved these modest improvements to their working conditions, the vestmakers' timing was terrible. Newly unemployed men and women numbering 2,000 represented perhaps

10,000 more residents of the Lower East Side without any means of support. Already a marginal population living and working in horrible conditions, and vulnerable to any disaster or disease, the vestmakers made the decision to begin their strike on a day when the official temperature hit 87 degrees—the lowest high temperature New Yorkers would see for another ten days.

II.
SLAUGHTER ALLEY

A FEW MINUTES before four o'clock on the morning of Wednesday, August 5, Sergeant White of the Classon Avenue police station in Brooklyn sat lightly dozing on his watch. A slight young woman appeared suddenly before him, dressed in white, and wearing a straw hat. "I've chopped my sister's head off with an axe," the apparition announced calmly, although her dress remained unstained by blood. *I'm dreaming*, White thought, willing himself to wake up, but he was not asleep.

Looking at the petite woman dressed in white, and remembering the heat of the previous day, White assumed he must be dealing with someone afflicted by the heat. Even at that early hour the temperature remained in the high 70s.

Still, he dutifully dispatched an officer to the woman's home, a tenement basement, the kind of dwelling occupied by the very poorest of New Yorkers. There the officer found Kate Larkin, a thirty-nine-year-old widow, unconscious and her head a mess of blood. The woman in white, her sister Alice Larkin, had struck her about the head with an axe seven times, breaking her nose, fracturing her skull in two places, and lacerating her scalp. According to doctors, her condition was grave.

Neighbors commented that while they liked Kate, they had never cared for Alice, whom they said "was of a peculiar disposition." When asked why she had apparently tried to kill her sister with an axe, Alice replied, "Sister had not been treating me well."

IN THE LATE nineteenth century, such stories were all too common. The very word "tenement" connoted to New Yorkers not just extreme poverty and disease but the worst and most senseless violence. Jacob Riis's account of "The Man with the Knife" describes "a poor, and hungry, and ragged man" who from hopelessness and desperation sprang into a busy street one day and slashed about him, "blindly seeking to kill."

Contemporary accounts of life in the tenements are marked by brutality: from domestic violence fueled by alcohol to the criminal violence of street gangs. The most famous case of domestic violence in New York was the case of little Mary Ellen, whose story led to the creation of the Society for the Prevention of Cruelty to Children (SPCC)—nearly a decade after the establishment of the American Society for the Prevention of Cruelty to Animals (ASPCA).

The Mary Ellen case was the first case of child abuse to reach a New York City courtroom, and during the month of April 1874, New York newspapers featured lurid details of Mary Ellen's abuse at the hands of her "mama," Mary Connolly. Having been orphaned as an infant, Mary Ellen was "indentured" to the Connollys by the

Commission of Charities and Correction, a crude form of early foster care. But Mary Connolly always suspected that the child was one of her husband's illegitimate children, and she beat Mary Ellen daily with a two-and-a-half-foot leather "cow-hide" normally used in the city for driving horses.

By 1896 the offices of the SPCC housed hundreds of records of child abuse in the tenements. In 1896 reformer Helen Campbell wrote in her exposé *Darkness and Daylight* of the "screams resound-[ing] through a tenement-house" as children were beaten. She documented just a few of the cases for her readers. Seven-year-old Antonia was found with her hair "matted with blood, and her face, arms, and body were covered with wounds around which the blood had dried and remained." Ten-year-old Patrick Lacey nearly lost an eye to beatings from his drunken father, and six-year-old Jennie Lewis was found by a police officer on her knees scrubbing her tenement apartment's floor: "Her face and body were much discolored and covered with bruises, and her emaciated arms were patched with red spots from pinches."

Criminality extended beyond the family and into all dimensions of life. The journalist Colonel Thomas Knox documented in detail street life among the poor of New York: from petty thievery among even the youngest children to gangs of con men, bank robbers, and murderers.

Like many observers of late-nineteenth-century New York, Knox blamed a combination of poverty, ignorant and brutish immigrants, and the evils of liquor. He also placed great blame on the nature of tenements themselves. "Whoever follows a case of distress to its abiding-place," Knox wrote, "finds it in part of one room of a tenement-house, and that one room duplicated in wretchedness by range after range of rooms from the oozy cellar to the leaky garret, and that house duplicated by streetsful of other houses, till benevolence stands aghast at misery miles in area and six stories deep." Knox referred to the individual born into poverty in New York's crowded and unhealthy housing as "the low tenement victim."

In Manhattan some wards on the Lower East Side were packed with 250,000 to 300,000 people per square mile. This was shockingly dense, unmatched even in London. By 1900, 1.6 million people would occupy 42,700 tenements in Manhattan alone, averaging 33.5 persons per tenement. By 1916, the Lower East Side would boast about 8,400 tenements occupied by over half a million people, for an average of 60 people per tenement.

The tenement was the breeding ground of crime. Knox wrote, "Ignorant, weary and complaining wives, cross and hungry husbands, wild and ungoverned children, are continually at war with each other. The young criminal is the product almost exclusively of these training-schools of vice and crime in the worst tenement-house districts." Against much of the common wisdom of the day, Knox asserted that necessity, more than any other cause, drove people to crime. "If one suffers from cold and hunger, and can neither buy nor beg food, fuel, and clothing, he must perforce steal it, for necessity is a master of human action."

Want, hunger, and the threat of violence were all constants for those who lived in a tenement. In such circumstances stealing food or coal became not only understandable but even a laudable means of scraping by. "Petty thievery by boys and girls who are not taught to discriminate between right and wrong, who are, in fact, led to believe it a virtue to steal in order to provide themselves and parents with comforts impossible to obtain otherwise, is a matter of course among the poorest classes."

Tenements not only bred and fostered crime, they were the very headquarters and clubhouses of New York's criminal element. For contemporary observers among New York's "better" classes, the term "den of thieves" might have been designed for the tenement house. The dark, twisting passages and numberless small rooms led many writers to describe tenements as warrens, lairs, or rookeries. These references to the feral, animalistic character of the tenements' inhabitants reflected the fears and prejudices of the middle and upper classes.

For Americans with Victorian sentiments, tales of families with young girls letting the second bedroom to strange men, or of several members of a single family sharing the same bed, fed the impression that tenements were dens of sin and wickedness. The tenements themselves were often used as brothels as well as safe havens for criminals of all sorts. "The various 'gangs' that have infested the city and given the police force no end of trouble for many years," Knox wrote, "are found in the densely populated districts. The tenement-houses afford them excellent hiding-places, and from them the gangs are recruited when a police raid has temporarily decreased their ranks and sent many of them to penal institutions."

In fact during Roosevelt's reign as police commissioner several of these gangs had been arrested while working in or preying on the tenements. During the summer of 1895 a ring of counterfeiters that for eight years had been putting out fake dollar coins was finally caught. Seven men and one woman, all members of the Horse Market Gang, were arrested working out of a tenement that acted as a counterfeiting factory, complete with molds, ladles, chemicals, plating apparatus, copper, tin, antimony, and about two hundred phony dollars. Police and Secret Service agents estimated that the gang was responsible for putting out four hundred counterfeit dollars per week. Another gang had been caught after terrorizing New York with a string of fires set in tenements to bilk insurance companies. In August 1896, several members of the gang were still on trial for murder, after one of the fires they set at a tenement on Suffolk Street killed a four-year-old girl.

With the central airshaft in many tenements allowing even the smallest fire to spread quickly between floors, a fire intended to destroy only a business or personal belongings could very easily consume an entire building and its inhabitants. On that day, August 5, the seventy residents of a tenement on Fifty-Sixth Street were considering moving out of their building because the night before, the *second* fire in a week had been set by an unknown person, who had soaked the wood with kerosene. Attempts to flee via the fire escape had been hindered by the boxes and barrels stored there. "My youngest child is only six weeks old," Mrs. John Lyons told a reporter, "but she has already passed through two fires. There are few infants with such a record." The arsonist was never caught.

Most tenements were little more than two-room flats with a kitchen and a single bedroom. Few people could really have been said to live "in" their tenement. Crowded, noisy, and filled with the stench of garbage, cooking, and stopped-up drains, most residents sought refuge on their fire escapes, front steps, or the roof—the "tar beach." Tenements also housed various kinds of industry, with people working in their rooms sewing clothes, taking in washing, or rolling cigars, adding to the noise, crowding, smell, and generally unsanitary and dangerous conditions. Wash lines hung between the buildings, with anything white soon turned gray by the ever-present soot, ash, and dust in the air. These lines also carried messages and small bundles between buildings. With the constant noise and putrid smell of the tenements, many residents simply kept their windows closed, some even going so far as to nail them shut, depriving them of any hope of a whiff of "fresh" air.

The East River was an important source of relief and diversion to children on hot summer days. Every street on the Lower East Side ended at a pier all the way up to the East Forties. Yet as one of the busiest waterways in the United States, drowning was common, as was waterborne disease. Pathogenic microorganisms found easy prey among the poorly nourished tenement children. During summer heat waves the resultant vomiting and diarrhea could prove fatal; "summer complaint" was often listed as cause of death among children.

The river was a nuisance for most New Yorkers. It refused to stay within its banks and frequently seeped into the basements of the poorest nearby tenements. Residents told stories of floating furniture and invading armies of rats at high tide. Even those lucky enough to live on higher floors—although their risk from fires was greater— were still forced to live with the constant smell of decaying fish.

With the tenements nearly uninhabitable, especially during a heat wave, when the temperature inside their apartments rose to 120 degrees, the entire population of the tenement districts crowded into the streets outside. With tens of thousands of horses plying the streets, manure and urine filled the gutters. The few garbage cans overflowed. For those not from the tenement district, the foul stench could be overpowering. New York streets during the summers were filled with hundreds of thousands of people, some peddling their wares, some selling fruit, some selling old scraps of clothes (the "rag pickers"), some gossiping, and some just hoping to catch the faintest breeze in the brick and asphalt valleys of the

Lower East Side. So many people filled the streets in front of the tenements that it was hard to imagine that all of them could fit back inside at night.

In 1890 Jacob Riis had described life in the tenements during New York summers:

> With the first hot night in June police dispatches, that record the killing of men and women by rolling off roofs and window-sills while asleep, announce that the time of greatest suffering among the poor is at hand. It is in hot weather, when life indoors is well-nigh unbearable with cooking, sleeping, and working, all crowded into the small rooms together, that the tenement expands, reckless of all restraint. Then a strange and picturesque life moves upon the flat roofs. In the day and early evening mothers air their babies there, the boys fly their kites from the house-tops, undismayed by police regulations, and the young men and girls court and pass the growler. In the stifling July nights, when the big barracks are like fiery furnaces, their very walls giving out absorbed heat, men and women lie in restless, sweltering rows, panting for air and sleep. Then every truck in the street, every crowded fire-escape, becomes a bedroom, infinitely preferable to any the house affords.

Riis took note of the horrible toll the heat took on the youngest residents of the slums. "Life in the tenements in July and August spells death to an army of little ones." While black streamers marked the deaths of adults, white ribbons marked the deaths of children. "When the white badge of mourning flutters from every second door, sleepless mothers walk the streets in the gray of the early dawn, trying to stir a cooling breeze to fan the brow of the sick baby. There is no sadder sight than this patient devotion striving against fearfully hopeless odds."

LONG BEFORE THEODORE ROOSEVELT was even born, Roosevelt Street in Lower Manhattan served as one of the most important arteries of downtown New York. Dating back to the days of New Amsterdam and named for one of his ancestors, Roosevelt Street anchored the Manhattan end of the Brooklyn Bridge. Off Roosevelt Street could be found some of the worst tenements that existed in 1896. To get to the rear tenements, the most thoroughly lightless, airless apartments inhabited by the very poorest New Yorkers, one had to turn off Roosevelt and walk down the perpetually dark and infamous "Slaughter Alley." The origin of the name was disputed, deriving either from the murders committed there, or, as Helen Campbell wrote, from "the slaughter of the innocents—the babies, who die here in summer like rats in a hole."

Accompanying a doctor, Campbell explored one of the rear tenements on Slaughter Alley off Roosevelt Street. She described entering the front room "of tolerable size, but intolerable dirt, where four little children sat on the floor eating bread and molasses." With the doctor she then entered a dark inner bedroom, which had a "heavy, oppressive smell . . . a fog of human exhalations."

The doctor had come to see a woman in the last stages of consumption—tuberculosis—by 1896 the most common disease among New York's poor. They found her propped up in bed to make breathing easier, "a deep red spot on each cheek, and her frame the merest skeleton." Back in the larger front room Campbell noted an old mattress in the corner serving as the bed for the four children, a few chairs, and "a closet, whose open door showed some broken crockery and one or two cooking utensils."

"Smells, filth, degradation, and misery," Campbell recounted, "old and young crowded together; evil, coarse, and suffering faces; tattered, faded, old clothes; dirty shops; drinking saloons right and left—these things are scarcely lacking in any quarter, and are plentiful in many."

For progressives, reformers, and mission workers like Campbell and Riis, the lack of running water in people's homes was a constant concern. While Theodore Roosevelt's boyhood home in Gramercy Park could boast piped-in water as early as the 1850s, even by 1896 most New Yorkers would have still viewed this as almost unimaginable luxury. Alleyway "hydrants" were the source of water for most tenements, requiring tenants to carry fresh water up stairs and dirty water back down—if they didn't throw it onto the street from an open window. A recent law had mandated interior sinks in hallways for newer tenements, but even these were usually filthy, rarely cleaned, and stopped-up.

Without reliable water sources, keeping clean was a difficult ordeal. The Tenement House Committee of 1894 had found that of the over quarter million tenement occupants whose living conditions were examined by its staff, only 306 had access to bathtubs in their homes. Unlike many other American and European cities, New York maintained no public bathhouses. Its citizens relied instead on free "floating baths," large wooden frames placed in the rivers to form pools. This was only an option during the summer, and even then was far from convenient for most of the working poor, requiring a walk of as much as a mile to the river in some cases. Still, the floating baths afforded some relief during the heat wave.

For those who could not make the trip to a floating bath, or had no fire escape on which to sit during the heat wave, the tenement roof offered the only respite from the suffocating heat. "One may see on any summer night many a roof crowded with restless and uneasy tenants seeking relief from the sickening heat of their airless quarters," Campbell noted. "If one climbs the stairs of any of these wretched tenement-houses on a warm summer night, the whole population seems to have sought the roof, and lies upon it in every uncomfortable attitude—men, women, and children huddled together, and all alike moaning in troubled sleep."

This was not just a matter of seeking comfort. With the extreme heat and poor air circulation inside their apartments, and with thousands already suffering from lung problems like bronchitis and tuberculosis, finding even a small space on a roof on which to spend the night could mean the difference between life and death. Airshafts were often piled high with garbage, and opening a window admitted only air rank with the smells of cooking.

Down at street level, many tenement dwellers tried to sleep on their doorsteps, on a garbage bin, in an empty cart, or even in an out-of-the-way spot on the street or in an alley. Yet the searing asphalt that continued to radiate heat throughout the night and baked the steaming garbage and horse excrement made these poor choices as well. Throughout most of the heat wave the city maintained its ban on sleeping in parks, although few parks even existed below Canal Street. The rooftops, as Campbell observed firsthand, offered "the only refuge from the heat, and the tenant who begins sleep on the doorstep is tolerably certain to end the night on the roof."

***

TENEMENTS WERE A BY-PRODUCT of New York's rapid growth, first appearing in 1833. As the population of New York doubled between 1845 and 1860, the mostly Irish immigrants sought cheap and immediate housing. Despite the cholera epidemics of the 1830s and 1840s that ravaged the occupants of the tenement districts, an

1857 report by the New York State Legislature called the early tenement a "blessing" as it afforded a cheap solution to New York's chronic need for housing for new immigrants.

But things soon changed. Owners of large houses downtown quickly understood the profit to be made partitioning their large rooms into apartments for multiple families, "without regard to light or ventilation, the rate of rent being lower in proportion to space or height from the street." These new tenements, the legislature's report continued, "soon became filled from cellar to garret with a class of tenantry living from hand to mouth, loose in morals, improvident of habits, degraded, and squalid as beggary itself."

With so many people living in buildings originally built for a single family, owners did not expect their property to last very long. To compensate, they fixed the rents high enough to cover the damage. What ensued was a cycle of disrepair and tenant slovenliness, with each condition reinforcing the other. Owners pocketed healthy profits without directing money back into their property, while dissatisfied tenants, already living amid dilapidation, did little to preserve or improve the condition of their homes. Later, as tenement horrors came to light, owners blamed the tenants themselves for the poor state of repair. "Neatness, order, cleanliness, were never dreamed of in connection with the tenant-house system," the legislature's report claimed, "while reckless slovenliness, discontent, privation, and ignorance were left to work out their invariable results."

The city faced a vast and growing web of tenements "containing, but sheltering not, the miserable hordes that crowded beneath mouldering, water-rotted roofs or burrowed among the rats of clammy cellars." Tenements were a profitable business. And as immigrants continued to arrive, back gardens continued to be dug up, and owners pioneered the concept of the rear tenement, whose apartments would be completely cut off from the street, from air, and from light. Faced with a vast increase of these breeding grounds of both crime and disease, official New York was forced into action.

The various laws enacted between 1867 and 1895 reflected growing concerns in cities about health, sanitation, disease, morals, fire, and crime. Yet they also illustrated the slapdash manner in which tenement reform was enacted. Airshafts were mandated, but not their size. Tenement laws reflected the concerns of the day, such as the 1895 prohibition against boiling fat in tenement cellars, a source of many fires. Loopholes were common. Fire escapes were required only if there were not some other means of egress provided. Thus a rickety wooden ladder might fulfill the letter of the law. A window to the outside normally required for hallways might be overlooked if there were some other means of affording light and ventilation. City officials were often given wide latitude in deciding such cases, yet even here the very oversight of the tenements frequently changed hands. At first the new Board of Health was made responsible for tenements in 1867. Simultaneously, however, responsibility for building laws rested with the Department of Buildings. Conflict between the jurisdiction of the two were inevitable. Was airshaft construction a "building" or "health" concern? The 1879 act sought to solve this problem by transferring most oversight to the Building Department, leaving only questions of drainage, light, and ventilation of old buildings to the Board of Health. Still, enforcing laws concerning fire escapes rested with *both* the fire and police departments, which were directed by statute to enforce provisions such as keeping fire escapes clear and free of encumbrance.

While much might still be made today of Theodore Roosevelt's foreign travels, his interest in nature, his historical writings, and particularly his time spent in the West, his brand of progressivism was clearly shaped by his intimate contact with New York's working poor. One of the great ironies of Roosevelt's life was that while he was the Harvard-educated, brownstone-born scion of one of New York's great old Dutch families, he knew the tenement districts and their inhabitants more intimately than any other prominent Republican politician of the day—certainly more than any other president of the Progressive Era.

Roosevelt had a long history of investigating the tenements. Beginning with his investigating the cigar-rolling trade conducted in the tenements while he was an assemblyman, followed by his midnight ramblings with guide Jacob Riis while police commissioner, Roosevelt balanced his evening-dress dinners at Delmonico's with forays into the most notorious, impoverished, and dangerous parts of Manhattan. There were perhaps few federal avenues open to Roosevelt while he was president to foster change at the local level in a city like New York. But as governor between 1899 and 1901, he became partly responsible for further tenement reform efforts, supporting the efforts of housing reformers, an assembly investigating committee, and subsequent legislation.

Roosevelt consistently supported tenement reform as governor. Right after his election in early 1899 he hailed the work of the Mazet Committee in revealing shoddy building practices and dangerous conditions. He backed Lawrence Veiller's Tenement House Exhibition in early 1900 by speaking at its opening. He sent an urgent plea to the state assembly to pass the Tenement House bill, which appointed a new commission to revise the laws. With past commissions dominated by real estate and building interests, Roosevelt ensured real progress in tenement reform by appointing reformers as well as health and safety experts.

All of this would occur in the few years following the heat wave and his time as police commissioner. That week in August 1896 would have tremendous impact on his knowledge of tenement conditions and the plight of the city's poor. His experiences during that time would have concrete results in the new Tenement House Law of 1901, and in general would help shape the opinions and actions of one of the leading figures of the Progressive Era.

ROOSEVELT'S INTEREST IN REFORM shaped his early political career, from the governor's mansion to police headquarters on Mulberry Street. By August, however, criticism of his saloon-closing crusade and the Parker-inspired deadlock on the commission had brought any efforts at reform to a standstill. On Wednesday, August 5, a meeting of the New York Police Board illustrated that the deadlock remained.

A precinct captain reported on the various ways liquor sellers continued to break the Sunday Excise Law forbidding the sale of liquor on Sundays, over a year after Roosevelt began this particular "crusade." In 1896 the new Raines law attempted to limit Sunday liquor selling to hotels. Now, however, phony hotels known as "Raines law hotels" were springing up all the time, and the number of fake private clubs was "increasing daily." Saloon owners often simply transferred their stock to these establishments in order to continue selling liquor on Sundays and late into the night. Even when arrests had been made, the magistrates or grand jury dismissed the cases.

Roosevelt could not have been happy to hear this. Here was the one aggressive stance he had taken to see that the law was applied evenly and fairly. He had been blamed for Republican losses as a result of the law's unpopularity, almost had his position on the Police Board legislated out of existence, and even been sent a letter bomb.

The Sunday saloon closing fight had probably ruined any future Roosevelt might have had in New York City politics. Now he was being told by a precinct captain that it had all been in vain, with little effect on the saloon keepers and, indirectly, their ability to pour money into the coffers of Tammany Hall. He was beginning to despise Parker. And the heat in the room was oppressive.

The official high temperature on Wednesday, August 5, was 89 degrees, a number probably kept low by a light westerly breeze. Still, from about 9:00 AM to 9:00 PM the temperature never dropped below 80. Struggling all day through such heat took its toll on one group of New Yorkers in particular: men of working age, all between the ages of sixteen and sixty-five. Edmund Doyle of the Street Cleaning Department died of sunstroke only a half hour after collapsing. Seventeen-year-old John Cunningham, a drug miller, succumbed after his body temperature reached 109 degrees, according to doctors. Frederick Neidlinger, age twenty-six, died at work in Ulmer's Brewery. A policeman, Patrolman Lawrence Goundie, was overcome by heat while on duty, and Edward Gaynor, twenty-two, was prostrated while selling papers along the Shore Road.

Though workingmen were the primary victims on Wednesday, other New Yorkers suffered as well. Della McCullough, age sixty-five, was riding into the city on the New Haven train due into Grand Central Station at 6:00 PM. Coming into the city through the long, hot tunnel was more than she could stand, and she died in one of the parlor cars before a doctor could even be called.

New Yorkers did not suffer alone. The heat wave settled over much of the Midwest and East Coast as well. The thermometer hit 98 in St. Louis, 96 in Chicago, and 100 in Springfield, Massachusetts. Out in Lincoln, Nebraska, with the Bryans about to depart for New York via Chicago, the intemperate weather made for grim news.

Having already made an eight-hundred-mile railroad trip from the Chicago convention back home to Lincoln, Bryan must have had some notion of the adversity he faced. The candidate would be expected to stop in every small, dusty town to give a speech, and the curious crowds were expected to be large. On the eve of perhaps the most important speech of his career, Bryan would arrive in New York thoroughly exhausted from his long, hot journey east. This was poor preparation indeed.

Indeed, the heat was already altering Bryan's trip even before he left Lincoln. On Wednesday, August 5, the top Democratic silver advocate Richard P. Bland, old "Silver Dick," had cabled Bryan that it was simply too hot for him and his wife to travel to Lincoln to accompany the Bryans for the entirety of their trip. It was a bad start for such an important trip.

***

AT ABOUT TEN O'CLOCK Wednesday morning, police officer Patrick Giblin chased Jerry the Tramp out of the Mechanics' National Bank on Broadway, put a gun to his head, and killed him.

Well-known along Broadway, Jerry had staked out a territory that stretched from Warren Street, just across from city hall, up to Houston. It was said he was known in every saloon and restaurant, occasionally coming in for a mug of ale. Before the Raines law took effect earlier that year, Jerry had lived in relative luxury, picking up scraps of food from the free lunches that saloons served as a way of enticing midday drinkers. But after the upstate temperance advocates abolished this practice, Jerry had suffered hard times. He had grown thin and emaciated. Now, driven mad by the heat, with wild eyes and his tongue hanging out of his mouth, Jerry—a small, black dog—ran up Broadway snapping and snarling, causing a panic among the pedestrians.

Inevitably the shout of "mad dog" went up. The truth is that poor Jerry was probably not mad at all, just suffering the effects of heat and looking for a cool place to lie down out of the sun. He was not a big, ferocious dog; in fact, he was tiny, "no larger than a big squirrel," one paper noted, "a little bit of a black dog, as devoid of pedigree as he was of friends."

Finding a bank door open, Jerry approached the attendant at the entrance, who aimed a kick at the dog. In a foul mood, Jerry snapped at the foot, which raised the cry from someone inside, "Look out, Mac! He may be mad!" This set off a panic inside the crowded bank, attracting the attention of Officer Giblin, who was "big and a great pistol shot."

"Kill the beast!" the crowd cried to Giblin. Not wanting to take too rash an action, the officer first studied the dog to see if it was really mad. The examination consisted of prodding the dog with his nightstick. Of course, poor little Jerry snapped at the club as he had the attendant's foot. "That was enough for Giblin," the *Herald* reported dryly. "The dog was mad, of course. It had resented his effort to ascertain the condition of its nerves, and necessarily the animal was a menace to the community." Giblin removed his pistol and readied to fire, at which point a clerk shouted, "Don't shoot him in here!" Giblin shooed the dog outside, put the revolver to the dog's head, and fired. "The little black dog rolled over and died," Joseph Pulitzer's *New York World* reported. "The crowd cheered. Policeman Giblin walked nonchalantly off."

This was not the end of Jerry the Tramp's undignified tale, however. Apparently the dog had run across the line between the beat of Giblin and that of fellow officer George Lewis from another station house. Having heard the shot, Officer Lewis rushed toward the scene and found the dead dog lying in the gutter. Without hesitation Lewis took out his own gun and also fired into the dog's head. "The dog was just as dead after Policeman Lewis shot it as it was before," one observer noted. But now Lewis, too, could return to his station house and report that he had dispatched a mad dog. "On the blotters at their stations and on the slips at Police Headquarters both Policeman Giblin and Policeman Lewis are given credit for having 'shot a mad dog at No. 261 Broadway.' Both are ready to swear that they did it."

Such an episode may have reminded New Yorkers of a new board game that had appeared in the city that very year. In *Rival Policemen: A New Comic Game*, players representing rival police precincts competed to capture the greatest number of crooks, moving lead police playing pieces over a grid representing city streets. In the game, though, no points were given for shooting mad dogs.

In fact Thursday, August 6, was a bad day for dogs in the city, as the cry "Mad dog!" was heard all over town. Policemen on this day shot another five dogs at 16th Street, 138th Street, 35th Street, Lexington Avenue, and 42nd Street. All the dogs were officially designated "mad," although they were probably just suffering through the early stages of heat exhaustion. For dogs the early symptoms include heavy panting, confusion, and heavy salivating, which might appear to be foaming at the mouth. During the heat wave countless dogs suffered these symptoms, with the unfortunate ones labeled "mad" and killed in the street by police officers.

Horses also suffered greatly during the heat wave. New Yorkers were utterly dependent on the tens of thousands of horses that plied the streets of Manhattan, drawing carriages, transporting goods, and pulling the passenger cars of the several aboveground railways. While the final human death toll from the heat would number around 1,300, the heat wave also took the lives of thousands of horses. One paper described the treatment of sunstroke in horses: "A pail of water dashed over the head, a couple of kicks to see how much life was really left in them—this was about the best the sunstruck horse got. And then a bullet put him out of his misery."

On a normal day perhaps two hundred horses might die. Their carcasses were routinely left on the street until removed by the city. During the heat wave, almost every street had a horse carcass rotting in the heat, and the city was unable to cart away the massive number of dead horses.

"THE THERMOMETER TODAY is said to be well up in the nineties," *Tribune* editor Whitelaw Reid wrote to a friend in Arizona on Thursday, August 6. "In New York the heat is oppressive enough to disturb even an Arizonian."

During the night of the sixth New Yorkers had received no relief from the heat, suffering through a sleepless night of continued high humidity and a temperature that never dropped below 74 degrees. In the morning a brisk northeast breeze had carried the promise of rain and a break to the humidity. But the rain did not fall, and both the temperature and humidity continued to rise.

The official temperature was deceptive. While the official high temperature for Manhattan on Thursday, August 6, was 91, only 2 degrees higher than the previous day, all New Yorkers agreed that it felt at least 5 degrees hotter, as the humidity rose to 87 percent. The *Tribune* noted that as the temperature reached its official high at 1:35 in the afternoon, "There were plenty of street thermometers that registered 101 degrees, and plenty more pedestrians who were willing to swear that it must be at least 120 degrees." Those pedestrians were not far off, as the temperature and humidity combined for a heat index of 123 degrees.

The *New York World* called Thursday "the worst day of the year." While the more staid *New York Times* dryly listed names of heat victims, the sensationalist yellow press seemed to relish the disaster, offering dramatic accounts of life, death, and insanity during the heat wave.

The *World* recounted the sad fate of George Kupfer, a truck driver in a lumberyard. With his wife ill and unable to provide her husband with breakfast or lunch, Kupfer went the entire day working in the oppressive heat without eating. He left work complaining that he felt "queer in his head." Returning home at 7:00 PM Kupfer told his wife he felt ill and began to cry bitterly before dropping to the floor unconscious. When he came to, he called for his wife, apparently unable to recognize her when she tried to calm him. Neighbors soon arrived at the Kupfer home, "where they found him lying there breathing like a horse that has finished a hot race." A little girl ran outside crying that a man was dying, and an ambulance was called.

Kupfer resisted help and became abruptly violent. When the police tried to subdue Kupfer so he could be loaded into the ambulance, he bit one policeman on the hand and hit another in the face. Finally the police and ambulance attendants were able to place Kupfer in a straitjacket and take him to Bellevue Hospital. The doctor diagnosed the heat as the main culprit affecting Kupfer's mind.

Amid the chaos caused by the heat, newspapers also reported continuing tragedy. Mrs. John Roberts suffered a double tragedy, losing her husband to the heat and all her belongings to a fire. John Roberts worked on the Hamburg steamship pier in Hoboken, New Jersey. He was overcome on his way back from work, and friends assisted him to his home, where he died in spite of a doctor's best efforts. Leaving her husband's body in their home, Mrs. Roberts went to the undertaker to arrange the funeral. Arriving back home after dark, she lit a small oil lamp to place near her husband. "The little woman's hands trembled so violently that the lamp fell," one paper reported. "In an instant the room was in flames." Firemen came and extinguished the fire, but Mrs. Roberts lost everything. Finally able to reenter her home, she collapsed on her husband's charred coffin, sobbing, "What next, oh Lord? What next?" The double shock now caused Mrs. Roberts to collapse, leaving her in critical condition.

Doctors at Bellevue Hospital—the large municipal hospital on Manhattan's east side—were already feeling overwhelmed. "I'll need the doctors' attention next," hospital superintendent Murphy told a reporter as a sunstroke victim was brought in by ambulance and four orderlies rushed out to meet it. The reporter then offered a detailed account of the unconscious patient's treatment. Doctors stripped the man and placed him in a large tub filled with as much as half a ton of cracked ice. A thermometer placed in the man's mouth registered the maximum: 110 degrees. Attendants grabbed large chunks of ice and rubbed the patient's skin. After ten minutes the man's temperature dropped three degrees. A few more minutes of rubbing, and his temperature was back down to a normal 98.6. Other methods of treating sunstroke in New York's hospitals included squirting patients with a hose, bleeding, and administering drugs, including sedatives, aconite to steady the pulse, and nitroglycerine to stimulate the heart.

The Bellevue patient was Charles Littman, a relatively young man at thirty-five, who fell unconscious at his carpenter shop. Littman was lucky that the ice bath worked. It was considered the best way to relieve sunstroke. Yet even at Bellevue doctors ran the risk of lowering Littman's temperature too quickly and causing hypothermia. The other treatments of the day indicated concern with regulating high blood pressure. Bleeding was intended to reduce the volume of blood in a patient's body and thus the blood pressure. Aconite, also known as wolfsbane (Germans once used the highly toxic herb to poison wolves), was used to slow the heart. All of these treatments, including the administering of sedatives or stimulants of any kind, are today considered ill-advised as cures for sunstroke.

Unfortunately, the ice available to doctors for treating sunstroke was not available to average New Yorkers. As home refrigerators did not achieve widespread use until the First World War, Americans relied on large wooden iceboxes, usually lined with tin or zinc, to keep food cool and fresh. Ice was bought from commercial producers or ice harvesters, who cut ice from the rivers during winter and stored it in large blocks insulated with sawdust to reduce melting.

By 1896 Charles Morse, an ice magnate from Maine, controlled most commercial ice production in the city. His business practices kept prices high and ice out of reach of the city's poor. Having no means of preserving food in the killer heat simply exacerbated the plight of the poor, already living in nightmarish conditions in the steaming tenements. Morse's hometown newspaper called him "the man who made millions while poor people suffered for ice" and claimed the high price of New York ice increased the city's death rate by 5 percent.

During the heat wave, hundreds of thousands of New Yorkers did not have access to a refrigerator or freezer. They could not drink a cool glass of water to relieve their suffering or rub an ice cube across their hot, dry skin. Brick tenements baked their inhabitants and quickly putrefied meat and curdled milk.

Ice became a precious, life-saving commodity. With this in mind the *New York Herald* initiated a Free Ice Fund, soliciting contributions for ice to be distributed in the Lower East Side tenement districts. As of Thursday, August 6, the Fund had raised nearly $12,000, with many of the contributions trickling in $1 or $2 at a time. The free ice stations run by the *Herald* had been besieged by the women of the tenements. "They went away," the *Herald* reporter observed, "lugging pans of ice, and followed by children who touched the cold tin as they walked along. To such as these, who had no means of preserving their food from the action of the burning heat, ice was a blessing." Simple and short-lived as it was, the gift of ice was crucial to the tenement dwellers' survival in the heat.

A similar charity designed to relieve the summertime suffering of the city's youth was the *New York Tribune*'s Fresh Air Fund. In 1877 New York clergyman Willard Parsons established the fund, placing sixty children with families in Sherman, Pennsylvania, for the summer. Parsons turned over the running of the charity to the *Tribune* the same year, and the newspaper ran the fund for the next eighty-five years. (An independent charity now, the Fresh Air Fund has provided free summer vacations to more than 1.7 million children from New York's poorest neighborhoods.)

In 1896 the Fresh Air Fund was especially active, sending thousands of mothers and children out of the city, if only for a day. During the week of the heat wave alone the fund sent almost 5,000 people to the country. About 3,800 mothers and children took part in day excursions up the Hudson River, while nearly 1,000 children were placed with families, mainly in upstate New York but also in Massachusetts, Connecticut, and New Jersey.

Charities like the Free Ice and Fresh Air funds worked in a vacuum, as officials did nothing. During the three years of this most recent economic crisis the city and state rejected all calls for poor relief. Any moves in the direction of helping the people, in defiance of the laissez-faire market economy smacked of socialism and anarchism. Business cycles corrected themselves, while families, churches, and ethnic fraternal organizations were expected to take care of their own.

On August 13, when the mayor finally called a meeting of his department heads to discuss the crisis, one suggestion was to distribute free ice to the poor—an idea proposed by the president of the Board of Police Commissioners, Theodore Roosevelt.

***

ROOSEVELT'S POLICE WERE kept busy during the early days of the heat wave. They were continually picking up unconscious men and women off the hot asphalt of the street and responding to cries of "Mad dog!" To the storeowners who complained about the rotting horse carcasses in front of their shops scaring away customers, all the police could say was "Wait."

At Mulberry Street the Police Board continued to be deadlocked by the feud between Roosevelt and Parker, a constant source of irritation to the board's president and to Mayor Strong. Meanwhile, in his crusade against the serving of alcohol on Sundays, Roosevelt faced a new challenge in the Raines law hotels. Dozens of saloons now called themselves "hotels" and rented rooms above the main bar.

The development was widely seen as seedy and unwelcome. Renting out the rooms above taverns struck many as a throwback to the days when prostitutes plied their trade only a stairway's climb from the saloon floor, while others saw the rooms as encouraging gambling and other liquor-related vices. In an August 6 editorial, the *New York Times* complained that in one precinct where there had been only two hotels before passage of the Raines law, now there existed fifty-one "hotels" that sold liquor Sundays "and all hours of the night with impunity and with a noticeable increase of drunkenness and disorder." Roosevelt may very well have had a personal motive in his campaign against Sunday liquor sellers. While no temperance advocate himself, he was something of a teetotaler, usually avoiding consumption of alcohol. This may have resulted from his younger brother Elliott's death brought on by alcohol abuse only two years before. Drink had turned the once athletic and vivacious Elliott into a wasted man, and the death of his playmate from youth had dealt a crushing emotional blow to Roosevelt.

OBSERVERS ON THURSDAY, August 6, noted the bluish-gray pall that hung over the city, obscuring the hot sun and limiting visibility from the tops of New York's tall buildings. It was the first time that year that such a "heat haze" had settled over the city. Its cause was the extreme humidity that resulted in so much suffering.

New Yorkers struggled day after day throughout the heat wave. How one coped often depended on one's resources, as access to a cool place and to cool drinks was often too costly for the ordinary person. Many simply stripped down to the least amount of clothes socially acceptable, even if it meant wearing clothing not quite appropriate for Manhattan during a workday.

A reporter for the *Herald* described the sight of people trying to keep cool. "It was a blistering, sizzling day," he wrote. "Humanity crawled into places where there were fans and iced drinks and stayed there. They put on their lightest clothes and took no heed of the remarks of the youngsters who decried duck trousers and yachting shoes. The negligee shirt was everywhere, and men with scrawny necks overcame their pride and wore turned down collars. The weather was a shade cooler than it was the day before, yet the humidity made existence almost unsupportable." The same reporter noted the "sickly blinding glare on the pavements and the walls of brick and stone" down on the Lower East Side, where the heat was "deflected by the skyscrapers on either hand, and reinforced by the furnaces and boilers under the sidewalks." The urban heat island effect was in existence already, and it would continue to bake New Yorkers for days to come.

III.
ENEMY'S COUNTRY

O N JULY 16, the day after Bryan won the Democratic nomination in Chicago, he received a long letter from Pennsylvania congressman Joseph Sibley. At the American
Bimetallic League convention in Memphis that June, Sibley, a fervent
silver advocate, had urged the creation of an independent silver party
to challenge both the Democrats and the Republicans in 1896. At the
time, Bryan had sided with outraged Democratic leaders and defeated
Sibley's motion, but not without offering the disappointed Pennsyl-
vanian an olive branch: "We say to all parties, go on with silver at your
front and we shall not envy you one laurel on your brow." With the
Democratic National Convention meeting the next month, such a
statement appeared a savvy piece of diplomacy on Bryan's part, since
he hoped to muster behind him the party's silver forces, Sibley included.
Indeed, after Bryan won the nomination, Sibley emerged as one of several serious contenders for the vice presidential slot on the ticket.

Having failed to secure the presidential nomination on July 15, Sibley had written a frank letter to Bryan about his candidacy and the upcoming campaign. Sibley opened by saying that he would have preferred to see the nomination go to Colorado senator Henry Teller, another dedicated silver man. If not Teller, Sibley would have preferred himself because, he said, "I felt confident that I had strength that you did not."

Sibley advised Bryan that in the current campaign, Pennsylvania would be a battleground state, and he urged the nominee to give speeches in Pittsburgh, Altoona, Harrisburg, and Philadelphia. "But do not waste your time in New England and New York," Sibley warned. Perhaps Sibley was addled by his defeat at the hands of Bryan, for he went on to offer the candidate completely contradictory advice. "The battleground is not in the South or the West; the battle must be fought in the enemy's territory, and it will be won in the enemy's territory." Bryan's reaction to Sibley's candid missive is unknown. Clearly he ignored the contradictory advice from a one-time rival who questioned Bryan's strength as the party nominee. Yet something about that phrase "enemy's territory" must have struck a chord with Bryan.

At two o'clock Friday afternoon, August 7, the Bryans boarded the train in Lincoln, beginning their slow journey east to New York. Although the Madison Square Garden speech set for August 12 would mark the official start of the Democratic candidate's campaign, by the time Bryan reached the city, he had already addressed thousands of people in half a dozen states. A genius at extemporaneous speaking, with the physical strength to stand for hours and the lung capacity to project his voice to the back of even the largest crowds, Bryan was never at a loss for words.

Before departing, accompanied by a pack of newspaper reporters, Bryan addressed the hometown crowd that had gathered at the depot. "In ordinary times I would have desired to have the notification take place at my home," Bryan said. "But this is not an ordinary campaign, and, feeling that the principles in which we are interested should rise above any personal preferences which we may have, I expressed the desire to be notified in New York, in order that our cause might be presented first in the heart of what now seems to be the enemy's country, but which we hope to be our country before this campaign is over."

Almost immediately that single phrase—"enemy's country"—went out over the wires and soon appeared in newspapers throughout the nation. Bryan would later complain that the phrase "was picked out for criticism by our opponents, and often used in a sense entirely different from the one intended by me." Later Bryan biographers, too, have complained that the eastern press in particular ripped the phrase out of context "and pointed to it incessantly as proof of his hatred and fiendish intent toward the propertied classes." Yet the context of the speech does not serve to make the phrase less explosive, and in truth, he was clearly echoing the widespread sentiment that followed his nomination, as expressed by Congressman Sibley: New York was the heart of the enemy's country.

Even if the press had taken the phrase out of context, it was still an inexcusable and embarrassing slip by a candidate so early in the campaign. This was the drawback of continually speaking off-the-cuff and the exact sort of mistake McKinley sought to avoid through his carefully orchestrated front-porch campaign.

The casual reference to "enemy's country" was also evidence that Bryan had yet to transcend his rural base and embrace a truly national political identity. While a national figure for years as a leader of the silver forces, he was nevertheless in many ways still a local politician, a man who had never represented a constituency larger than that of Lincoln, Nebraska. Even the silver issue was largely a regional issue, with little appeal for a national audience.

Bryan's trip to New York was also a political journey. He now addressed crowds drawn not only from the rural populations of Iowa, Illinois, and Indiana, but from the cities and towns of Ohio, Pennsylvania, and New Jersey. The experience of the reporters and national press pouncing on those two simple words must have deepened Bryan's resolve to depart from his normal form and read his acceptance speech in Madison Square Garden.

Not all New York papers wielded Bryan's words against him. Democratic papers like the *New York Herald* obviously relished depicting the upcoming campaign as a crusade against the moneyed interests. "Bryan Coming to Meet the Foe," a *Herald* headline declared. "The candidate goes East to conquer."

From Lincoln, Bryan's train stopped in Omaha and then crossed the Mississippi to Council Bluffs, Iowa. It stopped at all the small towns along the way, and Bryan obliged the crowds by giving short speeches. In almost every town Bryan did his best to shake hands with everyone, starting with the ladies. It was hard, hot work, getting his hands pinched and grabbed while standing in the meager shade of the last car's back platform. But Bryan was in his element, a natural campaigner who exuded sincerity and sympathy. "He wore his campaign hat of white felt," one observer noted, "a handkerchief was loosely knotted around his neck, and a linen alpaca coat and the absence of a waistcoat gave him the air of an easy going traveler who was ready to meet everybody along the route just as one farmer could meet another and stop for a little while to talk about the crop and the weather."

The effects of the heat were visible in Bryan's very appearance. The handkerchief around the neck served to protect Bryan's throat, while the absence of a waistcoat was a necessity. The heat wave that was settling on New York had already devastated the prairies and the Midwest. Before Bryan's departure, Nebraska had seen the temperature hit 94 degrees. Long before arriving in New York, Bryan suffered the full effect of the heat wave.

Meanwhile in the enemy's country, New York's sound-money forces continued to desert Bryan. Senator David Hill refused to attend the Madison Square Garden meeting, one of many prominent New York Democrats who planned to stay away that night. Other Democrats began actively working against Bryan's election. The Democratic Honest-Money League had established its headquarters at 15 West Twenty-Fourth Street and asked William Bourke Cockran to speak at a mass meeting on its behalf. The meeting would take place in Madison Square Garden just days after Bryan's speech. The Bryan campaign could not have received worse news.

BY AROUND FRIDAY, August 7, Roosevelt must have made the decision not to attend Bryan's speech and indeed to have as little to do with Bryan's visit to New York as possible. This was not merely a political decision, with Roosevelt the Republican seeking to avoid contact with Bryan the Democrat, Bryan the Populist, or Bryan the Silverite. In fact, during Bryan's visit to New York, and especially the night of the Madison Square Garden notification meeting, New York's Finest would be responsible for security.

As president of the Police Commission, Roosevelt might have taken the lead in preparing the police for Bryan's visit to New York, if not actually directing security himself. After all, the Bryan speech was shaping up to be a fairly enormous affair, with thousands of ticket holders expected to pack the Garden and thousands more listening outside. Providing adequate and effective security for so many people would be almost akin to launching a military operation, deploying perhaps hundreds of officers to man the doors, control the crowd, and watch for pickpockets. Furthermore, based on recent experience in the city, the night of the speech was going to be hot. Having an adequate police presence to prevent a crush of people might actually save lives.

Yet apparently Roosevelt was content to leave these matters to subordinates. It may have been a symptom of his general ennui with being police commissioner and his greater preoccupation with his political future. He planned to stay in New York Friday before departing for Oyster Bay, where he would remain for the duration of Bryan's arrival and big speech. In other words, while Roosevelt would be one of the few city officials to take steps to address the heat-wave crisis, he actually avoided the city during the worst of the weather in favor of cooler, breezier Long Island.

Friday morning found the police commissioner dealing with the tedious minutiae of his position. For a man with his sights set on Washington, it could be grim and demeaning work. In a short ceremony, Roosevelt officially commended Officer Charles Haas, a policeman who instead of shooting a mad dog had clubbed it to death with a cane. After giving a short speech, Roosevelt presented Haas with a cane a manufacturer had made for the policeman as a reward for his apparently heroic act.

During the night Roosevelt again conducted one of his midnight inspections of the city's police force. "Roosevelt Sleuthing Again," a *New York World* headline would announce the next day. At 11:00 PM he had walked in the rain to the Nineteenth Precinct Police Station, examining the records of several applicants for promotion and inspecting the station. Roosevelt shook hands with Mrs. Linner, the matron of the women's block, and conversed with a number of women "who were locked up for various offenses." After visiting the men's cells and declaring that he would visit several other police stations during the night, Roosevelt went back out into the rain.

***

WHILE THE UNITED States Weather Bureau representative marked down what would become the official record of New York temperatures during the heat wave, most New Yorkers probably paid more attention to the giant thermometer in Herald Square. The "Herald thermometer," a fixture of the *New York Herald* at Thirty-Fourth Street, offered thousands of pedestrians grim visual confirmation of what they already knew. At 6:00 AM the temperature was already 78 degrees, accompanied by high humidity. Over the next two hours the Herald thermometer registered an almost 20 degree rise in temperature, hitting 96 degrees at noon. "There was a rise in temperature and humidity until it seemed as though the safety valve of the weather would be blown sky high," one paper observed. Yet the temperature did not peak until about 3:30 in the afternoon, when according to the Herald thermometer it hit 101 degrees, exactly 10 degrees hotter than the official record of the day. Deaths were sure to follow the hottest day of the week so far.

Faced with the fourth day of blazing heat, the city might have taken some simple steps to save lives. One step would have been to limit working hours citywide. Commissioner Collis of the Department of Public Works issued an order altering the hours of work for his men. Instead of working the normal 8-to-5 shift, workers were required to report an hour earlier, at 7:00 AM, break from work during the worst of the midday heat from 11:00 AM to 3:00 PM, and complete the workday from 3:00 until 7:00 PM. Collis's move was based on an early insight that most of the victims of the heat wave were work-ingmen. Had Collis's order been copied on a wide scale, even only by city workers, many deaths might have been avoided.

As it was, laborers of New York continued to drop from heat-stroke. William Meehan, a longshoreman, died at St. Vincent's Hospital. Patrick Ronan, described by newspapers as "a laborer," was prostrated at work on Wednesday but died two days later. A twenty-six-year-old clerk named Thomas O'Brien was overcome on the side-walk and died before the ambulance arrived, his body then taken to the local police station.

Of the forty cases of heatstroke reported in New York City on Friday, August 7, nearly all were men under the age of fifty. Although the occupation of the victim was not listed in every case, those instances where occupation could be determined lend credence to the idea that mostly young men were struck down after working in the extreme heat.

For the following week, this pattern would be repeated on a daily basis. Relatively young men became overheated at work and either received treatment on the spot or returned home to their baking tenements. Because of their age and fitness, those who received immediate medical treatment still stood a good chance of recovering. For those who simply went home hoping to feel better with some rest, the prognosis was often poor, and the most common result was death.

THE FOLLOWING DAY, Saturday, the street-level Herald Square thermometer hit 103 degrees at 3:30 PM, with 90 percent humidity. "The sun did the broiling and the humidity did the basting," the *New York Herald* said. "Perspiration even gave up the terrific struggle and remained within the pores and boiled."

The police and hospitals reported that only ten people died from the heat, but this figure is deceptive. Overall, about forty more people died on August 8, 1896, than had died on the same date the year before. Once again urban laborers suffered a heavy toll. Henry Rapp, a forty-eight-year-old cabinetmaker, was overcome by the heat on the way home from work and died even before a doctor could attend to him. Twenty-seven-year-old Matthew Murphy died while working on Pier 35. Philip Frank, a mailman, died at Fordham Hospital after becoming exhausted along his route.

New York's travails on Saturday were not unusual, as much of the rest of the country continued to suffer as well. St. Louis reported twenty deaths from sunstroke; officials declared the morgue full, and hundreds of horses died in their harnesses. Evansville, Indiana, suffered its third day of temperatures 102 degrees or higher in the shade. Webster, Massachusetts, reported that the mercury hit 104. Kansas City, Missouri, also experienced a record-setting day of heat over 102 degrees. Perhaps the greatest suffering was in Chicago, which experienced a doubling of the death rate. Fifteen persons died of sunstroke, with nearly eighty people prostrated, many of these in serious condition and unlikely to fully recover. Moreover, with so much of the city's work having been suspended, garbage crews had not picked up the refuse that now sat and decayed in the alleys, "filling the air with fearful, deadly smells." The city's drinking water had been rendered largely unfit for consumption, contributing to the high mortality rate.

The situation in Chicago was dire as Bryan's train rolled into town.

***

THE BRYANS HAD risen at 5:30 that morning, and at seven o'clock they boarded the Rock Island train in Des Moines bound for Chicago. It was the start of a day that would see Bryan give nineteen individual speeches along the way, as the thermometers in Iowa and Illinois registered close to the 100 mark. A journey of only about three hundred miles, the trip to Chicago was scheduled to take thirteen hours. Bryan had intentionally chosen a train with a schedule that called for a stop at every station between Des Moines and Chicago.

In his speeches Bryan continually made reference to the fact that in previous elections eastern and midwestern states had a monopoly on producing presidential nominees. For him this was a clear illustration of the fact that American political and financial power was concentrated in the Northeast of the nation. In fact, this resulted from the practical realities of late-nineteenth-century America, more than from any conspiracy of elites.

The importance of the Northeast and apparent marginalization of the West was primarily the result of simple political geography. By the 1896 election there were still territories in the western United States that had not achieved statehood. Moreover, several states had achieved statehood only in the previous six or seven years: Washington, Montana, and the Dakotas in 1889; Idaho and Wyoming in 1890; and Utah in 1896. Even Bryan's own Nebraska had not entered the Union until two years after the Civil War. The 1890 census recorded just over a million residents in the entire state, a number that would barely budge over the next decade. By contrast, in 1896 four American cities—New York, Brooklyn, Chicago, and Philadelphia—had populations larger than the entire state of Nebraska. A state like New York, then, simply had more electoral votes and more seats in Congress than western states. This gave New York more say over laws and presidential nominations.

Yet Bryan maintained his simplistic hostility toward eastern interests and their most recent puppet, William McKinley. As his train stopped at the small town of Marengo at 10:20 AM, still only a few hours into the day's journey, Bryan could not help but draw a connection between the name of the town and his own campaign. In 1800 Napoleon had conquered much of northern Italy in the Battle of Marengo. During the presidential campaign friend and foe alike would often compare Bryan to Napoleon, and Bryan himself compared McKinley to Napoleon in his "Cross of Gold" speech: "Why, the man who was once pleased to think that he looked like Napoleon—that man shudders to-day when he remembers that he was nominated on the anniversary of the battle of Waterloo. Not only that, but as he listens he can hear with ever-increasing distinctness the sound of the waves as they beat upon the lonely shores of St. Helena."

Now Bryan took the Napoleonic mantle for himself. "I have been told by some of those who met me in the train," he told the crowd during his brief stop, "that the battle fought at Marengo was not more bitter a struggle than the battle that is going to be fought here for the purpose of restoring the gold and silver standard of the Constitution." While McKinley stayed at home in Canton, it was Bryan who on August 8 passed within only fifty miles of Waterloo, Iowa. Yet as the crowds clamored for Bryan, there was no hint of defeat in the air.

Bryan's pace was grueling, but he was driven to speak at every stop. Most of the small towns and villages where his train stopped had probably never hosted so great a celebrity as he, even if only for fifteen minutes. By the time the train crossed the Mississippi River around noon, he had already given about ten speeches.

The character of the towns began to change as they approached Illinois. The cities were getting larger and agriculture less prominent.

And Bryan was hot and tired. At Moline, Illinois, he and his wife were escorted to a truck from which he gave a short speech as sweat poured from his brow. Mrs. Bryan was handed a bunch of roses, which she began to distribute to the crowd, causing a "pushing, struggling enthusiasm" among the people. After Moline the train entered the coal-mining towns of the Spring Valley region of north-central Illinois. Only one hundred miles southwest of Chicago, miners with coal-blackened faces and smoky lamps on their hats lined the rails to watch Bryan go by.

The train rolled into Chicago at 7:40 PM, nearly thirteen hours after leaving Des Moines that morning and only twenty minutes overdue. The Bryans rode in a carriage to Clifton House, led by the band of the First Regiment. At their hotel, the couple took an hour and a half to wash and rest before appearing on the Clifton House's small balcony. Bryan gave a short speech, ending with "I am proud to have in this campaign the support of those who call themselves the common people." This was typical Bryan populism, and it was greeted with loud applause.

Finally the Bryans could return to their room for some much needed rest. It had been a long, hot day: He had given nineteen speeches and shaken thousands of hands. New York was still nearly a thousand miles away. At least tomorrow was the Sabbath, the day of rest.

IN CONTRAST TO Bryan's hectic Saturday, McKinley's day was almost somnolent. The Major greeted members of the Ohio Canal Commission and received a telegram of support from the 250 members of the McKinley and Hobart Club of Red Bluff, California: "No doubt about California. Such enthusiasm for Presidential candidate never before manifested." This was the extent of McKinley's front-porch campaign that day, in marked contrast to Bryan's triumphant and garrulous march to the sea. Bryan was a whirlwind; McKinley was barely a breeze. How could the Republicans hope to compete with the Bryan phenomenon sweeping across the country?

This was where Mark Hanna's organizing and fund-raising genius kicked in. True, Bryan was an army unto himself, taking his fight directly to the people in small towns and large cities, shaking every hand offered. Hanna, however, commanded an army of speakers numbering 1,400 men, who could be dispatched at will and with their expenses paid to counter the effects of Bryan's campaigning. Speakers did not just travel along the railway lines and address huge crowds but penetrated into every election district in the nation, holding small local meetings. Simultaneously, using the massive Republican war chest, Hanna and the National Committee sent out millions of pieces of campaign literature.

The Republicans relied on polls to tell them where the most work was needed. For instance, Bryan's August sweep through Iowa had galvanized much of the state behind the Democratic candidate. A canvass of the state in early September indicated to the Republican National Committee a majority of voters favored Bryan. Over the following six weeks speakers and campaign documents supporting McKinley flooded the state. In October, a new canvass convinced Hanna that Iowa was safe for McKinley. Hanna was right. On election day McKinley won Iowa by over 65,000 votes.

That Saturday, as Bryan headed to Chicago from the west, Hanna headed to the same city from the east, leaving New York to take control of the Chicago Republican headquarters. As the East was fairly solid for McKinley, much of the important work of the Republican campaign would be done out of this midwestern city. Over 100 million campaign documents would be shipped out of Chicago, compared to 20 million out of New York. Eventually 275 different campaign pamphlets would be printed, some as long as forty pages, in English, German, French, Dutch, Spanish, Italian, Swedish, Norwegian, Danish, and Hebrew.

Well aware of the power of print, Hanna and his staff also sent material directly to newspapers. Depending on the paper's circulation, the Republican committee would send out three and a half columns of material per week ready to be inserted directly into the newspaper. Still, no amount of campaign material or newspaper stories could match the efficacy of dispatching 1,400 prominent Republicans directly to small towns and cities throughout the country. Eager office seekers sought a place on Hanna's list. None was more eager than Theodore Roosevelt.

AFTER UNDERTAKING AN inspection tour of police stations the night before, Roosevelt attended a Saturday meeting of the Police Board.

These meetings had become a fruitless and frustrating annoyance for Roosevelt. He was forced to preside over a board that was deadlocked by a single member, Andrew Parker, who refused to vote in favor of Roosevelt's candidates for promotion. Roosevelt's attempts to remove Parker had been unsuccessful, and time and again the two men had squared off against each other, Parker maintaining an icy calm while Roosevelt grew increasingly flustered.

The Parker-Roosevelt rivalry had made for good copy in the yellow press and had subjected the police to derision. True, Roosevelt had successfully removed the previous corrupt police chief and had introduced a new level of professionalism to the force. Yet his efforts to enforce the Sunday saloon-closing law and the new Raines law, plus the daily spectacle of trigger-happy bluecoats gunning down small dogs in the city streets, had damaged the police department's reputation. Today's meeting might create more fireworks for the newspapers, and in light of how things had been going, chances were that they were the sum total of what it would produce.

The meeting was tedious. With the temperature in the room well over 90 degrees, Roosevelt led the board through the items on the agenda, including cases involving officers' conduct. Patrolman Edward Grey was commended for the arrest of Edward Berg, who, after shooting and wounding a man, then threatened the unarmed police officer with a revolver. Two policemen who had killed suspects, including the notorious James Cody of the Tenth Avenue Gang, were restored to duty after their mandatory suspensions were lifted.

Roosevelt also addressed violations of the Raines law, including the rapid multiplying of so-called hotels and private clubs seeking to serve liquor on Sundays. Roosevelt reported he had gone down to the Oak Street station one Sunday and asked the precinct captain, Vreedenburg, to write a report, which he now read to the commissioners. "Under the old law there were only two hotels in the Fourth Precinct," the commissioners heard. "Now there are just fifty-two, while others are being opened daily. In addition to this there are innumerable fake clubs. They are all chartered clubs, and in most cases the charter members are the proprietors and their bartenders." Captain Vreedenburg also noted that in a majority of the "hotels" no lunch was served or could even be discovered on the premises. In some saloons crusts of bread might be found on the floor, and a thin liquid called soup was available, but that was the only food to be seen. The commissioners agreed to send the captain's report to the chief of police.

By the time Roosevelt moved on to reading a letter of praise for the police from the American Bankers' Association, two hours had passed inside the sweltering police headquarters. Shirts and handkerchiefs were soaked through, and faces were flushed red. Roosevelt's fellow commissioners must have assumed he was close to ending the meeting and sending everybody home, or at least to Delmonico's for a glass of iced tea.

As the commissioners wiped their brows and looked at their pocket watches, Roosevelt surprised everyone by bringing up the sticky question of promotions. Perhaps he felt that the heat might have weakened Parker's resolve, or perhaps this was Roosevelt's natural belligerency showing itself. Whatever the reason, he seemed to be picking a fight and directed his remarks squarely at Parker. A reporter for the *Evening Post* recorded what followed:

> "Might we not take up the promotion of Inspectors?" [Roosevelt asked] And, looking at Mr. Parker, added: "Has anybody seen the eligible list?"
>
> Mr. Parker replied, without taking his eyes from the table: "I don't know; I haven't seen it."
>
> Commissioner Grant, who occupies the seat opposite to Mr. Parker, said: "I don't know that it would be a wise thing to do. Although, if it comes up, I stand ready to vote."
>
> Commissioner Parker hesitated a moment and said: "The reason I want the matter to lie over is that when I do vote I want to make a statement. That statement I have not prepared, and of course have not got with me."
>
> Commissioner Roosevelt then asked: "Do you intend to enter your statement on the minutes? For if you do and you have no ob-

jections, I may very likely wish to make a statement also, that, I suppose, will be all right."

"Oh, yes, certainly," answered Mr. Parker.

Roosevelt had made plain that he stood ready to answer Parker. The stage was set, then, for a showdown between the two men at the commission's next meeting—whenever that might occur.

In the meantime the police and the president of the Board of Police Commissioners had their hands full. William Jennings Bryan was due to arrive in only three days, and the heat wave showed no sign of abating.

***

JOHN HUGHES COULD not sleep. Like thousands of other tenement dwellers during the heat wave, he had taken refuge on the roof of his building at 202 East Ninety-Eighth Street. Hughes made frequent trips over the course of the night to the local saloon, where he purchased buckets of beer called "growlers," returning to the roof to drink. During one of these trips he met the building's janitor, William Froome. "This makes thirteen growlers of beer tonight, and I expect to make it eighteen before I get through," Hughes told Froome as he carried a fresh can in from the street.

After drinking the beer, Hughes stretched himself out on the roof's low parapet. A woman whose window looked out on the roof called to Hughes that he would roll over and be killed. Hughes drunkenly replied that his death "wouldn't cost the neighborhood much." Not long after, Hughes fell asleep on the parapet and rolled off the roof. He fell five stories into the concrete-paved courtyard of his building, where a police officer later found his crushed body covered with blood and the clothing from a wash line broken by his fall.

During the heat wave it seemed all of the Lower East Side could be found sleeping on rooftops or fire escapes. Inevitably people fell to their deaths. Certainly these strange and tragic accidents must be counted among the city's heat-related fatalities of that killer August.

John Hughes was not the only victim who fell from a great height that night. Two-year-old John Herman climbed to the windowsill of his home on the fourth floor to get a breath of fresh air and fell. Luckily he did not fall all the way to the ground but was caught only two floors below by the fire escape. At Harlem Hospital he was treated for two broken legs. Mary Lessie, tired from the day's work, fell asleep in her window on the third floor and fell to the yard below. She received severe injuries to her back and was taken to Bellevue Hospital. John Moxkam, overcome by the heat while walking along the embankment at 199th Street and Amsterdam Avenue, fell down the twelve-foot embankment and lay there unconscious until a passing patrolman discovered him. Although an ambulance was summoned, the man's injuries were so severe that he died before arriving at the hospital. An eleven-month-old infant named Lewis Citron was sleeping with his father on their building's fire escape when the child fell two stories to the ground. He died shortly after arriving at Bellevue.

One did not even have to fall from a height to fall victim to the heat. An unknown man fell asleep on the pier at West Thirty-Seventh Street, rolled into the water, and drowned. His body was not recovered.

Aside from fatal falls, the epidemic of heat-related mania continued to spread. "They Fought, They Drank, and a Few Landed in Jail," declared the headline of the *New York World* describing the "Haps and Humors of a Blazing August Day." After Henry Garsett paid ice dealer James Bracca ten cents for a block of ice, the iceman refused to climb the flight of stairs to deliver it to Garsett's residence on the sixth floor. As the two men argued, the ice rapidly melted in the sweltering heat. When Garsett, a clothing merchant, turned to pick up the ice himself, he found nothing but a pool of water. He demanded his money back from Brocca, who refused. Garsett began calling the iceman names, until Brocca hit him in the eye. Brocca was arrested.

During the heat wave many New Yorkers sought solace in alcohol, seeking to quench their thirst or at least escape the terrible reality of the weather. Returning home after consuming a prodigious amount of whiskey, James McNally quarreled with his elderly aunt, grabbed her crutch out of her hand, and knocked her down. He was arrested.

The combination of alcohol and heat can be dangerous. As a diuretic, alcohol promotes dehydration. Alcohol also hinders the body's ability to control its temperature. Both heat and alcohol dilate the blood vessels, making a person even more likely to become overwhelmed and pass out. On August 9 a thirty-year-old Irish laborer named Patrick Reilly died from the heat. Even so, the doctor listed "alcoholism" as a contributing cause of death. It can never be known how many more heat-wave deaths were caused at least in part by alcohol.

The heat continued to foster strange and aggressive behavior among New Yorkers. At the corner of Bleecker and Macdougal streets, Joseph Belinni drew a knife and stabbed John Carroll. Apparently Carroll was just a spectator to the row between Belinni and his friends caused by the question "Is it hot enough for you?"

Ralph Ethington beat coworker Henry Brown unconscious because he thought Brown had him fired. Jeremiah Donohue stabbed his friend John Cockley three times after an argument. William Hall received permission to drive his wagon through Twenty-Fourth Street, where asphalt was being laid, but one of the workers there, William Brodus, refused to recognize the permit. During the ensuing altercation Brodus slashed Hall with a knife across the cheek. At her restaurant on Greenwich Street, Sarah Jane Grant served a drunken Henry Britton dinner. When Britton demanded a drink, Sarah Jane replied, "You've had enough." "Oh! Have I?" Britton asked, scooping up the silverware and bolting out the door. He was swiftly arrested.

The combined stress on both mind and body from the extreme heat and humidity took its toll in various ways and in at least one case complicated assigning a cause of death. Thirty-year-old Ludwig Grobolowitz was overcome by the heat in the evening and died before the ambulance from Bellevue Hospital arrived. Although he seemed to be just another victim of the heat, the ambulance attendants soon discovered that the deceased also suffered from four stab wounds, one under each eye, one in the right temple, and one in the right breast. Days earlier Grobolowitz had fought with another tenant, Michael Franey, in the hallway of their Second Street tenement. Assuming he was the culprit in Grobolowitz's death, police arrested Franey, but though he admitted fighting with his neighbor, Franey confessed only to kicking the deceased in the leg and certainly not stabbing him. "Sunstroke or Homicide?" the *New York Tribune* asked, reflecting the macabre choice for citizens in the afflicted city.

By Sunday, August 9, New Yorkers were already suffering through their sixth day of temperatures in the 90s and suffocating humidity. While the Weather Bureau marked the official temperature at 90 degrees, thermometers throughout the city added several degrees as the humidity hit 89 percent. "It was the combination of heat and humidity that swept the town like a plague," one newspaper reported, "and while the sun was in the zenith it was unbearable." The combination of heat and humidity would have made the temperature feel like 130 degrees. Some found it too much to bear.

Lewis Pumper, a fifteen-year-old recent arrival from Poland, had joined his two older brothers in America only two weeks earlier. In the current economic climate, Pumper was fortunate to secure work in the bakeshop of John Schwartz on Clinton Street, where he took his meals before returning each night to his subbasement rooms in the home of Joseph Cobell. Arriving just in time for the heat wave soon turned Pumper despondent. The combination of living in nearly airless rooms at night and working in the burning heat of the bakeshop during the day engendered a deep depression that his brothers were not able to relieve. According to newspapers, the brothers had come from a part of Russian Poland "where neither the thermometer nor the spirits of the people rise very high." One journal mentioned that "the boy's vitality and courage were deeply sapped by the discomforts of the voyage across in steerage."

By August 9 the young man could not take any more. In the bakery's cellar Pumper tied a short leather strap to a water pipe overhead, stood on a stool, and hanged himself.

Cobell, his landlord, declared, "It was the heat that did it. Lewis came from a country where there is little or no hot weather, and to come right into this terribly hot spell and have to work in that hot bakery fairly drove the boy to desperation. There was no other reason for his act." Perhaps Cobell did not want to consider the effect on Pumper of living in his basement without access to sunlight or fresh air.

FOR THOUSANDS OF sweltering New Yorkers, the only sensible action was to flee the city altogether. Out on Long Island and at the Jersey Shore, hotels were filled to capacity, as were the excursion boats and trains bringing bathers to the region's beaches. Newspaper declared Sunday, August 9, the greatest day in Coney Island's history, with an estimated 200,000 people visiting the shore, dwarfing even the Fourth of July celebrations of the month before. Over 100,000 went bathing in the ocean, and the beaches were described as "black with people for a distance of three miles."

While Theodore Roosevelt was privileged with the ability to escape to his Long Island home to enjoy the breeze off the Sound, visitors to Coney Island were mainly the working-class families of New York. Fares on the steamboats and many railroad lines serving Coney Island were kept low to draw tourists who would spend money in the beachfront hotels, restaurants, bathing pavilions, and various amusements. Originally designed as an opulent playground for the wealthy, Coney Island had long ago transformed from a luxury destination to a popular one. Now visitors could espy the construction of a new amusement park being built along Surf Avenue. Steeplechase Park would be the first of three new large parks built over the next several years, with Luna Park opening in 1903 and Dreamland opening in 1904. By 1907 visitors to Coney Island were commemorating their weekend visits by sending 250,000 postcards across the country. In the meantime, the beaches and streets were dotted with many smaller concerns selling shaved ice, offering cold drinks, taking photographs, giving children pony rides, and even featuring vaudeville shows.

Yet during the heat wave, most people seemed to eschew the offered pastimes and stuck close to the shore and the surf. As one paper described it: "They went to the seashore to seek relief, not amusement. They wanted some little surcease from the awful heat of the past five days. The workers had been looking forward to a day's outing where it was cool. They awoke very early . . . to find it as hot as ever. Their first thought was of the breeze. When they saw that it was from the sea they knew that Coney Island would be cool and delightful." The number of people leaving the city was enormous, and the trolleys and steamboats were packed. "People fled as from a plague-smitten city," the same paper recounted.

With such overcrowding of the transportation network to Coney Island, and the crowds of people at the beaches that Sunday, it was a miracle that people did not collapse by the score on the railroads. Still, tragedy occurred. Reports of drowning came from all over the region. Fifteen-year-old William Brown was swimming in the Hudson with some friends when he suddenly threw up his hands and went under. As all the boys had been playing games and "cutting all sorts of antics," no one paid much attention until his friends noticed that he had not come back up for air. They tried diving for Brown, but unable to find him, they ran to a nearby police station for help. His body was soon recovered. Two died in Newark, bodies were found in the North and Hudson Rivers, and a little girl nearly drowned after wading in the East River.

The strangest drowning of the day occurred when F. R. Schultz, a baker, choked on his false teeth while bathing at Rockaway Beach on Long Island. Although he was swimming in shallow water at the time, he was unable to help himself and was dragged from the surf by a lifeguard. As the lifeguard tried to resuscitate Schultz, he noticed a bulging in the man's throat. Pushing his finger down his throat, the lifeguard found a plate with two false teeth on it. By this time Schultz was already dead.

Victims of drowning, of falling, of violence, of insanity, of suicide: All these must be included in the long list of heat-related deaths that Sunday.

As it was the Sabbath, a day of rest for most New Yorkers, some relief might have been found by the city's laborers, who had formed the majority of heat prostrations during the past week. Yet the day's heat-related deaths shot up to well over a hundred in the city itself, with another forty in Brooklyn. Once again the heat did not discriminate according to age, taking nineteen-month-old John Gleason and sixty-four-year-old Louis Garth within a few blocks of each other. Not surprisingly for a Sunday, most victims died at home, with at least one, John Bober, found dead on the roof of his residence. Several others died in the hospital after having been checked in for heat prostration. William McGuire had been checked into Bellevue the day before but died on Sunday. This suggests that many of that day's victims died from the delayed effects of exhaustion in the previous days or simply the cumulative effect of nearly a week of temperatures in the 90s.

One would hope that many lives were saved by simply having a day off work in the middle of the heat wave. Unfortunately for New York's laborers, work would resume the following day on one of the hottest days yet.

Newspaper reports came from around the country of the blistering temperatures and the victims of the heat. In Washington, DC, the official high temperature reached just over 97 degrees, "and the general impression is that to-day has been beyond all doubt the hottest and most uncomfortable of the season," the papers reported. The very architecture of Pierre Charles L'Enfant's plan for America's capital contributed to the heat, as the "wide asphalted streets and pavements reflected the heat, and as a general rule it was 10 degrees greater throughout the city than that officially recorded." The residents of Columbia, South Carolina, suffered through their third day of temperatures over 100, while Baltimore reported fifteen heat-related deaths. Out West the heat ravaged the corn crop, "and unless there is rain soon the situation in Southern Kansas and Oklahoma will become alarming." Des Moines, Iowa, reported two fatalities. In Springfield, Illinois, the Wabash Railroad shops, employing 350 men, were closed as a result of the extreme heat. Yet it was Chicago, hosting Democratic nominee William Jennings Bryan, that rivaled New York for the level of suffering and fatalities caused by the nationwide heat wave.

***

WHILE BRYAN'S VISIT to the city may have competed for headlines with the heat wave in the *Chicago Daily Tribune*, most of the city's residents seemed preoccupied by the simple ordeal of surviving the torrid day and suffocating night. If New York's yellow press indulged its taste for the macabre during the heat wave, the *Tribune* matched them for every rotting horse and dead dog. In particular the paper reported the situation among the city's poor, with one descriptive headline declaring, "WRITHE IN THE GUTTERS—Residents in Tenement Districts Suffer from the Heat—Thousands are Driven from Their Homes and Pass the Night in the Streets, Sleeping in Filth—Cobblestones Converted into Pillows—Babies Are Apparently Abandoned by Their Parents and Left to Shift for Themselves." Chicago was mirroring New York's misery. "All the horrors of hades were made real yesterday in the tenement house districts of Chicago," reported the newspaper.

In Chicago, heat had reduced people to animals, as the *Daily Tribune* reported people crawling on all fours through the streets. Hundreds slept in the gutters and in alleyways. At the heart of

Chicago's tenement district, the streets "were literally packed with half-dead human beings." Moaning people covered the sidewalks, "their faces in the dirt and filth," grateful for the occasional drop of rain that drenched them and eased the stench of the streets. The most pathetic sight, though, was that of a baby, "who could not have been more than a year old [lying] all alone in the gutter among the filth that had been dumped from a nearby fruit wagon." The baby's head rested on the curbstone where it slept soundly, oblivious to the misery around it.

By Sunday, after five days of blistering heat, Chicago's streets had become festering rivers of filth. With no rain to wash away the horse manure and urine, nor the organic refuse of the businesses and residences, the blistering heat made every street noxious and dangerous. Venturing out into the street at night to catch a breath of air meant making one's way amid animal feces, rotting produce, and discarded meat trimmings from butchers.

Ironically, the large rectangular garbage containers found on every street became sought-after perches for individuals and families to rest safely above the muck. "The garbage boxes were a godsend to those who found the streets too wet and filthy to lie in," a reporter from the *Tribune* observed. "Wherever one of the foul-smelling receptacles was, there was sure to be at least one person stretched upon it. Some of the boxes were covered with an old quilt, and babies, stark naked, lay stretched upon them without any one, apparently, having any fear of their falling off."

This was the situation in Chicago as the Bryans arose at 10:00 AM, with the temperature already 84 degrees. At the First Presbyterian Church of Englewood they attended a service given by their old friend from Omaha, the Reverend John Clark Hill, who had just been called back to Nebraska to become pastor of a church in Lincoln. Riding in a carriage to and from Englewood, on Chicago's southwest side, from their hotel at Madison Street and Wabash Avenue, Bryan must have been reminded of the time he had once lived in Chicago, attending Union Law College from 1881 to 1883. Although Bryan was familiar with the small cities of the American West, his nearly two years in Chicago, a city of over half a million residents at the time, constituted his first experience living in one of the country's truly large metropolises. Indeed it may have been those very years that impressed on him the transient and even corrupting role of the city.

For a number of personal reasons, Bryan's months in Chicago were most likely miserable. His father, Silas, had died in 1880, when Bryan was a junior in college, and twenty-one-year-old William left for his law studies while his family was saddled with Silas's debts. He also left behind his beloved Mary for two years. While his mother paid for tuition, Bryan was responsible for paying for his own room and board in Chicago, which he was able to do only by skimping and sacrificing, budgeting himself a mere $4 a week. He lived in a single, windowless room far from the city center. To save the 5-cent transit fare Bryan walked the four miles to school. To support himself he worked in the law offices of an old friend of his father's, the former United States senator Lyman Trumbull. Working part-time, Bryan swept the floors and managed the office's supplies of paper and ink.

Bryan had arrived in Chicago one decade after the Great Fire had devastated the downtown area. The city had rebounded with astonishing speed. Chicago was growing exponentially, from a population of 100,000 just before the Civil War to 500,000 when Bryan arrived as a student. It was a city of immigrants, with 40 percent of the residents the foreign-born and their children.

Chicago was foremost an industrial city, where huge corporations squeezed the independent businessman and exploited their own workers. Bryan visited the shops of the great Pullman Company, which made the famous sleeping cars for the nation's railways. He came away shocked at the wretched conditions of the workers and certain of the injustice of a system that allowed the vast majority to share so little of the great wealth being created around them.

It may have been in Chicago that Bryan first developed the ideas that would one day make him the Great Commoner. "History," he told one of the many discussion and literary societies he belonged to in Chicago, "teaches us that as a general rule, truth is found among the masses, emanates from them; a fact so patent that it has given rise to the old saying, 'vox populi vox Dei'" (the voice of the people is the voice of God).

But if those masses were exploited economically by the great robber barons, so too were they exploited politically by the great machine politicians. In Chicago, Mayor Carter Henry Harrison ruled absolutely over the Cook County Democratic machine. Harrison believed that Chicagoans had only two desires, to make money and to spend money, and he had special maps printed allowing tourists to find their way from brothel to brothel. In the face of manipulation of the masses by a corrupt elite, the "better classes" of Americans, Bryan believed, had a special duty "to assume the burdens of citizenship . . . To shirk that duty is treason."

Returning from church on Sunday, the Bryans received many callers at Clifton House, including George W. Peck, former governor of Wisconsin, and General A. J. Warner of Ohio, president of the

American Bimetallic League. Mr. Bryan sat for a short time to allow an artist to put the finishing touches on his oil portrait.

Mrs. Bryan, in a summer dress of unbleached linen with black dots, also received guests. When asked about the upcoming campaign and her husband's speech in New York, Mrs. Bryan spoke frankly. "I tremble sometimes at the thought of Mr. Bryan's succeeding," she said. Of the speech: "This speech will have to be entirely different from anything Mr. Bryan has said since the convention began. It will, of course, be more closely criticized and it must be a speech that will require no subsequent explanation."

Just before midnight, with the temperature still at 85 degrees, the Bryans boarded the slow train to Pittsburgh, due to stop at every town of any size. They would spend Monday night at Pittsburgh before arriving in New York on Tuesday, August 11, a day that would see the heat wave and the death toll reach their heights.

***

OUT ON OYSTER Bay Theodore Roosevelt enjoyed a Sunday with his family, yet these days he was giving a great deal of thought to the upcoming presidential race and Bryan's pending arrival. Just days before, Roosevelt had written to his British friend Cecil Spring-Rice: "If Bryan wins we have before us some years of social misery, not markedly different from that of any South American Republic. The movement behind him is most formidable, and it may well be that he will win. Still, I cannot help believing that the sound common sense of our people will assert itself prior to the election, and that he will lose. One thing that would shock our good friends who do not really study history is the fact Bryan closely resembles Thomas Jefferson; whose accession to the Presidency was a terrible blow to this nation."

In comparing Bryan to Jefferson, Roosevelt meant that both men saw the American yeoman farmer as the foundation of both the spirit and the economy of the United States. In the same letter Roosevelt observed that the "semianarchistic" free silver movement had the Anglo-Saxon or Scandinavian farmer as its backbone, not the wage-earning immigrants of the cities. In other words, the current revolutionary threat to American democracy came, ironically, from property-owning, native-born Americans, not from the property-less immigrant workers of American cities.

By 1896 Roosevelt had become something of a student of American cities. In 1891 he had published *New York*, a book that traced the history of his native city from its discovery by Henry Hudson in 1609 to the present. For Roosevelt, the city was the capital of American art, architecture, and commerce, as well as a crucible of different races from which the "True American" might arise.

An adherent of social Darwinist notions of the "survival of the fittest," Roosevelt saw New York as the place where only the brightest and strongest would survive. While New York could not take the lead in all respects of American life and politics, nevertheless, "its life is so intense and so varied," he wrote, "and so full of manifold possibilities, that it has a special fascination for ambitious and high-spirited men of every kind, whether they wish to enjoy the fruits of past toil, or whether they have yet their fortunes to make, and feel confident that they can swim in troubled waters—for weaklings have small chance of forging to the front against the turbulent tide of our city life. The truth is that every man worth his salt has open to him in New York a career of boundless usefulness and interest."

Indeed, according to Roosevelt's vision of America, cities might be seen as a mark of civilization itself and engines of progress for all nations. If William Jennings Bryan resembled Thomas Jefferson, then Theodore Roosevelt might well be compared to Jefferson's ideological nemesis, Alexander Hamilton.

Bringing together a varied population in a small and dense island such as Manhattan might create its own unique problems, but it also bred art, ideas, innovation, and wealth. Americans were living increasingly in cities, Roosevelt noted, making the United States largely an urban, not a rural, nation. He foresaw a time when most Americans would live in cities and large towns, and that this would present the country with both unique problems and opportunities. Roosevelt saw that, for better or ill, the American future was an urban one.

Over the next few days Roosevelt would move easily and comfortably from the shores of Oyster Bay to the crowds of Manhattan. Not so Bryan, who having crossed the Mississippi had already entered hostile terrain and was approaching one of his greatest defeats.

IV.
INFERNO OF BRICK AND STONE

THE CITIZENS OF New York had already suffered a week of killer temperatures. There was no relief on Monday, August 10, a day when the thermometer failed to dip below 90 until 9:00 PM. The tortured inhabitants of the city's tenement districts gasped for breath in the brick and mortar ovens they called home.

The *New York Herald* described how, as the day dawned, people desperate for a cool place to sleep were found virtually everywhere. "The sidewalks were lined with men, women, and children. Cellar doors were their mattresses and beds were made in trucks and wagons." The rising sun revealed a wretched scene: "From block to block long rows of baby carriages filled the gutters, and from street to street there went a wail of misery and discomfort."

Had he seen them, such sights would have only confirmed for Bryan the hellish nature of American cities. In both Chicago and New York people spoke of little other than the weather, while the cities' newspapers ran apocalyptic headlines describing the wide-spread suffering and death. It would be Bryan's monumentally bad luck that his New York arrival coincided exactly with the height of the heat wave.

MEANWHILE, MCKINLEY'S hometown received an unexpected group of visitors on Monday. With Bryan's train due to arrive in Canton later that day, about sixty members of the Pittsburgh reception committee traveled to the Ohio town to escort the Democratic nominee into Pennsylvania. While at the train station someone suggested they call on McKinley, since his house was just a short walk away. Forming a line, the Bryan supporters marched to the McKinley home on Market Street.

A surprised McKinley greeted his visitors on the veranda. A spokesman for the Bryan men said, "Major McKinley, we believe that every candidate for the Presidency is worthy of the highest respect, regardless of his political affiliations. The members of the committee, therefore, have called to pay their respects to you as an American citizen." It was a display of respect and esteem for the opposing party's candidate rarely seen in American politics.

McKinley returned the proffered words of respect: "We are all of us proud of our country's history, and we should all be determined to make this Government in the future as in the past the best Government in the world. Of you who disagree with me politically, it is very grateful to have assurance of your personal good will." The Bryan men applauded and pressed forward to shake McKinley's hand before returning to the station.

Two Bryan supporters, however, stayed to speak to McKinley and his wife. Richard "Silver Dick" Bland of Missouri, the likely Democratic nominee before Bryan gave his "Cross of Gold" speech in Chicago, had finally caught up to Bryan's train. Originally he and his wife were scheduled to depart from Lincoln with the Bryans as a show of support from the most important silver advocate of the day, not to mention a senior Democratic Party leader. But Bland had begged off several days ago, citing the extreme heat. The Blands had also failed to appear in Chicago to meet the candidate's train, even though the Bryans had stayed overnight in order to attend church on Sunday.

Their failure to meet before the halfway point of Bryan's trip, in Ohio, was open to interpretation. Was Bland distancing himself from a Bryan candidacy? Did he feel robbed of the nomination and now took revenge by way of a small slight? As temperatures throughout the Midwest and the East approached 100 in some places, Bland's original excuse for not catching up to the Bryan train rang true: The sixty-one-year-old Bland and his wife simply thought it too hot—and dangerously so—to travel, accompanying the Bryans on a slow, exhausting, and uncomfortable train trip halfway across the continent. But a half hour sitting in the McKinley parlor chatting with the enemy allowed the press to speculate about Bland's motives. After their visit the Blands returned to the station to join the Pittsburgh reception committee as it prepared for Bryan's arrival.

By the time the train arrived, Bryan had already had a busy and eventful day—and night. "Night is supposed to be a season of rest," he would later write, "but I found during the campaign that the rule could not always be observed." The Bryans had departed from Chicago on the Pittsburgh-bound train just before midnight, planning to sleep for the duration of their trip through Indiana. But just as they did during the day throughout the trip, supporters and the merely curious had turned out in every town along the way. At South Chicago a large crowd, including a brass band, prepared to give the candidate a rousing reception, even though it was past midnight. The beat of the bass drum must have resounded in the exhausted Bryan's head, while the shrilling of the trumpets flayed his nerves.

At Delphos, Ohio, the next morning, disaster nearly struck. The train arrived just after 7:00 AM, and already the crowd was too large. The streets around the station were jammed, and people packed the rooftops. Bryan emerged from the train only to offer his apology that he could not make a speech. Just as he finished, the wooden awning of a store only twenty feet from him collapsed with an enormous crash, sending nearly a hundred people tumbling down with it. As people in the crowd began to panic, threatening a crush, Bryan shouted, "Stand still, don't move." Incredibly, no one was hurt, and he joked, "If you would get on our platform it would not fall down." Recovering from their fright, the spectators laughed and cheered as the train moved off. Platform collapses became a common hazard of Bryan's groundbreaking cross-country campaign, which attracted record crowds.

The next day at Crestline, Ohio, an onlooker snapped a picture of the Bryans. Both William Jennings and Mary Bryan look directly into the camera. Mr. Bryan wears a dark suit with his trademark kerchief tied around his neck, and his hat tilts back from his face, slightly covering his bald pate. A watch chain hangs from his waist, and his hand is being gripped by an enthusiastic well-wisher, although Bryan does not seem even to notice it. His smile is wry and tight-lipped, while Mary Bryan gazes into the camera with a broad smile and bright eyes. Her hat is slightly askew as she tries to balance a large bouquet of flowers in her left hand. A man described by Bryan as "an enthusiastic silverite" shakes her right hand, pulling her slightly toward him. Having been on the campaign trail for only a few days, Mary Bryan looks a little dazed and overwhelmed.

In Mansfield, Ohio, Bryan addressed an issue that would dog him throughout the campaign. Less than seventy miles from the Republican stronghold of Canton, he touched on his relative youth and lack of military service. "Here [in Canton] are some who believe that only in times of war can people prove their patriotism," Bryan began. "I was too young to prove my patriotism in the time of war, but I glory that in a country like this every year presents a battlefield and every day gives those who live in the country an opportunity to prove their devotion." It was a fair attempt to puncture this particular criticism. In a nation only a generation removed from the Civil War, Americans continued to define themselves and their country in the context of that great conflict.

The heroes of 1896 were, to a man, Civil War heroes, and America's most ubiquitous war memorials commemorated that war. Bronze statues and Civil War veterans could be found in every town in America, including those along Bryan's route that week. Some veterans wore their threadbare uniforms every day, while others hobbled along streets missing an arm or leg. Other men like McKinley continued to wear their Civil War ranks as badges of honor. That simple title "Major" in front of McKinley's name spoke volumes to the average American in 1896. Bryan knew this, knew the impossibility of competing with it, and could offer only the excuse of his age and the claim of devotion. These were poor substitutes.

Men like Bryan and Roosevelt, born just before the war, were doomed to live in its shadow, which created in them a sense of inferiority and incompleteness that bordered on emasculation. No wonder that when war broke out with Spain in 1898, both Bryan and Roosevelt jumped at the chance to prove their worth and their manhood.

THE CLIMAX OF Bryan's August 10 trip came at Canton, where cheers of "Hurrah for McKinley!" competed with cheers of "Hurrah for Bryan!" Rolling into McKinley's hometown at just around 1:00 PM, Bryan could not have failed to note the many McKinley banners displayed by the crowd. If the East was the "enemy's country," then Canton perhaps constituted the front lines. A speech there was bound to be interrupted by cheers for the Major, and Bryan, in the gentlemanly style of nineteenth-century politics, would continually be forced to shower praise on his Republican opponent. Nevertheless, Bryan stood atop the platform and launched into a speech in front of a hostile crowd numbering in the thousands.

From the beginning of his speech, Bryan referred to McKinley as his "distinguished opponent" and declared himself glad to be able to testify at his home "to his high character and great personal worth." This elicited loud cheers from the crowd of locals. The Democratic candidate noted that while McKinley was their neighbor, Bryan himself sought to be a neighbor like the Good Samaritan. "In this contest I hope to be the neighbor of those who have fallen among thieves," Bryan boomed. "He is a neighbor who, in the hour of distress, brings relief."

Turning to the free coinage of silver, he declaimed that whether in Omaha or Canton, he trusted that the neighbors of the two candidates would vote as they saw best, "although it may result in keeping your distinguished citizen among you as a neighbor still," he joked. Some of Bryan's supporters in the crowd jeered, "That's where he belongs!"

As his speech ended, so ended the stop in Canton. No one suggested they march to McKinley's home, and the train readied to leave. The train rolled out of town and toward Pittsburgh.

Bryan arrived in Pittsburgh just before 7:00, exhausted from his trip. Once again, thousands met the candidate's train at Union Station, and the police had to force a path through the crowd to the Central Hotel. Bryan emerged briefly onto his hotel room's balcony, bowed to the cheering crowd, but said nothing. He was saving his already strained voice for a large rally to be held that evening in the Grand Opera House.

After dinner the couple made their way to the opera house, and Bryan began to speak at 9:30 PM. One observer called his voice "husky," saying it "showed signs of failing under the severe strain of the past few days." The immense gathering in one of America's biggest cities made this an important campaign stop, but Bryan could squeeze out only fifteen minutes of campaign boilerplate before heat and exhaustion made him stop. Flanked by representatives of the mine workers' and steelworkers' unions, he said little that was new, repeating his belief in the people of the United States and in their ability to make the correct judgment on every subject.

Despite his brief Pittsburgh speech, Bryan displayed his inexperience in a national campaign. Even in his foreshortened remarks, he repeated his jarring reference to the East being "enemy's country," an odd thing to say in any city east of the Mississippi. While the Republican press had enjoyed repeating this phrase on the eve of his arrival in New York City, portraying it as the sort of gaffe a young, inexperienced demagogue might make, in fact he seemed to like this particular turn of phrase. Furthermore, he lapsed once again into the martial rhetoric of one who had never experienced battle, pledging that during the campaign "not a single private in the ranks will stand nearer to the enemy's lines than him in whose hand is the standard." And once again he almost guaranteed a frosty reception in New York

City. How many times would he refer to that city as "enemy's country" before arriving to give perhaps the most important speech of the campaign? This was but one of the factors conspiring to make his New York visit a difficult one.

In the Grand Opera House that evening, with his voice failing and the exhaustion of the day taking a physical toll on him, the temperature inside the packed hall reached extreme levels. While there were no reports of heat prostration in the audience, every observer noted that "the heated atmosphere was almost unbearable." It was a grim foreshadowing of what awaited Bryan inside Madison Square Garden.

**

IN NEW YORK, as of Monday, August 10, frantic preparations were still being made for Bryan's big speech only two days away. One reporter described the situation at the Democratic headquarters at the Bartholdi Hotel as being "a mixed up mess," as campaign officials ran about on different errands and no one could answer reporters' questions. All the journalists could report was that New York's Democratic leaders hoped to host a giant, loud rally like the one that accompanied Bryan's nomination in Chicago. If they could pull it off, such an event would illustrate his popularity among New York's working class and maintain what they referred to as his "boom," or what later political pundits would call "momentum."

The Democrats planned to pack the Garden with an unprecedented 10,500 seats, with as many as 7,000 more standing. Such a crowd had been seen but once before at the Garden, on its opening night in June 1890. That event had occurred on a mild early summer night. To pack the same hall in 100-degree heat was madness.

No other locale in the United States during the heat wave would have dared bring together such a mass of humanity, while headlines screamed the daily death toll. But the date had been reserved, Democrats from all over the country were even now pouring into town, and Bryan himself was but a day away. "Madison Square Garden," the *Times* warned, "promises to be the most uncomfortable, and, some think, the most dangerous place in the country." The consequences of packing so many people into the Garden on such a hot night "can only be guessed."

Democrats at the Bartholdi were so absorbed with the planning of the meeting, and so intent on keeping away from the throng of perspiring ticket-seekers, that they overlooked the arrival in town of the vice presidential nominee. To Sewall's surprise, no reception committee was on hand, and not even a carriage awaited him as he stepped off the train from Boston at Grand Central Station. A solitary figure among the crowd at the busy station, he made sure his luggage was claimed from the train before hailing a hack to the Fifth Avenue Hotel. At the hotel, nobody looked twice at the man with a face begrimed with soot and ash from his five-hour train ride into the city. He wore the common summer wear for gentlemen of the day: light trousers, tan shoes, a yellow alpaca coat, a straw hat, and, like Bryan, a handkerchief tied loosely around his throat. After handing his coat to a bellboy, he registered and then gently put off the newspapermen who approached him. "Wait till I get a bath and a shave, and I'll be glad to see you," he said as he headed toward the hotel's barbershop.

An hour later he sat smoking a cigar, discussing some details of the campaign with reporters, and admitted knowing little of the following night's meeting. The vice presidential nominee said he did not know who would preside over the meeting, New York senator David Hill having already declined. Sewall said he had not even finished his speech. He did not know when the Democratic presidential candidate would come to Sewall's home state of Maine, nor how many speeches Bryan would give there if he did. He did not know if Bryan would accept the Populist nomination. He did not know where Democrats planned to establish their permanent national headquarters for the campaign, and he expressed no preference. The only thing Sewall seemed certain of was that he planned to leave the city and return to Maine as soon as possible, probably the day after the speech. With the temperature just outside his hotel room a balmy 90, even at 5:00 PM, such a sentiment was understandable.

THEODORE ROOSEVELT HAD already fled the heat. As of Monday, August 10, he planned to stay out at Oyster Bay on Long Island for the duration of Bryan's stay in the city. Both the heat and party politics probably contributed to this decision, although as police commissioner he certainly would have had his fair share of work to do the evening of Bryan's speech. Even so, with the Police Board deadlocked, and his sights set on a McKinley victory and subsequent appointment out of New York, the president of the Board of Police Commissioners stayed home to conduct a letter-writing campaign.

His targets, as ever, were the Storers, the friends of McKinley who had bailed the Ohioan out of financial trouble after the 1893 Panic. Just a week before, Roosevelt had rowed Maria Longworth Storer across Long Island Sound, almost pleading for her to use her influence with McKinley on his behalf. Now he addressed letters to both Bellamy and Maria Storer, noting his own efforts to secure for McKinley's close friend a cabinet post or ambassadorship to France.

Roosevelt also gently reminded them of his own ambition. Both Bellamy Storer and Henry Cabot Lodge had discussed his taking the position of assistant secretary of the navy in a McKinley cabinet, perhaps even in a Navy Department led by Bellamy Storer. To Mr. Storer Roosevelt reiterated his willingness to accept such a post but at the same time demurred that "the really important thing is to get you in the Cabinet or at Paris. This is what we must strive to accomplish." To Maria Storer Roosevelt composed a longer note explaining in detail the way he had pressed Mark Hanna on her husband's behalf. "I spoke of Bellamy as *the* man for the Cabinet, either for War or Navy, or else to go to France," he wrote, saying that "my personal feelings did not influence me, but that for various reasons, ranging from his vote on the Gold Bond Bill to his whole record in Congress and his standing with Catholics, I felt no appointment would do more to strengthen McKinley." While this might have been a bit of flattery on Roosevelt's part, it was also good politics. Roosevelt was absolutely right that Storer had a reputation as a sound gold man, as opposed to McKinley, whose pet issue remained his beloved tariff. And the support of the Storers as leading Catholics could help mitigate Democratic support in the cities, especially among immigrants.

Unfortunately, Roosevelt's first meetings with Hanna had not gone exactly as planned. With any possible McKinley administration still seven months away, Hanna had apparently given Roosevelt— and probably every other office seeker—something of a brush off. Now he tried to explain this to the Storers. In his letter to Mrs. Storer, Roosevelt related that Hanna had said "at present he was considering nothing but how to elect McKinley . . . I thought it wise not to press the matter further at the moment." Even so, Roosevelt tried to make clear he had made his best effort. Clearly it was not up to him alone to secure a post for Bellamy Storer, an Ohio lawyer and congressman whom McKinley had known well for years, as opposed to the young police commissioner from New York. Roosevelt's goal, instead, was to secure a quid pro quo from the Storers. Now that he had raised the topic of a Storer appointment with Hanna, it was up to the Storers to bring their own influence to bear with their close friend McKinley.

WITH THE STREET temperature hitting 95 and the humidity at 70 percent, the heat settling over the city on this seventh day of the heat wave felt like 120 degrees. Hospitals reported twelve infant deaths from the heat, although many more died inside the suffocating tenements. Sixty death certificates were filed that day in Manhattan for children under the age of two, including Charles Bellman, age seven months, and Gladys Shields, age six months.

Before departing the city for Long Island on August 10, Roosevelt had issued an order that may have saved many lives during the last few days of the heat wave. With the city hospitals complaining to the police that their ambulances were "taxed to the utmost caring for heat cases," Roosevelt ordered that police wagons be pressed into service.

Like flushing the streets or changing work hours, this was a seemingly simple order that nevertheless depended on the individual judgment and initiative of a city official like Roosevelt. Quick treatment for heat victims in a hospital's ice baths was the best way to save the heat-stricken. Making enough transportation available to carry the sick to hospitals, or to cart away dead horses, might have been the most basic of measures taken by the city, thus saving lives and removing the "flavor of pestilence" that Roosevelt would later describe to his sister. This did not happen—even Roosevelt's order to provide police wagons was not adequate to handle the body count. Supply wagons, coal trucks, and even the morgue's "dead wagon" ultimately had to be pressed into service taking heat victims to the hospital.

Meanwhile the heat wave continued to dominate newspaper headlines. "An Epidemic of Sunstrokes," the *Herald* declared, as the *Tribune* announced "DEATHS BY THE SCORE." Every paper on Monday, August 10, dedicated several pages to the tragedy, listing the victims and often giving an hour-by-hour accounting of the temperature. "The plague of high temperature and high humidity on the city," the *Journal* reported, "is eating out its life at a never before equaled speed." Outside of New York, much of the country continued to suffer through the heat wave. Across the Hudson in New Jersey, many people died from the heat, and the Botany Worsted Mills in Passaic shut its doors so as not to endanger the lives of its 3,000 employees. Even in the farming districts it was reported that farmers had left their fields to escape the heat. With the streams drying up, cattle and other livestock were suffering gravely. In Connecticut deaths were reported in Hartford and New Haven, while Providence, Rhode Island, registered the record temperature of 97. Philadelphia reported a slight easing of temperatures, from 97 degrees the day before down to 93, with a total death toll from the week approaching a hundred. More deaths were reported in Baltimore, Boston, Washington, DC, Pittsburgh, Atlanta, Cleveland, St. Louis, Chicago, and as far north as Michigan and Minnesota.

New York, though, remained the capital of despair. "Manhattan Island was an inferno of brick and stone," the *Journal* observed, "radiating heat deadly in its intensity. And over all, gray as the presence of death which it held, was the pall of humidity." Like the fabled desert city of Is, the sound of whose bells could be heard at sunset, rising up through the sand, New York from a height also seemed to be "in the depths of an opalescent sea." "But the sound that came from this city under the gray sea was not the vague music of bells," the paper concluded, "but the heart-stirring dissonance of bereavement and anguish."

Death and suffering had greeted the Weather Bureau's man Dunn every day of the heat wave. After a week of unbearable heat, he had altogether stopped answering his phone to give the hourly official readings to the newspapers. In fact, it was reported that on August 10, he had left the city altogether. A reporter had observed him out at Montauk Point on Long Island. The same reporter dryly observed that relatively cool Montauk Point is "at the extreme easterly end of Long Island" and "swept by ocean breeze." Officially Dunn was out at Montauk Point to inspect the instruments of another weather observer there. However, he had been seen in the company of two boys "riding a tandem." At that very moment, scores of people were being treated for heat exhaustion in the city hospitals, while city coroners were working overtime on the dead. "When Dunn quits his post things must be in a bad way," the reporter for *New York World* wrote. "And they are."

CONSIDERING THE HUNDREDS of deaths and hundreds more prostrated in the street daily, the hospitals and ambulances were severely overtaxed. Roosevelt Hospital sent word to all of its affiliated physicians to assist the ambulance corps, and medical students were pressed into service. Even after Theodore Roosevelt arranged for police wagons to serve as extra ambulances, one-third of the calls for ambulances still went unanswered. At Roosevelt Hospital every wagon and ambulance that rolled up contained two victims of the heat. The superintendent noted, "We have sent word to the police to get sufferers here by any conveyance at hand—trucks, wagons, cabs, and even wheelbarrows if they cannot do better." The superintendent of Hudson Street Hospital also admitted that ambulance calls were going unanswered, "but we are finding great relief that our suggestion that carriages be used as much as possible is being freely followed."

The coroner's office was tragically overworked. Coroners and their staff were working from sunrise until two in the morning each day. On Monday, August 10, one of the clerks in the coroner's office collapsed from heat prostration. Amid such heat, the examinations of the dead were necessarily cursory—the quickly decomposing bodies had to be buried, and fast.

A week into the heat wave relatives of the deceased were beginning to complain that no official from the coroner's office was able to come to their home and issue a death certificate until the body was in the first stages of decomposition. When a reporter asked Coroner O'Hanlon about this complaint, he countered by criticizing the habit among the poor of seeking relief at night on their tenement roofs. "The people of the lower east side especially, think that after a day of torture, relief is to be found on the roofs of houses that have been baking for a day and perhaps, as in the present case, a week," the coroner observed. "They and their families go to the tin roof and sleep, or try to, and the heat that is pouring up all around them, the residue after the sun has finished his day's roasting, either makes them victims at once or prepares them for destruction in a day or two."

O'Hanlon's grim mood was understandable. On Monday, August 10, alone he had seventy-seven cases on his list for investigation, with over fifty of the cases requiring climbing more than two flights of stairs. The situation had deteriorated such that Coroner Fitzpatrick was moved to write an emergency appeal to Mayor Strong asking for more staff. A further request illustrated the dire situation the city faced: Fitzpatrick asked that the law requiring bodies to be left uncared for until viewed by a coroner be suspended, "as the force of Coroners is altogether inadequate, and the enforcement of the law only works hardship on the friends of the dead and endangers the health of the survivors."

WITH NEW YORK'S press continuing to mock the efforts of William Dunn of the United States Weather Bureau, including his "fleeing" the city, not to mention his cool aerie on top of the Manhattan Life Insurance Building, and especially his low temperature readings during the heat wave, the *New York Journal* turned to Dr. Thomas Draper of the New York Meteorological Bureau. For twenty-eight years Draper had manned a set of thermometers, barometers, and wind gauges atop the Arsenal in Central Park.

On August 11 the *Journal* gave Draper center stage in an article entitled "WHY SO MANY HAVE DIED: Dr. Draper Explains the Conditions of the Long Heat Plague." "Because of the high temperature, abnormally high humidity, and the absence of wind," Draper explained. "The temperature has been higher before, but not for so long a time. This heated spell began on August 4," he noted, giving a table of temperatures that was markedly different from the official temperatures collected by Dunn. Draper observed temperatures both in the shade and in the sun. Even his "shade" temperatures were several degrees warmer on any given day than Dunn's observations. On August 5, the second day of the heat wave, the official temperature hit 89, while Draper observed a temperature of 95 in the shade. On the same day, he observed a temperature of 131 in the sun. This pattern repeated throughout the heat wave. On August 7, the fourth day of the heat wave, the official temperature hit a high of only 91. Draper, however, recorded 97 in the shade, and 132 in the sun. On August 10, Dr. Draper noted a temperature of 137 in the sun.

Draper emphasized the importance of high humidity and lack of wind, two key characteristics of the heat wave that were absent from Dunn's observations. "The wind charts show that during the hours of sleep there has not been a strong breeze any night this week," Draper said, "and on some nights the speed has been less than a mile an hour." Because wind aids evaporation, humidity reached its highest, most suffocating levels at night. On most afternoons during the heat wave the humidity was only around 50 percent. Yet during the early mornings, from 2:00 until 8:00, the humidity soared to the 80 percent and 90 percent levels. On August 7 nighttime humidity hit 94 percent, and on August 9 humidity reached an unbearable 97 percent. Using a modern heat index calculation, this meant that even during the coolest moment of August 9, when the temperature, according to Draper, sank to 82, the temperature a body would feel still sat at an uncomfortable 94 degrees. During such a night, almost a week into the heat wave, New Yorkers attempting to get a restful night's sleep were thwarted. With high humidity and no wind, there was no relief. The night of August 11, the eighth night of the heat wave, would prove to be little better, with a low temperature of 81, but with humidity at 85 percent. Workers continued to die by the score, and tenement dwellers continued to bake and gasp on the Lower East Side.

Even the *New York Times*, a paper usually loath to dramatize the plight of the city's poor, offered a grim picture of the day's suffering. "In the tenement-house districts yesterday the suffering was most intense," the paper observed, "and helpless women and children, enervated by days and days of hopeless, squalid, sweltering, sat or lay drowsily on stoops."

The writer had apparently walked along Cherry Street, just a block from the East River, and noted how heat-induced torpor had settled on this normally bustling lane. "The motley throng was there like so many dogs impounded in a place of awful heat, where every breath meant a struggle and every struggle a pang. And whatever puff of wind that moved bore heated odors to add to the misery of the sufferers." Comparing the "motley throng" to a pack of panting dogs was classic *New York Times*, as was the complaint of the foul-smelling air in the tenement districts. When it came time to sleep, families "sought the heat-belching roofs, or lay, sleepless, panting, on the heat-soaked stones." As the coroner had noted, in a desperate attempt to draw in a breath of air, tenement residents climbed to the roofs, a practice that continued to sap their strength and contribute to heat exhaustion. "The days of death continue," the *Times* announced. "The sun is still unwearied of its scourging."

The city papers noted that the hottest and most dangerous place on Manhattan Island was the stretch of asphalt in front of city hall. Each day, that overheated part of the city claimed several victims, including a man who threw up his hands and collapsed shortly before noon on August 10. At that moment a thermometer on the steps registered 112 degrees.

Only individual department heads took action. Commissioner Collis of the Public Works Department had already established shorter and earlier work hours for his men. In the public stores, the bonded warehouses belonging to the New York Customs House, sixteen men had been too ill to come to work that day, and the collector issued an order closing the warehouses during the middle of the day.

**

THE BRYANS' OVERNIGHT stay in Pittsburgh gave the Democratic candidate an important gift: six hours of continuous sleep. Exhausted and hoarse, and with his hands purple and swollen from shaking thousands of hands during his trip across America, Bryan was already in poor shape for his big speech the following day.

The trip east was just a taste of what he would face during his groundbreaking cross-country campaign in the months to follow. Indeed, weighed against the potential impact of the speech in hostile New York, the train trip itself was probably the more valuable campaign tool. True, perhaps 17,000 people would attend the Garden speech Wednesday night. But many times more people had heard Bryan speak either from the back of the train platform in small towns or in the auditoriums of the big cities like Chicago and Pittsburgh when the party stopped for the night. And millions more read his speeches in the newspapers.

Yet New York was still the key. The Bryan campaign sincerely hoped that a rousing speech in New York City would win over skeptics and make inroads into the urban East. A success there on the scale of his "Cross of Gold" triumph would resonate throughout the country. And New York remained the most important swing state in the Union: Winning it in November would give Bryan the White House. With this fact in mind, he planned to spend the rest of the journey largely silent and would not give any speeches that would further weaken his voice.

The residents of Altoona, Pennsylvania, packed windows and balconies overlooking the station, as railroad workers sat atop nearby boxcars. Bryan and Bland appeared on the rear platform to cries of "Bryan!" and "Speech!" When Bland took on the duty of addressing the crowd, his words were drowned out by cries of "Bryan, Bryan!" People had not left their homes and businesses to crowd onto the train tracks and hear old Silver Dick Bland speak a few rusty platitudes. To repeated demands for a speech, Bryan shook his head, placed his hand at his throat, and called out in a husky voice, "Can't boys, I can't." Understanding there would be no speech, the crowd rushed the train so that both Mr. and Mrs. Bryan could again undergo the hand-shaking ordeal. Throughout the day Bland took over speaking duties as the Bryans shook hands.

The final destination for the day was Jersey City, New Jersey, where the Bryan party would take the ferry across the Hudson to Manhattan. In its coverage of the campaign's arrival at the train station, the pro-Bryan *New York Journal*, organ of thirty-three-year-old William Randolph Hearst, made it seem as if every New Yorker had turned out to welcome the candidate. Indeed, the paper had a record of offering wildly exaggerated estimates of the crowds that greeted Bryan all throughout his trip. The entire trip East, asserted the *Journal*, "was one continuous ovation for the Democratic candidate for the Presidency." The Bryan party themselves estimated the crowd at Harrisburg that day at only 5,000, while the *Journal* claimed 20,000.

Even so, the paper trumpeted its inflated figures as proof of a wave of support for Bryan—and, consequently, for free silver. "Unless all the evidence is misleading," the paper stated, "the silver sentiment throughout Pennsylvania, in New Jersey, and even in New

York, is as intense as in the Western States. It may be that the people of the East have not, until quite recently, caught the enthusiasm upon the silver question. But undoubtedly it is strong in the East." His New Jersey arrival was depicted as a "Riot of Enthusiasm," in one headline, a "Maelstrom of Cheering Men and Women" that almost engulfed the candidate. The *Journal* also said that the police drew their clubs in order to regain control but were restrained by Bryan himself. Whether true or not, it was certainly a wonderful example of the Great Commoner's common touch.

While the *Journal* tried to turn the near-riot to Bryan's advantage, most New York papers used it to criticize the arrangements for Bryan's visit. The large police presence itself was cause for comment, as well as the lack of organization and of a coherent plan to escort the candidate and his party. Before the train arrived, police officers had lined up behind a rope that stretched across the waiting space of the station. A sergeant for the Jersey police told a *Times* reporter that they had been ordered to keep the crowd away from the candidate. "All men seemed heartily ashamed of their work," the *Times* reported. One policeman supposedly said of Bryan, "I thought he was a man of the people, and here he has called out nearly half the Jersey City force to keep the people from seeing him." Another likened the protection that might be given to the Prince of Wales or the czar of Russia. After the police had stood along the rope-line for half an hour, they were split into three groups: one to keep a path clear for the train, one to keep a passage clear for the Bryan party once they had alighted, and one to act as bodyguards. Several detectives also mingled with the crowd and arrested two pickpockets, causing some commotion before the crowd returned its focus to Bryan's imminent arrival.

Unlike the cheering *Journal*, the other city papers depicted a more subdued greeting for the candidate, although they did acknowledge the enthusiasm of the small crowds. Estimates of the crowd from papers hostile to Bryan ranged from 1,500 down to only a few hundred, while the "regiment" of Jersey City police was estimated to be between seventy and a hundred men. About thirty reporters awaited Bryan's arrival. Also on hand were vice presidential nominee Arthur Sewall, national chairman James K. Jones, and national treasurer William St. John, at whose house the Bryans would stay. Arriving at about 8:30 PM, Bryan stepped down from the train and turned to help Mrs. Bryan down the steps. She then took Jones's arm as he escorted her through the crowd. The *Times* called the crowd's cheers "feeble" and gave an unflattering description of a travel-weary Bryan: "His face was travel-stained, and he seemed very much fatigued. He looked almost like a sick man and not like an Alexander seeking new worlds to conquer."

In order to avoid the crowd, the Bryans were conducted to the elevator used for lowering baggage to the ferryboat landing. Yet people simply made a dash down the stairs to the landing and were already awaiting the candidate when he emerged from the elevator. Bryan acknowledged the repeated cheers by waving his hat in the air, as Mrs. Bryan, "with a flush of pleasure," bowed to each side of her.

During their short walk to the ferryboat to Manhattan, however, things became dangerous. The crowd pressed in on all sides, and the members of the Bryan party became separated from one another. Mrs. Bryan was pushed away from Jones, and if St. John had not come to her rescue, observers said, "she might have been badly crushed." Mr. Bryan fared little better.

Despite the large police presence meant to protect the candidate from just such a situation, the police had obviously failed to make plans among themselves. Instead of forming a box around Bryan and clearing a passage to the ferryboat, the police became mixed with the crowd. One observer called the police arrangements "execrable" and said that "by their disorganized efforts [they helped] to create even worse disorder."

The Bryans finally boarded the ferry *Hudson City* with a small remnant of their party. Deck stools were brought for them, "and perspiring and upset by their struggles Mr. Bryan and his wife sat down with the remark that they were glad the struggle was over."

Suddenly a panic arose when the group failed to find Mrs. Bland among them. It took the aid of two policemen to extract her from the crowd at the rear of the boat and bring her forward. All the while the ferry passengers continued to cheer Mr. and Mrs. Bryan. One young man so attracted Mrs. Bryan's attention that she handed him her bunch of roses. "This work of favor was the young man's downfall," the *Tribune* said. "Instantly he was set upon by the people around him and in the fierce struggle for the flowers they were totally destroyed." Ultimately, all parties boarded the ferry without injury, but according to one observer, the reception had been "a gross failure."

The near-disaster shook Bryan's host, William St. John. For the remainder of their New York stay, St. John would ring William and Mary Bryan with a large amount of security. He would insist on a vast police presence wherever the candidate went, supplemented by a force of private detectives. St. John would even act as a sort of bodyguard to Mary Bryan, rudely shoving well-wishers out of the way. All this would serve to cut the Great Commoner off from the citizens of New York.

CROSSING FROM JERSEY CITY to Desbrosses Street in Lower Manhattan, Bryan followed one of the most traveled paths across the Hudson, one that dated from the time Native Americans used rafts and canoes centuries before Europeans arrived. Later the Holland Tunnel would open onto the city just a few blocks away, the longest underwater tunnel in the world when it opened in 1927. But with the Brooklyn Bridge still the only major span across the Hudson and East rivers, New Yorkers were absolutely dependent on ferries and had been since the years of New Amsterdam. Indeed, Bryan now crossed at the site of the very first chartered ferry serving Manhattan, the Netherlands Council granting its charter in 1661. After that, the number of ferry services and their passengers increased dramatically, and two hundred years after the first ferry 50 million New Yorkers were taking the ferry every year. By the time Bryan rode the *Hudson City* across the river, the common saying held that when there was fog in the harbor, half the business population of New York would be late for work.

Bryan's trip across the Hudson by ferry invited more comment than if he had simply ridden into the city like candidates in later years. Some papers called the Hudson Bryan's Rubicon; others referred to it as his Delaware, the river George Washington crossed into New Jersey before the Battle of Trenton.

Perhaps writers for the New York journals were too jaded to comment on it, but for Bryan and his wife, there must have been a certain drama to the river crossing. Approaching the city across the relative calm of the water, and watching as the thousands of lights of Lower Manhattan slowly drew closer, must have made a great impression on the two residents of Lincoln, Nebraska. Suddenly after days of hurtling toward the city, covering hundreds of miles a day by rail, the journey seemed to have slipped into a kind of slow motion, as the outlines of new "skyscrapers"—a word already in common usage—hoved into view. Such an arrival into the city was perhaps particularly fitting for the populist Bryan. As a man who made his career railing against the Money Power, of which railroads were one of the most ubiquitous examples, abandoning the train for a ferryboat ride possibly appealed to his sense of right. Bryan was probably unaware that the Pennsylvania Railroad also operated the *Hudson City.*

After the fiasco in Jersey City, it was a relief to the arriving party that police arrangements were more satisfactory on the New York side. Police held the crowd back until Bryan left the boat, and he was taken out a side door to the entrance of the neighboring ferry slip. Three carriages drove the party two miles to the St. John home, where a small crowd of about 150 people waited. In fact the crowd seemed drawn more by the large police presence than any foreknowledge that Bryan was soon to arrive.

One cabman driving by suddenly brought his horse up with a jerk and asked, "Wat t'ell's goin' on here?" "Bryan's coming," called out a policeman. "The devil he is," the cabman replied, as he whipped his horses and drove off. "Just tell him that you saw me." The Bryans' carriage soon arrived, and the party walked rapidly into the house, ignoring the cheers from the street. After the door had closed, a loud voice across the street tried to revive the enthusiasm of the disappointed crowd by calling out the first part of the old campaign chant, "What's the matter with Bryan?"

At that very moment Bryan emerged from the house again and walked out on the steps. A hush fell on the crowd, and the broad base of the stone steps lit by the electric lamps gave the impression of an actor stepping onto the stage. "His pale face was outlined by the electric glare," one witness described, "his tangled hair fell down over his shoulders, and his eyes seemed to flash in the light, and, as he drew himself erect the audience caught just for an instant a fleeting glimpse of a magnetic pose, such as he might have brought into play when he carried the hysterical and emotional Convention at Chicago along with him."

Bryan stood on the step and looked both ways down the street, perhaps looking for more people, as the situation in the street below was one to which he was unaccustomed: Here he was in the largest American city, faced with a small and completely quiet crowd of fewer than two hundred people. Unlike his reception in other cities, the crowds that had greeted his arrival in New York, both at the ferryboat and at St. John's house, numbered under three hundred total. What hope did he have, then, of filling the 15,000-seat auditorium of Madison Square Garden? Bryan turned back toward the house as if to go back inside, and now the crowd erupted into applause and cries of "Speech!" But Bryan only shook his head and stepped back into the house.

By prior arrangement, Bryan had agreed to meet with newspapermen at 10:00 PM, but as the train had been delayed, this meeting did not take place until nearly 11:00. It promised to be a short meeting, since before Bryan appeared, St. John lectured the newspapermen, "Now, with Mr. Bryan, this is going to be 'How-de-do,' and 'Goodby,'" one of the reporters present recounted. "The man is thoroughly tired out. You must not ask him a question. If you have any questions to ask, you may ask them of me, and I will answer so far as I can, or get the answer from him."

"Now," said St. John, with a hint of theatricality, "you may see Mr. Bryan." He then opened a set of sliding doors, revealing Bryan, washed, smiling, and perfectly attired in evening dress, standing amid a bower of flowers sent by well-wishers. To proffered hands Bryan held up his, showing them to be badly discolored and swollen. "You see," Bryan said in a whisper, "I have had a hard time of it shaking hands from the rear of the cars. They would give me a hearty clasp, and I tell you that the number of times that hand has been wrung has been enough to make me wince." Noting his rasp, one reporter cautioned him against speaking more and suggested a certain liquor-based cure. "The remedies suggested for my throat," Bryan laughingly replied, "are limited only by the number of people that I have talked with within the last two days. I will be all right tomorrow." With that, the meeting with New York reporters was over. St. John announced that the candidate would see no one and give no further interviews or speeches before his appearance at the Garden the following night.

As BRYAN HAD entered New York, the Democratic National Committee had finalized arrangements for the meeting at Madison Square Garden at last. Over 30,000 applications for tickets had been made, with most of them turned down. Organizers worried that many New Yorkers assumed that the Madison Square Garden meeting was a political rally and thus open to all. They still remembered Grover Cleveland's notification in 1892, when a crush of people seeking admission had caused women to faint and almost led to a mass panic. To avoid such a calamity, organizers had requested a large police presence, and Chief of Police Conlin had also announced the presence of a police surgeon to care for anyone stricken by the heat.

On the stage with Bryan would be a scattering of leading Democrats, with many prominent absences such as Senator Hill and Tammany politicians. Their places would be taken by leading silver advocates, like Richard Bland, Senator Joe Blackburn of Kentucky, and Senator Ben Tillman of South Carolina. Indeed the city seemed to be awash in southern and western politicians. "The buffalo herd is coming," one fervent free-silver advocate shouted in the Fifth Avenue Hotel corridor. "The stampede is making its way east!"

V

BRYAN FELL WITH A BANG

Come along get you ready wear your bran, bran new gown,
For dere's gwine to be a meeting in that good, good old town,
Where you knowed ev'ry body, and they all knowed you,
And you've got a rabbits foot to keep away the hoodoo;
Where you hear that the preaching does begin,
Bend down low for to drive away your sin   .
And when you gets religion, you want to shout and sing,
There'll be a hot time in the old town tonight, my baby.
FROM THE SONG "A HOT TIME IN THE OLD TOWN," 1896

D URING THE 1896 campaign Mary Bryan recorded in a small
notebook the many gifts her husband received from well-
wishers. These included: "One pair of suspenders. One
cane. One band wagon. One mule. One silk bed quilt. . . . One os-
trich egg."

Canes were the most frequent gift, made from materials such as
petrified wood, fish vertebrae, and antelope horn. The head of one
cane represented an eagle with diamonds for eyes—after one large
public reception the Bryans found the diamonds had disappeared. A
fungus that bore a resemblance to Bryan was sent, as well as an egg
with a shell formation that suggested the candidate's initials. Rabbits'
feet arrived in large quantities. "If there be virtue in the hind foot of
a rabbit procured under the most favorable circumstances," Mary
wrote years later, "Mr. Bryan should have won this election. It is difficult to imagine that his opponent was more adequately supplied

with rabbits' feet; plain, furry little feet, feet mounted in every in-
genious form . . . came to us with such frequency that they are not
included in the notebook record." As a Christian, William Jennings
Bryan likely rejected such totems, although at the speech on the night
of August 12 he would need help from every quarter to "keep away
the hoodoo."

In Brooklyn, the Russell family of Huron Street particularly suffered on the day of the big meeting. Patrick Russell, seventy-three
years old and a retired merchant, visited his eldest daughter in Manhattan on one of the hottest days of the year, returned home, and died.
His youngest daughter, Mary, was prostrated in the city and taken
to Presbyterian Hospital, where she later died. Finally, Russell's son,
Patrick Russell Jr., a clerk in Brooklyn's Hall of Records, stayed
home from work to attend to his family and to funeral arrangements.
His wife became prostrated, and after fetching a doctor for her,
Patrick himself succumbed to the heat and died. His wife was not
expected to recover, which would make four deaths from heat in one
family within twenty-four hours. It is quite possible that as a clerk
in the Hall of Records, Russell had been exceedingly busy with filing
death certificates. The day before he died, Brooklyn recorded 178
deaths, more than twice the number of deaths on August 8, and
nearly three times the more normal number of 64 deaths recorded
on August 4. Now the Russell family death certificates would be
among the 147 filed that day in the Brooklyn Hall of Records.

With the Herald Square thermometer again hitting 103 degrees,
while the official reading by Mr. Dunn reached a laughable 92, New
Yorkers suffered through their ninth day of killer heat. Perhaps 200
New Yorkers perished from the heat in Manhattan alone, with the
total number of deaths easing only slightly from the record of 386
the day before. New York's laborers continued to bear the brunt of

the heat wave, although fifty infants under age one died on Tuesday, August 11.

As the airless, windowless tenements baked their inhabitants, the heat wave decimated entire families, like the Russells of Brooklyn. At 228 West Nineteenth Street, one black and white crepe streamer and one deep black streamer hung from the doorbell, announcing to visitors the double tragedy that occurred. The five members of the Abbott family—the widowed mother, two sons, and two daughters— occupied an apartment on the second floor. By all accounts they were an exceedingly close and happy family, especially the relationship between the mother and her son Edward. Thirty-four years old and a driver for the milliners H. O'Neill and Company, Edward had returned home from a hard day's work on Saturday feeling tired but not seriously ill. No one in the Abbott house was particularly worried as Edward was young, with a strong physique and excellent health. The next evening, however, Edward suddenly fell ill from the heat and lost consciousness. The summoned physician tried to revive him, but after only five hours Edward Abbott passed away. Within only twenty-four hours, then, the young Abbott went from feeling merely tired to dying. It was a shocking example of how quickly the heat could claim an otherwise healthy young man.

With the family gathered around Edward's bed, sixty-two-year-old Mrs. Abbott now complained of feeling ill, and a physician was once again summoned. With their mother in bed and attended to by a doctor, the remaining Abbott children made arrangements for their brother's funeral to take place the morning of August 12 at St. Francis Xavier's Church. At eight o'clock the evening of August 11, Mrs. Abbott died. In the morning a 10:00 AM mass for the repose of the souls of both mother and son was said, and their bodies were later buried together. Until the time of the mass, the bodies of mother and son lay side by side in the stifling tenement they had called home. Flowers and small tokens brought by friends and relatives lay on the two coffins. One observer noted that between sobs of grief the mourners asked one another, "Who shall be next?"

The treacherous swathe of pavement in front of city hall, recently come to be known as "Death Pass," continued to claim victims that day, as a "shabbily dressed" man succumbed on the hot asphalt. His identity was unknown, as was true for many victims. New York Hospital alone recorded four cases of deaths without any names associated with the bodies. One man who died suddenly at Broadway and Murray could only be described as having "dark hair and sandy mustache" and wearing a "dark coat and vest and striped trousers." It was a telling commentary of life in the rapidly expanding city, one filling up with tens of thousands of additional immigrants every year.

While the city fostered associations of every kind, from fraternal orders to reading clubs, from St. Patrick's for Irishmen to the Harvard Club for alumni, the vast metropolis simultaneously cultivated isolation and alienation. For every club that collected those of similar ideas or origins under its roof, there also existed in the city a charitable organization that ministered to the "fallen" and "destitute." The famous Water Street Mission was said to have been a "profound benefit to thousands of outcasts," transforming "fallen men and women" into useful members of society. The House of Mercy and the House of the Good Shepherd tended to "fallen women and girls," while the Invalids' Home and Home for Incurables gave shelter and comfort to those awaiting death. A dozen homes existed for the aged, "for men and women suffering from friendlessness and penury." Even so, for every man or woman indeed saved from homelessness or destitution, countless others slipped through the cracks. The dozen nameless victims of today's heat provided ample evidence of this sad reality of American urban life. During the past week over one hundred bodies of unclaimed dead had been taken to Potter's Field on Hart Island. The boat responsible for taking the bodies from the city normally made only three trips to the island each week, but several extra trips had been required during the heat wave. Still, so many unclaimed bodies remained at the morgue awaiting burial that extra staff had to be hired.

While New Yorkers could not help but see the bodies of the dead horses that festered in every city block, other animals suffered as well. The oldest American buffalo in the Central Park menagerie, "Uncle Bill," died in the intense heat. His body was taken to the Museum of Natural History, where his skeleton would one day be on display. The other animals at the zoo survived but showed signs of stress. "The polar bear immersed himself in the tank of water at the bottom of his cage, and did not look happy. The lions and tigers crawled into the shade. The seagulls and penguins gasped for breath, and the hyena laughed dryly."

Dogs continued to be gunned down in the street by policemen summoned by nervous pedestrians, frightened by the sight of a staggering and salivating cur. Like the horse corpses littering the streets, not every dead dog enjoyed a speedy burial. On Sunday afternoon a police officer of the Thirty-Seventh Street station shot and killed a dog, and then promptly reported the incident in order that the Board of Health might remove the body. On every night afterward, the police officer reported the incident, as the dog's dead body remained untouched in front of a Broadway apartment house. After three days of lying directly in the sun, the dog's rotting body created a fearful stench. Someone had covered the corpse with straw, but the smell remained. The owner of the apartment building had made re-peated requests to the Health Department for the dog's removal, but with hundreds of horses still lying uncollected in the streets, the body of one small dog was a low priority.

In the midst of such heat, ice continued to be a precious com-modity. Crowds of children clustered around stopped ice wagons begging for the smallest chip of ice. Most deliverymen were generous with their load and disposed of any ice that would be wasted anyway. Yet ice wagon driver Isaac Franklyn wasn't so generous to laborer Jacob Gorschkovitch. Gorschkovitch stepped on Franklyn's wagon to obtain a morsel of ice, and Franklyn responded by shoving the man so violently that he fell and broke his arm. Franklyn was charged with assault. In another part of the city, a ten-year-old boy was knocked down and run over by an ice wagon driven by John Von-stettin. Knowing all the city ambulances were busy, a policeman hailed a passing cab and sent the boy to the Hudson Street Hospital, where he was listed in grave condition. The driver was being held by police to await the result of the boy's injuries.

With the heat affecting New Yorkers' minds in such ways, Bryan may have been in more danger than he realized. Over the previous weekend, Martin Broderick, a twenty-five-year-old brickmason from Hudson, New York, and father of two, left his home and family without a word to anyone. From Hudson he traveled to Albany, where he bought a revolver. He then traveled to Chicago to await the arrival of the Bryan train. Upon the Bryans' departure from Chicago, Broderick boarded the same train and traveled with his revolver all the way to New York. His motive remained unclear. If he had any intention to harm Bryan, he had ample opportunity during the sev-eral days' trip from Chicago to New York. In the age before the massive protection afforded presidential candidates, and only five years before McKinley himself would be felled by a man carrying a revolver under a handkerchief, Bryan constituted an easy target for even an unskilled assassin. One paper identified Broderick as a "Bryan man," perhaps indicating that he hoped to protect the candidate from injury.

Whatever his motive, Broderick disembarked from the train with Bryan and made his way to the New York home of his brother James on Ninety-Eighth Street. Martin told his brother his story, exhibiting the revolver. Much alarmed, James Broderick finally convinced his disturbed brother to retire and get some rest. The following morning James secured a promise from Martin to remain inside the house while he went to work. Feeling anxious for his brother, at home alone with a revolver, James soon returned from work to find a large and excited crowd surrounding his home. In his absence his brother Martin had shot himself in the breast, inflicting a critical wound. As Martin was being taken from the house, James told a reporter that he believed his brother's mind "was affected by the heat."

This strange episode of the 1896 campaign has been entirely forgotten, perhaps because of its enigmatic nature. Was Broderick's story true or just the fantasy of a disturbed mind? Did he really travel on the same train as the Bryans, and if so, how close did he come to the candidate? Was this an assassination attempt? Bryan may very well have been lucky to avoid an assassin's bullet, part of the charmed existence he had been leading since his nomination. Madison Square Garden would bring his lucky streak to an end.

***

I N 1932, Franklin Roosevelt became the first candidate of a major party to accept the presidential nomination in person at the national convention. With politicians still worried about appearing too ambitious or power-hungry, tradition held that they exhibit some restraint when notified of the nomination.

By 1896 there was little precedent for a candidate to accept the nomination at a huge rally like the one planned for Madison Square Garden that night. Abraham Lincoln had been notified of the 1860 Republican nomination at his home in Springfield and took a couple days to write a letter of acceptance. In 1868 the Democratic nominee, Horatio Seymour, had addressed a room full of people at Tammany headquarters in New York. For the next twenty-four years candidates accepted the nomination of their parties at their homes, in the clubrooms of hotels, or in the legislatures and governors' mansions where they served. There was only one clear precedent for the Bryan notification ceremony at Madison Square Garden in 1896. It occurred four years before, when Grover Cleveland accepted the nomination on a dangerously hot night in Madison Square Garden.

July 1892 had been so hot that those New Yorkers who were able to had fled the city for the cooler climes of the Long Island and New Jersey shores. Many believed that the seemingly empty city could not provide enough spectators to fill Madison Square Garden for a political rally. Yet on July 20, an estimated 15,000 enthusiastic Cleveland supporters filled the still-new auditorium to hear the ex-president accept the nomination.

It was the first rally of its kind, part of the slow erosion of the republican restraint and decorum dating back to George Washington that kept candidates from "running" for office or openly seeking the nomination. The 1892 meeting also offered a number of contrasts with Bryan's notification ceremony four years later. Cleveland was a hometown boy addressing the most sympathetic audience in the country. Even the normally Republican *New York Times* greeted his candidacy with enthusiasm. Every prominent New York Democrat was present that July night, including Tammany men like Richard Croker. That night Police Commissioner Martin not only was present but personally cleared a path for Cleveland. Cleveland gave such a short speech that the text did not even fill a full column in the next day's papers. Yet he gave his speech without reference to notes, and the *Times* called it "excellent." Even so, Madison Square Garden was dangerously crowded and overheated.

Right from the start the meeting was out of control. When the doors opened that July night, approximately 5,000 people dashed into the auditorium to get first pick of seats. One paper likened it to a dam bursting, and noted that women and old men were part of this "sprint" for seats. That some spectator was not trampled was nothing short of a miracle. At another point during the rally the crowd surged forward and actually snapped a guardrail directly in front of the speakers' platform. Men sprang onto chairs in preparation for leaping onto the platform itself, and one man fainted in the crush. A panic almost ensued, and only the cool demeanors of Cleveland and the other speakers calmed the crowd. In spite of the chaos, New Yorkers of all political shades were unanimous in calling the historic meeting a great success.

Four years made a big difference for the Democrats. Cleveland's name and portrait were nowhere to be seen even at the national convention in Chicago, let alone at Madison Square Garden. Indeed, Bryan's nomination and the very Democratic platform were repudiations of the sitting president.

Partly as a result, Democrats themselves were especially divided. Before Bryan's arrival in the city, many New York Democrats had publicly split with their own party's candidate, and Senator David Hill refused even to take part in the ceremony. Tammany Democrats like Cockran were conspicuously absent. New York did not seem a hospitable environment for Bryan at all.

The Bryan campaign had chosen New York City for largely the opposite reason Cleveland had four years before: not because it would generate a sympathetic and enthusiastic hometown crowd, but because it was the "enemy's country" and needed to be turned to the Democrats' cause that year. The size and nature of the crowd that greeted the candidate outside the St. John house seemed to have shocked Bryan. He had expected a cheering and adoring throng numbering in the thousands. When faced with a handful of silent gawkers instead, he had quickly retreated through the front door. No, the Madison Square Garden speech was never really for the skeptical and merely curious New Yorkers, but for the country in general. This is why Bryan made the controversial decision to read a long and complicated speech. Combined with the heat wave, it doomed Bryan's big night from the outset.

"The next day [after arriving] was spent resting and getting my speech into print," Bryan later recalled. By seven o'clock that night his voice had largely—although not completely—recovered. Even New York's sympathetic press, such as the *New York World*, noted that his voice still remained husky and that after only ten minutes of reading his speech his breathing became labored. The effects of the train trip clearly lingered.

While starting the campaign before the official notification had worked wonders for Bryan's apparently booming popularity, the exhaustion caused by giving several speeches a day in extreme heat took its toll. Simply staying in William St. John's home resting for twenty-four hours did not allow for the deep recuperation he needed. On the eve of embarking on a campaign the likes of which the country had never seen before, his trip to New York that August may have served as a primer on what not to do. Even the young, powerful Bryan had limits, and he had clearly reached them by the time his train screeched to a halt in Jersey City.

WHILE BRYAN PREPARED for the rally that evening, the New York police made the final arrangements at Madison Square Garden. In addition to keeping order and watching for pickpockets, New York's Finest prepared for the inevitable victims of heat. A temporary hospital had been established in the basement under the supervision of Dr. Charles E. Nammack, chief police surgeon. The police department had supplied a dozen cots, while a representative of the Department of Charities, on hand at the Garden that evening, had arranged for blankets and air pillows to be sent from Bellevue Hospital. A moveable bathtub, tubs of ice, aromatic spirits of ammonia, and special caps made with ice were readied for victims of the heat.

Inside the auditorium itself four policemen were stationed at various points, armed with white flags bearing a red cross. In the event of an audience member falling victim to the heat, the policeman would give the signal to other teams of policemen armed with stretchers and accompanied by one of the Bellevue doctors. While the press would later criticize the police for barring some reporters' entry, their precautions for victims of heat appeared thorough and professional.

In spite of the total police presence of 275 men inside the Garden, disaster almost struck when the doors were opened at 7:00 PM. Harkening back to the Cleveland meeting four years before, thousands of people immediately rushed through the doors and raced for open seats. "The crush of human beings was frightful," one observer noted. "It was a panic to all intents and purposes," said another, "and the weakest was sent to the wall." As the police tried to "stem the tide," Patrolman Andrew Devery was struck so violently in the stomach that he had to be taken to the basement hospital, the first casualty of the evening. Another policeman was knocked down by the crowd, and yet another pressed by the crowd so hard against the interior glass doors that he nearly broke through.

Twenty-five policemen had been stationed at the entrance to deal with the crowd, and they attempted several times to form a wedge and cut the crowd in two. Just outside the doors the situation was the same. Acting Deputy Chief Moses W. Cortright commanded the policemen attempting to control the stampede of people. A powerful man of strong build, he took an active role in trying to press the crowd back to prevent injury, and after fifteen minutes of extreme exertion, he became the first heat victim of the evening. Led to the basement by one of his men, Cortright had aromatic spirits of ammonia and an ice cap administered to him by Dr. Nammack. Within the hour Cortright had recovered and wanted to return to duty, but the doctor kept him in the hospital until ten o'clock.

In the end, no case of heat prostration was severe enough to warrant the ice bath, and all of the cases of heat exhaustion came early in the evening during that initial crush at the entrance. Once inside the vast auditorium, the panic subsided. "Strong men drew aside to adjust their garments after the wild stampede," one reporter observed, "and women gasped their relief at so narrow an escape from physical injury."

The Garden was hot. One observer noted a temperature of 97 degrees, with the sticky humidity caused by the close-packed thousands. In fact the heat seemed to make more of an impression on the audience than Bryan's speech. "Sweltering," was a common word. "Furnace-like," one person said.

The audience's suffering was prodigious. "Anything for Comfort," a *Tribune* subheading announced, in a special section dedicated to covering only the spectators' actions in the heat. A number of observers noted that with every coat and vest removed, the audience appeared as a sea of white. "The south gallery which stretched its length opposite the rostrum looked not unlike a laundry with its washing hung to the breeze after the crowd had disposed itself for the season of refreshing," the *Tribune* reporter wrote. "Every man elbowed his neighbor with freedom as he wielded his enormous palm-leaf fan after the awkward fashion peculiar to the male sex when in a hurry to cool off after a period of undue exertion, and every fan-wielding arm was innocent of a coat-sleeve. Coats and waistcoats had disappeared. Negligé was the order and it was pressed to the limit of respectable possibilities."

Right on cue at 7:30, the band began to play, but few in the audience took heed. "The vast majority were looking for a breeze that cometh not from the business end of a brass horn in operation," the writer for the *Tribune* continued. "It was not a melody but a blizzard that your New-Yorker wanted, and if Mr. Bryan, instead of bringing his speech, had carried a Rocky Mountain zephyr in his handbag and poured it with unstinting hand upon the perspiring mob he might have counted more surely on ultimate success in this campaign than from any possible effect his speech as a finality made for him." "The movement of three solid acres of fans," said the *World*, "was like the gentle surge of the sea."

Everyone was aware that this was not an ordinary Democratic rally. The *New York Times* printed a long list of "Prominent Democrats

Not Swallowed by the Populists," including Grover Cleveland, David Hill, William Bourke Cockran, and Roosevelt's politically active uncle, Robert Roosevelt. As members of the Democratic National Committee began entering the auditorium, no one let out a cheer, and vice presidential nominee Arthur Sewall's entrance sparked no interest at all. One newspaper recorded the first cheer occurring at exactly 7:57 PM, when a man in one of the highest galleries shouted, "Three cheers for Bryan," although the reporter swore the man actually said "O'Brien." The band then struck up with the song "My Girl's a Corker":

> My girl's a corker, she's a New Yorker
> I buy her everything to keep her in style
> She's got a pair of legs, just like two whiskey kegs
> Hey boys, that's where my money goes-oes-oes

It was a ribald burlesque song that included lyrics such as "She does the teasin', I do the squeezin'," and "She wears silk underwear, I wear my latest pair," not to mention couplets like "She's got a pair of hips, just like two battle ships." It was at this unfortunate moment that Mrs. Bryan chose to appear on stage. She gazed out at the vast auditorium and seemed to enjoy being the focus of the small tumult that accompanied her appearance. It was unlikely that she was familiar with the lyrics of "My Girl's a Corker."

As Mrs. Bryan and members of the National Committee took their seats on the stage, a man took up position at the rear of the rostrum with an oversized American flag. He waved it at every opportunity, and when Bryan finally appeared, the man carried the flag down and "tried to insert the staff in the resisting palm of the Presidential candidate, who looked unmercifully bored at this effort to make of him a male Columbia posing in a grand tableau for effect." If planners wanted Bryan to take the flag, they certainly hadn't warned the candidate. This attempt at theatricality marked an awkward beginning to the proceedings.

The task of introducing the candidate fell to Governor William J. Stone of Missouri. He read his speech from a little notebook and was constantly interrupted by calls for Bryan. The curious New York audience had not come to listen to the governor of Missouri. The high point of Stone's speech came when he laid into England and asked rhetorical questions that received such "machine-like" responses that one reporter suspected the audience participation had been orchestrated. "Shall we be bound in financial servitude to England?" Stone asked. "No! No!" came the reply. "Shall we follow or lead?" "Lead! Lead!" "Shall we be sovereign or vassal?" "Sovereign! Sovereign!" Finally, the opposition from the crowd overwhelmed his words, and throwing the little notebook aside, the governor lifted above his head a white scroll representing the Chicago platform. "Take this," he exclaimed to Bryan, "assume leadership, and we will follow!"

Finally, Bryan's time had come. To the roars of the audience he repeatedly raised his hands to command silence. He moved his jaws nervously as though chewing something. He sat down again, and only when the chairman pounded the edge of the platform with his gavel did the noise cease. Bryan rose again, and one reporter described the candidate in close detail:

He is a tall, powerfully built and strikingly handsome man. His brow is broad and high and his large, firmly curved nose, the mark of ambition and command, juts out between dark, hazel eyes that kindle and flash.

His head is thickly covered with black wavy hair, which curls over and conceals the tips of his finely formed and characteristic ears. His hair is so long at the back that it curves upward from the coat collar. His jaws are wide and strong. His chin is massive, the chin of a born fighter. His upper lip is long and his mouth is large and mobile, almost too large. Mr. Bryan's mouth is the least pleasant feature in his face. When he speaks he uses his lips as though his teeth projected and there is a curious lisping or hissing sound from many of his words. His neck is thick and sinewy.

His head is massive and high, the sign of a reverent nature. His arms are very long and his hands are big, sinewy hands, carpenter's hands, practical hands, with strong spatulate fingers, a curious thing to find in an idealist. Mr. Bryan's hands are not those which are usually owned by imaginative men, and they go far to prove his wife's often-repeated assertion that he is a deliberate, slow-thinking and laborious man. His legs which were hidden from the audience by the pulpit, are thick and muscular. His feet are broad. He was dressed in a black suit, with a sack coat and a white tie. A tiny diamond sparked on his shirt front.

Bryan held up a thick sheaf of pages, his face pale and his hands shaking, and began to speak. He held the pages close to his face, lowering and raising the manuscript again and again. Perhaps not used to standing in a fixed spot during his speeches, he swayed from side to side as he shifted his weight from one foot to the other. He did not attempt oratorical techniques of any sort and was hardly recognizable as one of America's greatest public speakers. "It was not the old Bryan of dash and fire, but a careful man, treading unknown soil," one man observed.

Within five minutes the crowd began to leave. Bryan appeared not to notice, but Mary Bryan watched the exodus closely and with a worried expression. For the first twelve minutes of what would be a hundred-minute speech, no one in the audience even applauded. Within fifteen minutes, perhaps 2,000 people had left the auditorium, although one New York paper estimated departures at over 5,000. With hundreds of people leaving every minute, the very din of so many shoes made his speech almost impossible to hear.

In the midst of unbearable heat, as it became clear that there would be no repeat of the much-heralded "Cross of Gold" speech, few saw any reason to stay. Some speculated that perhaps as many as two-thirds of the seats were empty by the time Bryan sat down. Others suggested that some people stayed out of "pity" or that so many silverites had come East for the big speech they could not leave before it was over. Many papers noted that the Garden was packed by Tammany "heelers," loyal party men who had been ordered to stay. Clearly, though, the mass of New Yorkers who had come for the big show was disappointed.

The decision to read the manuscript had been a strategic one, as Bryan knew the text would be reprinted nationally the next day. Yet it was also a tactical error. His success at the Chicago convention had resulted less from the actual text of the speech than from his oratory and its frenzied reception. Had he caused an equivalent stir in hostile New York, *this* would have been the main story across the country the following day. As it was, he might have indeed given a "temperate and masterly effort," according to one paper, but most would have agreed with the *Tribune*'s editorial headline, "MR. BRYAN'S LABORIOUS FAILURE."

With Bryan's words overshadowed by the departure of his audience, the significance of the speech has been almost lost to history. Those who listened to him before leaving the Garden that night complained that he was too timid and apologetic. Gone were the attack against the Money Power and the violent rhetoric of burning cities and crucifixion that marked the Chicago speech. Instead, he presented himself as a moderate, even a conservative, ready to defend property rights and the status quo.

Bryan actually began by quoting his ideological opposite, Andrew Jackson: "'Distinctions in society will always exist under every just government. Equality of talents, of education or of wealth, cannot be produced by human institutions. In the full enjoyment of the gifts of Heaven and the fruits of superior industry, economy and virtue, every man is equally entitled to protection by law.'" Bryan's purpose, then, was not to level society or divvy up the spoils of industry. "Our campaign has not for its object the reconstruction of society," he proclaimed. "We cannot insure to the vicious the fruits of a virtuous life; we would not invade the home of the provident in order to supply the wants of the spendthrift; we do not propose to transfer the rewards of industry to the lap of indolence."

A laundry list of all those things a Bryan administration would *not* do was in itself a recipe for somnolence. Anyone attending that night's performance expecting a fiery attack on the robber barons and their political allies in Washington had to be disappointed as they listened to him calmly announce, "Property is and will remain the stimulus to endeavor and the compensation for toil." People not knowing better might have believed they had stumbled into a McKinley rally.

The rest of the speech was a long and dreary defense of bimetallism. Bryan offered nothing new, and certainly nothing as exciting or memorable as the "Cross of Gold." In fact, the text he read from was really suited only for print and did not allow for passion. One paragraph began: "The theoretical advantage of the bimetallic system is best stated by a European writer on political economy."

One could barely even call this a speech. It was a treatise, almost an academic paper, and it stimulated a predictable response from the 15,000 men and women sitting elbow to elbow in near-100 degree heat, fanning themselves with "Bryan Silver Fans." There were no references to the rest of the Democratic platform shaped in Chicago, and students of the 1896 election will be excused from assuming that silver was the only issue discussed there. The platform that year included references to the Monroe Doctrine and sympathy for the rebelling Cubans, references that might have provoked some applause if Bryan had made them. There was a plank against the "importation of pauper labor" as a way of protecting American labor. The Democratic platform's condemnation of "centralization of Governmental authority" and "the arbitrary interference by Federal authorities in local affairs" might also have highlighted the "Democratic" character of the Democratic platform, while illustrating that Bryan had ammunition in his arsenal other than a single silver bullet. As it was, however, Bryan spent over an hour discussing bimetallism, as New Yorkers by the thousands made for the Garden's exits.

When Bryan finished, he sat down to enthusiastic but scattered cheers. The next day the sympathetic *New York World* had the headline: "The Effect Marred by the Vast Auditorium and Terrific Heat—Only Half the Audience Stayed to the End," and recounted: "When the young orator arose to speak the temperature in the building was 97 degrees of Fahrenheit. But before he finished the thermometer showed a fall of two degrees. The scientific explanation of this fact is that at least 4,000 persons had left the hall. Within five minutes after the beginning of the speech at least a thousand men departed." This was, the paper said, partly as a result of the "depressing effect of the heat," leaving Bryan "demoralized by the spectacle of thousands of his hearers marching slowly out of the doors." Arthur Sewall then stood for a short speech, and the meeting was over.

ONLY THE MOST rabid pro-Bryan supporters claimed victory after the Garden speech. Certainly many blamed the extreme temperature inside the auditorium, a killer heat that had claimed hundreds of lives in New York by the time Bryan addressed his audience. Others blamed his choice to read from a manuscript or his exhaustion from his long, hot train trip east. Still others blamed the entrenched hostility of the East to Bryan's brand of rural populism. Probably all of these conclusions were correct, and they combined to leave Madison Square Garden half-empty at the end of a speech Bryan himself had called his "greatest opportunity."

The glee among Republicans was almost transparent as they discussed the speech in their letters. Joseph Foraker, the former governor of Ohio who would win a seat in the U.S. Senate in this election, said, "Mr. Bryan made himself by one speech, and now he has unmade himself by one speech." Mark Hanna relished the fact that Bryan had talked only of silver during the speech. "He's talking silver all the time and that's where we've got him," he said.

To his friend Henry Cabot Lodge, Roosevelt wrote that Bryan "fell perfectly flat here in New York, his big notification meeting has simply hurt him." To his sister Roosevelt wrote a longer evaluation:

> Bryan fell with a bang . . . In his speech he tried to do the "dignified statesman" business, and he merely lost what little renown he had

as a wild-eyed popular orator; his only chance was with the people who care for neither dignity nor statesmanship, and this he threw away. He not only hurt himself very much here in the east, but also in the west. I believe the tide has begun to flow against him. The educational work done about finance by the distribution of pamphlets has been enormous, and it is telling. It is hard to reach the slow, obstinate farmer; but all who can be reached are being reached.

The police commissioner's letter reveals as much about Roosevelt as it does about Bryan's speech. For Roosevelt, Bryan was a classic demagogue, a "wild-eyed popular orator" who could manipulate the ignorant masses. Yet Roosevelt, despite his anti-Bryan bias, remained a keen observer of American politics. He rightly noted that by going the "dignified" route Bryan had thrown away his advantage as a skilled orator. He was correct that the New York speech marked the exact moment when the tide began to flow against him. Roosevelt was no admirer of Bryan, but he respected the threat that Bryan represented to Republicans that year. After the Garden speech, that threat appeared to have significantly diminished.

As Roosevelt remained out on Long Island during Bryan's meeting, he must have gleaned most of his information from the newspapers. This included how well the police performed that evening. In fact, the police preparations were recounted by every New York paper, with mixed evaluations. Most papers gave the police good reviews, noting that they were out in force, well-prepared, and "good-natured." The fact that a fatal crush did not ensue was directly credited to the police, as was the absence of any heat-related fatalities. The *New York Tribune* said, "Rarely before in the history of anything belonging to earth and demanding police protection has there been such elaborateness and perfection of detail as were plainly manifested at this meeting." Many observers noted the wise decision to cordon off the Garden at a two-block radius to prevent a deadly crush at the doors. Only ticket holders, then, would be able to pass this first line of 1,000 policemen still two blocks from the Garden.

The shabby treatment of some reporters resulted in bad marks for Roosevelt's police. Chief of Police Conlin himself had personally signed entry orders for the benefit of newspapermen, but not every policeman received the message clearly. When the *Tribune* reporter showed a "burly sergeant" the order signed by his chief, the sergeant asked, "Who the divil's that?" It took the reporter an hour to cross the police line and enter the Garden. The reporter from the *New York Sun* was also turned away and wrote a blistering attack on the police the next day.

Roosevelt wrote his friend Lodge with an explanation. "As I know you will see the *Sun*," he began, "I wish to say that every other paper in New York, no matter of what politics, spoke in the highest terms of the way the Police handled the crowd at the Bryan notification meeting. The trouble with the *Sun* was that its reporter got there after the house was full, the notification people having issued just twice the number of tickets that there were seats, and after the house was filled the Police of course had no other alternative than to turn every one back." The *Herald* actually defended this policy of the police as well, calling it a "wise" decision, "for had the rush within been permitted to continue there would have been many heat prostrations and a possible panic."

With the Garden meeting finished, Bryan, Sewall, and their party departed for the Democratic headquarters at the Bartholdi Hotel. There Bryan gave a short, impromptu speech that had more passion, religion, and humor than his two-hour Garden speech. "Some of your financiers have boasted that they favor gold," Bryan told the small crowd from the hotel balcony, "but you shall teach them that they must carry their ideas far enough to believe, not in gold, but in the golden rule that treats all men alike. I commission you as soldiers to fight and as missionaries to preach wherever you go from now on until election day."

Bryan declared himself unafraid of the threat of a gold-standard Democratic Party organized to oppose him. "You will search the pages of history in vain to find a battle that was ever won by generals," he asserted. "They have not a private in their ranks." He ended with a rousing affirmation that in the United States "every citizen is a sovereign," and every citizen owed it to himself and his country to exercise the right of suffrage.

The Bartholdi speech, although only a few minutes in length, contained all the religious militancy that the Garden speech lacked. Some in the Garden that night had paid $10 a ticket for the privilege of sitting inside for two hours on one of the hottest nights of the year, packed together with 15,000 other New Yorkers. Those standing for five minutes in the street in front of the Bartholdi Hotel heard a vastly more rousing and "Bryanesque" speech. It cost them nothing.

**

THE MUCH-ANTICIPATED Garden speech had been almost overshadowed by the week's heat wave, and the heat wave itself contributed to Bryan's failure in New York. Now just as the speech finished, the heat began to ease. Thursday, August 13, marked the final day of the heat wave. New Yorkers welcomed slightly cooler temperatures, as the official high recorded by Dunn dropped below 90 for the first time in seven days.

Still, deaths in both Manhattan and Brooklyn occurred at almost double their usual summertime rate, with approximately 170 deaths over the norm. Certificates were still being filed on August 13 for deaths that occurred on August 11. The death certificate for Garret Stephenson Kirwan noted that he lived in a tenement at East 143 Street with his parents, immigrants from Ireland. The doctor who had been attending Garret since Monday listed as the direct cause of death: "Exhaustion from Heat." Garret was forty-four days old.

Eleven-month-old Mamie Brandy also died on Thursday, the daughter of Italian immigrants living in a tenement at East Thirty-Second Street. Her death was caused by "Heat prostration due to exposure." The use of the term "exposure" was not at all common on death certificates during the heat wave, and it conjures very serious and heart-rending possibilities. The common late-nineteenth-century use of the word indeed meant "abandonment" of an infant, but the doctor may have simply meant that Mamie had been left in the sun or exposed to the heat in a particularly dangerous way. The coroner chided tenement dwellers for taking to the baking asphalt roofs every night; it is certainly possible that Mamie's parents had in fact been trying to give their little girl access to some fresh air but instead had exacerbated her heat exhaustion with tragic results. Whatever the explanation for Mamie's death, she and Garret Kirwan were only two of the eighty-five infants under the age of one to die in New York that day.

Even as the heat wave departed, it continued to devastate the city. The delayed effects of hyperthermia meant that even as temperatures dropped, New Yorkers continued to die by the score. The lower temperatures only gave the illusion that the crisis had passed. Meanwhile, in the tenements, those laborers who had taken to bed sick with the heat days before only now began to die. Continuing deaths among lower temperatures was one of the heat wave's cruelest tricks.

Thinking the worst was over, New Yorkers began to step back and assess the crisis. The "terrible spell of hot weather," Whitelaw Reid noted in a letter to a friend on Thursday, "has left everybody in a dispirited and demoralized state." In a special section the *New York Journal* noted in a headline, "THE HEAT MORE DEADLY THAN A GREAT DISASTER." The paper referred to the heat wave as "the greatest plague of heat ever visited in this vicinity, the longest and most fatal," and compared the five worst days of death to other American disasters. Individual days of the heat wave had killed more people than the Great Chicago Fire, the Great Blizzard of 1888, and even the St. Louis tornado of 1896.

Nevertheless, like every other paper of the time, the *Journal* greatly underestimated the actual number of deaths. The paper claimed that only 39 had died from the heat on August 9, when the actual number was closer to 170. August 10 was listed as having seen 71 deaths, but the number was closer to 250. Even the most deadly day of the heat wave, August 11, witnessed only 213 deaths, according to the paper. The number was actually closer to 340. The total number of heat-related deaths given by the *Journal* was approximately 600. This represented well under half the actual number of heat-related deaths during the heat wave, yet still an enormous figure. Even this number would have made the New York heat wave of 1896 one of the worst natural disasters of the nineteenth century. Still, within only a few years the tragic week seemed to have been lost to history.

The fall of even a few degrees of temperature was front-page news in a city enduring ten days of killer heat. "When the heat has been so terrific for so many days," the *Tribune* observed, "a slight fall in the temperature is most welcome and readily noticed and appreciated. . . . The change was apparent early in the day. The early riser noticed at once that the air was not so dead and enervating as it had been for the week past. There was a little breeze stirring, too, while in the distance could be seen clouds that held out a hope of rain later in the day." Except for a few drops falling uptown, however, the promise of rain was not fulfilled. "The great difference that a fall of even a few degrees makes in the comfort of the community when the mercury has been over 90 degrees for more than a week was well illustrated, for the sufferings of the inhabitants of this city were visibly less than they had been Wednesday."

Yet the city was still in the grips of extreme heat and still coping with the aftermath of the deadly week. One indication of this was the great traffic jam at the East River ferries caused by the eighty-three hearses awaiting transport. The Thirty-Fourth Street, Twenty-Third Street, Tenth Street, and Astoria ferry houses were completely "blockaded" from eight in the morning until eight at night by funeral processions. Police tried to keep the processions in line and orderly, but no sooner had one funeral procession departed by ferry than another one turned off First or Second Avenue bound for the ferry houses. Some hearse drivers even tried to work their way through the crowd heedless of leaving the mourners behind them. The funeral processions spilled out onto First Avenue, blocking a section of that major city thoroughfare for part of the day, as both truck drivers and passengers sought alternative ferry routes or abandoned trying to cross altogether. Just after noon, when both the crush and the heat were at their worst, two women and a driver were overcome, and their carriages were detached from the line and used to convey them home. Several hearses ended up crossing without an attending funeral procession of carriages as the mourners had either become lost or simply worn out by the heat and went home, "leaving the last offices for the dead to the undertakers."

From the beginning the tailors' strike had unhappily coincided with the heat wave, making their suffering all the more acute. Now it looked as if the heat wave would assist in ending the strike. Reports today indicated that all the men planned to be back at work the very next day. The tailors had achieved some success as many contractors had signed new agreements with the tailors' union. Moreover, tailors had opened several "co-operative shops" that received work directly from manufacturers, perhaps frightening some of the contractors. Almost 3,000 men were still on strike as of Thursday. The *New York Times* noted that "many of these have suffered from insufficient good food during the heated term and the closely packed mass meetings they have daily held, often for hours at a time." With the contractors caving, the suffering of the tailors had not been in vain.

Violence was still a problem: A "small riot" had broken out in the shop of Samuel Klein, as strikers had tried to oust nonunion men. And the combination of the heat and the strike may have pushed one tailor over the edge. Christopher Prausch had been suffering greatly for days. Wednesday night, unable to sleep like so many New Yorkers, Prausch had instead paced the apartment he shared his wife, holding his hands to his head. Early in the morning, as his wife made breakfast, Prausch suddenly rushed at her, seized her by the throat, and stabbed her with a penknife in the arm and abdomen. He then ran into the street with the knife and confessed his crime to a policeman, saying that a crowd was following and trying to kill him. Officer Logan at first did not believe the clearly demented man, but when they returned to Prausch's apartment, Logan found Mrs. Prausch faint from loss of blood. While a doctor tended to the wife's wounds, Christopher was taken away. As he was presented to the magistrate, Prausch suddenly shrieked and threw up his hands before collapsing in convulsions on the floor. The examining doctor declared him "crazed by the heat," and Prausch was taken to the hospital.

Although the small break in the heat lessened the toll on horses, New Yorkers continued to complain about the remaining carcasses littering the streets. In many cases they had been left to rot in the street for several days while the city tried to keep up with the demand for removal. Public health concerns still existed, and the *Tribune* optimistically predicted that with falling temperatures, the city would be able to "cope with this peril successfully." This was optimism indeed, as for over a week the city had done virtually nothing to respond to the grave health crisis created by the heat wave.

VI.
STRANGE AND PATHETIC SCENES

O NLY WHEN THE heat wave had reached its end did New York City's government make even the smallest efforts to relieve the plight of the poor. As the heat wave had settled on the city, Mayor Strong had done nothing, not even calling an emergency meeting until almost the very end of the ten-day crisis.

If there were two public officials who might be considered the heroes of the heat wave, they were Charles Collis of the Department of Public Works and Theodore Roosevelt of the Board of Police Commissioners. Right from the beginning Collis experimented with altered work hours for his men. He also instituted the practice of "flushing" the steaming streets of the Lower East Side using teams of men with fire hoses. Roosevelt, too, took some individual initiative in responding to the crisis. He ordered that police wagons be pressed into service as ambulances to take the stricken to city hospitals. And at the mayor's meeting on August 13 he recommended, in concert with Wilson of the Board of Health, that the city purchase ice and distribute it for free in the city's poorest districts.

Not only did Roosevelt go along with this course of action, but he took it on himself to personally supervise the distribution via police precinct houses, attempted to stop any fraud from taking place, and made a point to see how the city's poor used the ice. Through his distribution scheme Roosevelt in effect busted the ice trust controlled by Charles Morse, and he came into intimate contact with the poor's suffering during the height of the heat wave. The heat wave, then, had a profound effect on the future progressive president and trust buster.

Hundreds of victims of sunstroke and heat exhaustion filled the city hospitals during the week. Bellevue Hospital reported its busiest day in years. Its Sturgis Pavilion, generally used for operating cases and closed during the summer, was opened specifically to deal with heat cases. Soon it was filled with patients wilting on cots and buried in ice baths. Students from the Training School for Nurses left their classes to assist Bellevue's doctors. Meanwhile, the coroner's office could not keep up with all of the new cases being brought in and soon had a backlog of sixty bodies awaiting examination and determination of death.

Still, the official response to the heat wave remained almost non-existent. Only Commissioner Collis seemed to understand that the city must adjust to the crisis, temporarily change policies, and perhaps introduce new ones.

Pulitzer's *New York World* took credit for another of Collis's innovations during the heat wave, one that certainly brought some relief to the working poor of Lower Manhattan. The commissioner's son Lloyd, the *World* claimed, had read the paper's "graphic accounts of midsummer misery among the dwellers in tenement districts," and had devised a plan to hose down the streets of the Lower East Side, cooling the burning asphalt and flushing away the rotting and stinking detritus. The commissioner had approved the plan and had passed it along to the acting commissioner of Street Cleaning, Captain Gibson, who served in the absence of Colonel George Waring. With Gibson's approval, Collis had marshaled the twenty-five men of his department's hydrant gang and split them into five divisions of five men each, with each group equipped with a horse and wagon and fifty feet of hose.

At eight o'clock on Monday evening, August 10, the teams assembled at the corner of Canal and Ludlow, near William Seward Park. Collis addressed his troops: "By 12 o'clock tonight we shall have thoroughly washed every street in this section between Houston and Division streets. Let each gang take a street. Hitch on to every fireplug and don't spare the water. It's a terrible night, and many lives may depend upon the way you work. Flood the streets and cool the air. Now go ahead." With hundreds of boys playing in the hoses' streams and their parents watching from the sidewalks and tenement windows, the street cleaning men washed down five miles of streets by midnight, cleaning the gutters and cooling the air. "Down went the mercury a good ten degrees," the *World* claimed. The next night three times as many men were to be employed flushing the streets around Mulberry Bend and Chinatown.

Collis sent Mayor Strong a report regarding the "flushing" of the streets the night before. "It was a great boon to the poor people in the tenement district," Collis wrote. "Parents literally brought their children in the street to have the water poured on them and there was at least 50,000 little ones to whom it was a perfect holiday. Many of the adult citizens thanked me and everybody seemed to think it was a good thing."

Collis's department continued its plan of watering the streets on the Lower East Side. During the night, about ten miles of asphalt below Houston were hosed down. "The work thoroughly nullified the retentive heat in the paving stones," said the *Tribune*, "and made existence more tolerable for the dense population of the territory during the night." "Monday and Tuesday nights in the tenement-house district will not be soon forgotten by the East Side," the paper continued in another place. Yet as gleeful as the overheated women and children seemed as they wallowed in the water, the desperation that made them lie down in the filthy torrent of these street-borne rivers actually seemed to border on the pathetic.

COLLIS'S IDEA TO shorten the workday and confine working hours to the coolest parts of the day was not repeated citywide. Only the mayor could have issued such an order, and there is no evidence that other department heads followed Collis's lead. In fact, New York City displayed a sort of bureaucratic inertia in response to the heat wave.

When a reporter suggested that the Parks Commission should also limit the work hours of its men, Commissioner McMillan, rather than taking action, consulted the counsel for the city about the legality of permitting men to work fewer hours while charging for a full day. The literal-minded parks commissioner acknowledged it would be "an act of humanity" to cut down the hours of manual labor but doubted that this would be accepted by the city comptroller, as state law mandated an eight-hour day. Corporation Counsel Scott replied that he did not believe the city comptroller would "quibble over such a matter" as "a man could not be driven to his death, even by an act of the Legislature." Scott even cited the example of Collis and the Department of Public Works, illustrating Collis's leadership in making an emergency decision during the crisis.

Still, most city departments made no changes, and city workers suffered terribly as a result. Roosevelt's police were among them. The overworked police force, constantly responding to calls of prostrated citizens and helping remove horse carcasses, had not been allowed to make any changes in their heavy regulation summer uniform. On Monday alone 208 officers had been sent to the hospital and another 85 sent home ill. In the past few days 6 policemen had died. Theodore Roosevelt's end-of-the-year report to Mayor Strong would note that doctors had been called to station houses to treat sixty cases of severe heatstroke in 1896. In 1895 the number was only ten. Moreover, Roosevelt reported ten police deaths during the two-week August heat wave, more than in any other entire month that year.

During the ten days of the heat wave, the city refused to lift the ban on sleeping in parks. On August 8 the drunken John Hughes fell from his roof, while baby Lewis Citron fell from the fire escape where he and his father were sleeping. Both died. Desperate New Yorkers had little recourse but to seek comfort on the tenement roofs or down at the piers. On August 10 several people drowned, and others continued to fall from their buildings' rooftops and fire escapes. All of these victims of the heat wave were seeking the slightest relief from their suffocating apartments. The *New York World* noted the problem and the city's ultimate responsibility for these deaths. "The suffocating heat at night has driven thousands of people to piers on the East and North Rivers," the paper said, using the Dutch name for the river on Manhattan's western shore before the British renamed it Hudson. "It is not permissible to sleep in the parks at night. Over in Brooklyn the park officials have suspended their regulations so that thousands of men and women, in whose apartments the temperature approaches that of a Turkish bath, have been allowed to take quilts and pillows into the parks and stretch themselves under the trees for a cool sleep."

The paper held out the slim possibility that "the sleepy Park Commissioners of this town may awake to the fact that humanity demands something of them in this emergency." It continued, "There was a record yesterday of more than a dozen persons who fell from roofs and fire-escapes, whence they had gone to gather whatever breeze was blowing and to secure a night's sleep. Some of these folks were killed and the rest were seriously injured. Many who went to sleep on the piers fell into the water and were rescued with difficulty. Three or four of them were drowned."

Lifting the ban on sleeping in parks constituted perhaps the simplest gesture the city might have made in response to the heat wave and one that could have saved lives. Not only had the "sleepy Park Commissioners" done nothing, few city officials had taken steps to relieve the plight of New Yorkers during the crisis. "Up to this time the only city bureaus which have taken any cognizance of the heat plague are the Street Cleaning and the Public Works departments," the paper noted, referring to the flushing of the streets specifically. "When men, women and children are forced to the roofs and the fire-escapes and to the hard planks of a pier in order to obtain a night's rest," the writer concluded, "it certainly seems as if the time had come to throw away 'Keep off the grass' signs in the parks and to suspend any rules or regulations which prevent the public from resting in the parks after dark." It was a rare call for government action during the heat wave and might have pressed the mayor to finally call an emergency meeting of departments the very next day.

Other city departments had been dealing with the demands of the heat wave all week. In the twenty-four-hour period ending at noon on Wednesday, August 12, more deaths were recorded than ever before in New York's history. The filing of these 335 death certificates placed a great burden on the two clerks in the coroner's office, who themselves risked prostration from their increased workload. "The filing of certificates," said the city registrar, Dr. Tracy, "is somewhat a matter of physical capacity. Most of the time we have two clerks busy writing burial permits. They can write so many permits and take in so many certificates in twenty-four hours and no more. Their full capacity is taxed now, and many persons are waiting in line for permits most of the time."

Desperate measures had to be taken to get the job done. Even the coroners had been drafted into doing clerical work, simply to allow families to bury their dead. In a poor bit of timing, Coroner Hoeber was on vacation during much of the heat wave, making even more work for the personnel who remained. Hoeber's secretary, Joseph Cassner, pitched in to take up the slack, and by noon on Wednesday had worked thirty hours straight. Throughout the city funerals were delayed as the four coroner's physicians could not keep up with requests to visit every home with a corpse and make a ruling on the causes and circumstances of death. The four men made heroic efforts to crisscross the city, visiting tenements often miles apart while climbing hundreds of flights of stairs. All of this exertion, of course, occurred during the most extreme heat any of them had ever experienced.

The dedication of the men of the coroner's office illustrated the readiness of some city officials to make sacrifices and even risk their own health to address the current crisis. While there was no central authority directing efforts from the mayor's office, virtually every city department was forced to accommodate itself and its personnel to the heat wave in some way. With the Board of Health's contractor responsible for removing dead horses completely overwhelmed, the city's sanitary superintendent, Dr. Charles F. Roberts, was forced to take other extraordinary measures. On Wednesday, August 12, he wrote to the chief inspector of the Division of Contagious Diseases, Dr. Charles S. Benedict, with instructions to have the entire disinfecting corps of his division stop their normal work around the city and focus instead on disinfecting and deodorizing the bodies of dead horses. Clearly Roberts worried that the current "heat epidemic" might lead to a true epidemic and an entirely new health crisis. With a great pile of twenty-seven dead horses at the Second Avenue car stables, this was a real and frightening possibility.

Other city department heads continued to make small but important decisions affecting the lives of New Yorkers. By order of Commissioner Collis of the Public Works Department, the free baths in the East and Hudson Rivers were ordered to remain open all night to provide relief from the heat, with separate times given to men and women. "The City's Free Baths to Be Never Closed," one headline announced on Wednesday. This was another move by the city that reflected the seriousness of the heat wave, as the floating baths in the rivers were designed expressly for hygiene and not recreation. For now, the ability of the poor to find some relief via the floating baths all night long, although counter to their original hygienic purpose, probably saved lives. Once again, a small step made by a single department head, without reference to the mayor, made a significant difference in the quality of life of New York's suffering poor.

Commissioner Collis continued to take the lead among city officials in addressing the heat wave in other areas. On Wednesday, August 12, he doubled the number of men in each of the five "gangs" to ten, and they continued their work hosing down the blistering asphalt over almost an entire square mile of streets and alleys between Houston and Grand. Moreover, Collis maintained the changed work hours for his men, limiting work to the coolest hours of the day and suspending any work that necessitated laboring in the sun. Unfortunately for this hero of the heat wave, in later years inefficiency in road repairs along Park and Fifth Avenues, as well as his close association with the Platt political machine, would leave the commissioner of Public Works open to harsh criticism.

ALTHOUGH POLICE COMMISSIONER Roosevelt remained at home on Long Island during the height of the heat wave, his police continued to be in the vanguard of city employees responding to the crisis. When a man or woman fell in the street due to heat prostration, a policeman was called to attend the victim and find some conveyance to a hospital, putting serious stress on the heavily dressed police force. On August 11 alone six patrolmen and one police captain fell victim to heat exhaustion while on duty.

The police continued to hunt down "mad" dogs in the street, while turning a blind eye to the frolicking of small boys in the city's public fountains. They also responded to the many strange incidents that accompanied the heat wave. On August 11 police had been called by Mrs. William Grimm to a tenement on West Forty-Second Street. Mrs. Grimm had left her baby in its carriage on the sidewalk as she went to get her husband his supper in their ground-floor apartment. When she returned, the carriage was empty. A neighbor, David Wheeler, passing by the carriage sitting in the sun on one of the hottest days of the year, believed the infant on the point of collapse. He took the baby up to his room one floor above, stripped it, and placed it in a bath.

When another neighbor told her that Wheeler had taken her child, Mrs. Grimm ran up the stairs and found her baby lying naked on a cot in Wheeler's room. Although Wheeler told his downstairs neighbor of his good intentions, Mrs. Grimm refused to believe him and summoned the police to report her baby's kidnapping. The judge hearing the case dismissed it after hearing of Wheeler's benevolent actions, and the *New York Herald* agreed with its article title, "Samaritan After All." It was not recorded whether the judge reprimanded Mrs. Grimm for leaving her baby unattended on the sidewalk on a day when the temperature in the sun hit 135 degrees. Inside or outside of the tenement, the heat wave meant suffering and death for New York's children.

Even so, many observers noted great improvements in caring for the very young as representatives of the Board of Health went door to door checking on children's health. Only on Tuesday did the *Times* give credit to the Board of Health for "securing the improvement in the construction and sanitary appurtenances of tenement houses." The "terrible mortality among young children," the paper asserted, had been greatly relieved by "the close inspection of food supplies, and especially of milk, by the Board of Health." Riis, too, noted that fifty so-called summer doctors were dispatched into the tenements, with free advice and medicine for the poor.

Despite these efforts, and despite the aid of charitable institutions, the city's gravediggers "work over-time, and little coffins are stacked mountain-high on the deck of the Charity Commissioners' boat when it makes its semi-weekly trips to the city cemetery." Sadly, the coffins of little Mamie Brandy and Garret Kirwan joined dozens of other little coffins making their final journey.

***

WHEN ROOSEVELT ATTENDED meetings in Mayor Strong's office, as he did on August 13, he may well have contemplated that this was an office he might have occupied. After all, Roosevelt had been offered the chance to run for mayor in 1894 as he had in 1886. Only his wife's concerns about money stopped him from running as a reform Republican. Instead the mantle had fallen to William Strong, a millionaire merchant and banker who had no such financial restraints. Strong, too, was a reform Republican, and he won the grudging support of party boss Thomas Platt. Strong's election was aided by the Lexow Committee's report on city corruption, especially in the police department. Vowing to run the city on business principles and heedless of patronage, Strong's appointments of Colonel Waring to the Street Cleaning Department and Roosevelt to the Police Commission signaled to the Good Government Clubs and Citizens' Committees a commitment to reform. Various forces would conspire to unseat Strong after only one term, including voters' grave displeasure with Roosevelt's own war on Sunday drinking.

Strong came to the conclusion to call a meeting only after speaking to the Health Board's president, Wilson. Wilson recounted for Strong the death statistics of the previous week, noting that they were comparable only to the epidemic of Asiatic cholera that had struck the city forty years earlier. Apparently it was Wilson who first raised the subject of distributing free ice to the poor. At the mayor's meeting an emergency appropriation of $5,000 was made in order to purchase ninety-five tons of ice. As Roosevelt occupied seats on both the Board of Health and the Police Commission, it is quite possible that he had a hand in the decision as well.

Aside from the ice appropriation, however, little that was new came from the meeting. Flushing the streets, keeping the floating baths open all night, and the changed work hours in some city departments were steps already taken by individual department heads. The only other new decision possibly resulted from the critical *Tribune* article of the day before attacking the city's "sleepy Park

Commissioners." Now the city decided to throw open the parks at night and ordered the police not to prevent people from going on the lawns or stretching themselves out on park benches. "This order refers, of course, to persons seeking relief from the excessive heat," the order sent to police stated. "Officers are instructed to be vigilant in preventing mischievous boys and disorderly persons from abusing the privileges set for them in this order."

Responding to the criticism directed at the Park Commission for lagging so far behind its counterpart in Brooklyn, Park Commissioner Samuel McMillan told the press that day that the city was only formalizing what had been unofficially understood by police for some time. McMillan said that the Commission had long ago instructed police officers that if people wanted to sleep in the parks during the "hot spell," they should not be discouraged from doing so. "Why, we've been doing this ever since the hot weather set in," McMillan told a reporter. "We don't intend to make a practice of it. We were in a position where we could afford to be lenient with those who were sufferers from the heat. But we are not going to throw the parks open for the benefit of those who are covered with disease and vermin. It won't do to have such persons sleeping on the benches." Echoing the order to police, the policy to throw open the parks was merely a temporary remedy during the heat wave and not meant for those who had no other place to sleep. While McMillan may have asserted that this had been the city's policy since the heat wave began, most New Yorkers remained unaware of it until his announcement. A Central Park policeman noted that the number of people sleeping in the parks had been relatively small, as it was "not generally known that they would be permitted to sleep among the cool breezes which are supposed to blow among the trees there at night."

Most of the responses to the heat wave had not challenged the basic tenet that charity must be left to private interests. Flushing the streets, changing work hours, and leaving open the parks and public baths constituted fairly mild responses that fell squarely within the purview of the city departments. Giving away free ice was an exception.

Private interests, including a city newspaper, had been giving away free ice for some time. For the city to enter the field previously occupied only by private charity, and to actually *give* something away, was new in its history. Certainly this foray into public charity reflected the seriousness of the heat wave. It also reflected the growing belief that would mature during the Progressive Era that government did indeed have a duty to address the suffering of the city's poor, whether through tenement reform or health and sanitation measures. Finally, the decision to give away free ice probably had something to do with the recent establishment of a New York "Ice Trust" that had raised the price of ice to the level of a luxury for the city's poor.

Never in its history had New York City witnessed such a sight. Roosevelt had instructed policemen to inform local residents of the ice distribution as they made their rounds. Roosevelt, the police, and the journalists who covered the giveaway were shocked at the turnout. Hours before the ice even arrived at the precinct houses, hundreds of men, women, and children crowded around the stations clamoring for free ice. "It was to them better than bread to the starving," the *Journal* said. "Mothers with sickly babes in their arms jostled with weary men, while children begged for a piece of ice to take home to the sick room." The *Times* estimated that 20,000 people had been served ice, so that managing the enormous crowds became a tricky task for Roosevelt's police.

Such vast numbers desperate for ice complicated the logistics of the giveaway. At first the police had tried to give away the ice on the sidewalk, but they soon moved the ice down into the cellar to better manage the crowds. "The applicants for the ice came with towels, aprons, bags, boxes, baskets, tin and wooden pails, and in fact any and every sort of receptacle," one witness noted. "A man drove up to the Eldridge Street Station in a wagon, evidently expecting to get all the ice he wanted. He found that it took him nearly two hours to get twenty pounds."

Roosevelt was right in the thick of things during the evening's distribution of ice. He made his rounds from station to station around the East Side, including Eldridge station, the precinct house for the neighborhood of the striking tailors. There the police found it difficult to spread the five tons allotted them among the massive crowd of people gathered around the station. In less than half an hour, the entire amount had been distributed. If each person received on average a twenty-pound block, then approximately five hundred people went away with ice. This represented only a tiny fraction of the residents of one of Manhattan's most densely packed tenement districts.

Near the end of the distribution, the situation became a bit dicey. When the crowd was told that the ice was gone, they refused to leave. Women begged for even the smallest piece of ice for their sick children at home. The scene was repeated throughout the Lower East Side, as ice supplies quickly ran out before even a small portion of the people could be served. Witnessing this firsthand led Roosevelt to ask that the following night's ice purchase be more than doubled. Over on the West Side at the Charles Street station, only two people appeared asking for ice, and for a time nearly two tons of ice remained, slowly melting in the heat. Apparently the men of that station's six o'clock shift had not been told by their superiors to inform "the poorer classes" that the ice at the station was meant for them.

Roosevelt was obviously moved by what he saw that night. In an August 15 letter to his sister, he recounted the "strange and pathetic scenes when the ice was distributed." Such scenes would be repeated the following day as the ice giveaway reached 250 tons. Moreover, as Roosevelt had spent much of the heat wave out on Long Island, touring the Lower East Side that night while overseeing the ice distribution was his first opportunity to witness the suffering of New York's poor from the heat.

He must have been shocked by the suffering of the police force as well. At Eldridge station he was perhaps told of the collapse of Patrolman William Williamson, who lay unconscious at Bellevue Hospital. He must also have seen a report that Patrolman Walter Bray of the West Forty-Seventh Street station had died only a few hours after suffering prostration. Black bunting and streamers marked the homes that had suffered deaths, as scores of hearses plied the streets. Roosevelt's position as police commissioner offered him a unique perspective on the heat wave, as he witnessed the suffering of both the poor and his own police officers as they coped with the emergency.

Ice was not the only item in short supply. Alarmingly, newspapers reported a citywide shortage of coffins. In the New York factory of the Brooklyn Casket Company, clerks had been pulled from their desks to help manufacture new caskets. Nearly two hundred men had been working night and day to keep up with demand during the heat wave. Of these men one had been prostrated at work and died, and another lay critically ill from heat exhaustion. Still, the workers had not been able to keep pace with the orders from city undertakers. And the morgue was so overcrowded with bodies that many lay on the floor. Perhaps half of these bodies would not even require a fancy casket from the Casket Company, as they were destined for a mass grave at Potter's Field. Of the more than fifty bodies at the morgue awaiting interment on Wednesday, twenty-eight of them had received a pauper's burial. This was but another sign of the toll the heat had taken on New York's poorest and most vulnerable residents.

***

BY THE TIME of the ice giveaway Thursday evening, a full day had passed since Bryan's speech. Only now was the full enormity of what had occurred at Madison Square Garden dawning on pundits and politicos in New York and across the nation. While city newspapers had exhausted their vocabulary describing the heat wave—"blazing," "scorching," "searing," "broiling," "baking," "burning"—they now turned to cooler terms to describe Bryan's New York reception. The *Evening Post* noted the "chilling effect" of his failure on his managers, while the *Times* proclaimed in a headline: "FROST FOLLOWS MR. BRYAN." (The headline for the *Chicago Tribune* read: "BRYAN GETS A FROST.") New Yorkers continued to dissect the failure of his Madison Square Garden speech. The *Nation* mockingly noted that Bryan had now revealed his twin character, "that of a demagogue and that of a solemn economist." The journal lambasted his "gross" and "incredible ignorance," which placed him in the "booby class in business." "He would do much better to stick to his crown of thorns and cross of gold," an editorial concluded.

All observers blamed Bryan's reading of his speech, and many noted the effect of the terrible heat. The *Tribune* noted the great surprise New Yorkers felt on hearing of the speech's failure. "No one could remember a case where a man of prominence ever came to here with a similar reputation for the possession of great oratorical gifts," one writer said, "and fell so far short of meeting the expectations of his audience and the public." As the *Post* commented, "The great length of his address evidently wearied him as much as it did his audience, suffering as both were from extreme heat."

The following day, in a short talk to reporters, Bryan himself addressed the question of his having read the speech from a manuscript. "I wrote the speech with the distinct purpose of reading it," he claimed. "I did not care to trust myself to declamatory effect, because I feared I might be tempted to lose sight of the main issue. I knew I was in a gold country, where every word would be analyzed with close scrutiny. I gave my reasons analytically and logically, and I trust my future to that speech, as affording the millions of readers who peruse it an opportunity to judge what the silver question is."

Bryan was falling back into his old habits. Referring to New York as "gold country" came very close to again labeling the city "enemy's country." In fact his next utterances constituted a fairly harsh criticism of the East. "The trouble with many in the East," he continued, "is that they regard the silver question as a fad, like the measles, to run its course. They will not study it and they regard the West as incapable of forming solid judgment. This is all wrong."

Bryan was speaking once again as a regional, rather than national, candidate. As he spoke to reporters, he recalled once being quizzed along his train journey by an audience member about the authority for some his statements, when "laboring men" in the audience were able to answer on his behalf. For Bryan, this showed that "ignorance is no characteristic of the West." While standing in a New York City hotel, he criticized the East while defending the West. As can be imagined, New Yorkers did not appreciate men from west of the Mississippi coming to their city and pointing out their deficiencies.

As WILLIAM JENNINGS and Mary Bryan, joined by Arthur Sewall, spent part of the day greeting visitors at the Windsor Hotel, their reception revealed New York's tepid feelings for the Democratic candidate and his ideas of free silver. Expecting a large crowd, William St. John had arranged for Bryan to address the crowd from the front stoop of the hotel, guarded by forty policemen. He was to be disappointed.

One reporter counted "exactly 163 persons" including "several small children, and idle pedestrians, in front of the hotel gazing at the stoop." With such an embarrassingly small gathering for a street demonstration, the reception moved inside. At this point most of those awaiting Bryan's arrival simply left. Inside the empty halls, St. John and others paced the rooms with "an air of chill disappointment." Even after Bryan arrived, very few people approached the candidate and his wife—certainly no one of note attended the reception. Not a single Tammany politician attended.

After the first group of people waiting for Bryan had shaken his hand and greeted Sewall and Mrs. Bryan, there occurred long periods of time when no one entered the reception room at all. Bryan was described as glancing "darkly towards the door," while Sewall's "usual gravity would deepen into gloom." During these stretches the Bryans and Sewall fell into conversation with one another, while just outside the parlor door Bryan supporters tried to entice people into the room in the manner of carnival touts. "Walk right in," one urged. "Go in and tell him your name and he'll introduce you to his wife," said another. "Don't stand out here; there he is; go right up and speak to him."

Those who approached Bryan were rewarded with a handshake and a few words. Gone was St. John's previous warnings against shaking the candidate's bruised and swollen hands. "Mr. Bryan gave a hearty pressure of the hand to every one as he approached," one man observed. "His grasp was warm and friendly, and he had a pleasant word for each person." In the end, only about three hundred people shook hands with the Bryans, and after a short time, St. John called off the reception. Once again the New York trip smelled of failure. The only kind words for Bryan that day were reserved for his wife.

If William Jennings Bryan failed to take New York by storm, at least Mary Bryan was warmly received. "MRS. BRYAN CHARMS ALL WHO GREET HER," exclaimed a *Journal* headline. While Hearst's *New York Journal* continued to support Bryan and free silver even after the debacle at Madison Square Garden, laudatory remarks about the speech were conspicuous by their absence. Instead the paper offered three full columns to Mary Bryan, in warm tones echoed by much of the rest of the city press. Except for some women who apparently did not approve of her black straw hat, "Mrs. Bryan won the hearts of all the women who called on her yesterday." Men and women who greeted her came away saying, "She's just lovely!" "How can Bryan help winning when he won such a wife!" "How magnetic!" "How charming!" When asked about the Madison Square Garden speech, and the subsequent press reports that she had looked "anxious" as people fled, Mary Bryan disputed the claims. "I didn't feel in the least anxious," she said and indicated that Bryan's first speech to Congress had caused her more anxiety. The crowd she called "a grand, noble one." When someone showed her the morning headlines describing Bryan's failure, Mary protested, "Don't ask me to say anything about them, please. I am satisfied with the reception accorded Mr. Bryan, and grateful for the splendid demonstration of enthusiasm. There wasn't an incident to mar the meeting, and I shall always remember with pleasure this visit to New York." It was a diplomatic response, more tactful than her husband's continuing references to "enemy's country" and his statements about "the East." When she was asked about Madison Square Garden, the pride of New York, Mary replied that it was "a superb building, especially the exterior."

While William rested, Mary continued to hold receptions, the last one occurring at 4:00 PM in the hotel's ladies' parlor. Dr. Ella Jennings, who at one time operated a dispensary for working women on Tenth Street, had a short chat with the candidate's wife and came away believing that Mrs. Bryan's prominent role in the upcoming campaign signaled the changing status of women in politics. "I regard it as the most hopeful sign of the future," Dr. Jennings said, "that the candidate for the Presidency accords full recognition to his wife. It is a harbinger of the time when a woman shall occupy the Executive chair." Also among Mary's fans at the reception was Clara Foltz, the first woman admitted to the California bar, who later moved to New York. "I believe the comradeship shown between Mr. and Mrs. Bryan will have a tremendous influence on social conditions and family life," Foltz said. "Think how much more of a help a woman thoroughly educated in legal matters as Mrs. Bryan is, can be to her husband, than a mere fashion plate." Perhaps Foltz was really talking about herself, as Mary Bryan had received no education in legal matters whatsoever.

At the end of the reception, as the wives of Senators Stone and Stewart escorted Mary to a private parlor, she received the best news of the day. She had lost her wedding ring in Pittsburgh while riding to Union Station a few days before; the man cleaning the carriage afterward had found it and returned it to the Bryan campaign. Now at the end of a long and tiring day, in which she played the dutiful and supportive wife to the Democratic presidential nominee, the potential first lady again slipped on her wedding ring. The leader of the silver forces had given his wife a traditional gold wedding band.

As of that afternoon, the Bryans still planned to continue with their tour of the East, leaving for Boston at noon the next day. Their stop in Boston was to be followed by a trip to Maine, Arthur Sewall's home state. Both Bryans spoke of their impending trip with anticipation. Someone asked Mrs. Bryan whether she intended to "carry the war to Bunker Hill." "We do not intend making an incursion and devastate the country," Mary replied—"with a sweet smile," according to one witness, "that was symbolic of peace and good-will." "We are on our mettle," she added, "and will do our utmost to conquer convictions." To the question as to whether she felt confident, Mary Bryan replied, "Why certainly. I feel sure we will win."

But if Mary was certain, those managing the Bryan campaign were not. Apparently the failure of the Madison Square Garden speech, coupled with the sparse attendance of today's public receptions, prompted an emergency meeting among Chairman Jones, Senator Gorman, Governor Hogg, Governor Stone, and others on hand to manage the campaign. Just as both Bryans spoke of their imminent departure for Boston, the Democratic leaders were on the point of rejecting a further tour of the East. In particular, some worried that with statewide elections scheduled for Maine the next month, a Bryan tour of that state followed closely by a Republican victory would be a national embarrassment for Democrats. "The evident chilliness that has fallen on Bryan men in this city since his essay reading Wednesday night," the *Times* said, "had added to the solicitude of these leaders. The three receptions that failed so lamentably at the Windsor Hotel settled the matter."

When the campaign managers finished their conference, they announced that the tour of the East had been cancelled. Instead, Bryan would retire to some quiet place for the next two weeks to work on his letter of acceptance. The campaign would not start again until September 1.

While later historians of the 1896 campaign might dispute the relative success or failure of Bryan's Madison Square Garden speech, Roosevelt and others had it right. The canceling of a further tour of the East, and the suspension of the campaign for an entire two weeks, with less than three months until election day, strengthened the perception of failure even within die-hard Democratic circles. The *Tribune* called the campaign's managers "despondent, dubious, and disgusted." The paper also noted Bryan's desire to completely abandon the New York party headquarters in the Bartholdi Hotel in favor of a national headquarters in Chicago. Some portrayed this as essentially conceding New York, the most important state in late-nineteenth-century national politics, and even much of the East Coast to McKinley. The *Nation* characterized the decision to not campaign for two weeks "sad news" to Republicans, since Bryan was losing votes every day that he spoke. "The folly of allowing him to go to Maine and make a lot of speeches which might be followed by a large Republican majority at the State election next month," the paper noted, "was so obvious that even less wise men than those who are managing the Democratic canvass must see it."

Now Bryan would retire to some quiet place to write a letter of acceptance, only days after his Madison Square Garden speech. The question had to be asked: If Bryan planned to write a letter of acceptance, then what was the point of coming to New York and formally accepting the nomination at a massive public rally? Why read a speech from a manuscript meant for publication if the candidate planned to write an acceptance letter anyway? The Democrat campaign was in poor shape, and the obvious contradictions only underscored the disastrous ramifications of his decision to read the speech.

***

EVEN WITH THE heat wave over, New Yorkers continued to suffer and die. On Friday, August 14, the high temperature reached only 80 degrees, bringing the heat wave formally to an end. Because of the delayed effects of heat exhaustion, however, scores of New Yorkers continued to die from the effects of the heat wave. Robert Ferguson, the former telegraph operator at the Mulberry Street Police Headquarters, died from the heat, while Mary Tierney actually died at the Elizabeth Street station house.

Still, with the summer almost over, it seemed likely that the "heat plague" had run its course. In fact, for the rest of the month the official high temperature would only once more reach 80, as New Yorkers enjoyed milder temperatures in the 70s. On August 22 the high reached only 69.

As the heat relinquished its grip on the city, New Yorkers once again focused on the dangers of industrial society. Two more trains collided over in New Jersey. An electrician of the Steinway Electric Railroad got caught in the powerhouse's machinery and was "crushed in a terrible manner." In Cleveland, a group of strikers ambushed the strikebreakers at the Brown Holsting Works, killing two. Closer to home, at Ninety-Seventh Street, a two-year-old girl rolled off a pile of sand next to her house and into the path of an ice wagon, which trampled her to death. While the heat may have finished killing innocents, the industrial city, with its rushing trains and whirring machinery, retained its capacity to murder and maim.

Rain broke the heat wave decisively. "After more than a week of drought and death-dealing heat," the *Times* said, "rain fell early [this] morning and again in the afternoon and brought to the suffering millions of the Greater New-York the first relief they have had since the hot wave's arrival." On Thursday night, New Yorkers had watched the clouds gather and produce frequent flashes of lightning. But no rain fell, as the humidity rose and threatened to make Friday another killer day of heat. Finally, at 3:00 AM the rain began to fall, the air cooled, and a breeze swept the streets. "It was not a boisterous breeze," the paper observed, "but it was stronger and fresher than had been known in a week, and people were grateful." The breeze actually penetrated into the open windows of the tenements, and cleared some of the foul and dead air that had long been trapped inside. The rain stopped by morning, and as men and women left for work, clouds still blocked the sun. It was a good omen for a cooler day.

City department heads gathered again on Friday in Mayor Strong's office to hear a report from Theodore Roosevelt on the previous evening's distribution of free ice. Roosevelt said the ice had been distributed "in a satisfactory manner" and called for the city to purchase and distribute more ice that day. After the experience of Thursday night, President Charles Wilson of the Board of Health came to the conclusion that ice need not be distributed in every precinct. Based on Thursday's demand, Wilson drew up a schedule of the amount of ice to be distributed at each station house. Wealthy "brownstone" precincts, such as the Fifteenth, Seventeenth, and Nineteenth, would receive no ice, while more sparsely populated districts, such as around Liberty Street downtown, would receive only three tons. In contrast, the poorest and most densely populated districts would that night each receive as much as eleven tons of ice. Cut up into approximately ten-pound pieces, this would mean the station houses at Eldridge Street and Delancey Street would each be able to serve more than 2,000 people.

Roosevelt reported the difficulty his policemen had detecting fraud among the applicants for ice, unless the police were personally acquainted with them. Roosevelt noted instances when several children from the same family were sent for free ice, which was subsequently resold by their unscrupulous parents. Roosevelt also cited two cases of children of affluent parents applying for ice. One was the daughter of a wealthy plumber, and the other the daughter of a contractor. To prevent such deception, Roosevelt had ordered patrolmen to search out the poorest families on their beats and give them tickets for the ice. Roosevelt ordered that widows with large families be given priority.

That evening, the ice distribution commenced at 6:00. In all the precincts the supply of ice was exhausted by midnight. In the more crowded districts, such as the Seventh, Eleventh, Twelfth, and Thirteenth, although each received ten or eleven tons of ice, supplies quickly ran out. As early as 4:00, the neighborhood children began to gather around the station houses. They carried tin pans, pails, baskets, wash boilers, and similar receptacles. The *Times* gave a detailed description: "These children were a study. Some were fairly clean, more were very dirty. Some were neatly dressed, but the majority wore ragged clothing. Half-fed children, barely able to drag themselves about, were sent by their parents to carry away ten pounds of ice. Nearly all of the applicants were children." While condescending and nearing caricature, this description was not necessarily inaccurate. Not only were these children the city's poorest, but after a long, hot summer day and without access to adequate bathing facilities, even better-off children might be seen in torn and dirty clothing. At the Madison Street station, which served the very poor and crowded Seventh Precinct, one observer estimated that five hundred children were waiting at the appointed hour of distribution. All carried tin pails and pans for the ice. When the ice was late arriving, what did these hundreds of children do? Of course, they began banging them together. The "din" that these "unruly" children made, the *Times* said, was "deafening."

At the Seventh Precinct station house Roundsman Hulz was in charge of the distribution. A large man, "he showed that his heart was in proportion to his size." From time to time Hulz lifted small children from the crowd and gave them their ice allotment to prevent them being crushed. Sometimes he addressed harsh words to children he knew did not qualify for free ice. One woman who applied for the ice Hulz recognized as being the proprietor of a "street stand" and the owner of a house. Police took to asking children what their fathers did for a living. "He's a boss tailor," one little girl replied. "Then you run home and tell him to buy his ice," Hulz replied. "This ice is for poor people." When Hulz asked one "neatly-dressed, but delicate-looking" little girl, "Where is your father?" the girl replied, "I don't know, sir. We haven't seen him for six months, and mother is sick and can't work." "Come right along," Hulz said, and picked out a good-sized piece of ice for the girl.

With the ice again rapidly depleted, Roosevelt returned to his office on Mulberry Street. Back at police headquarters by 9:00 PM, he had a long interview with the reporter from the *Evening Post*. He recounted some of the scenes he had witnessed and some of the ideas he had put into practice. At the Elizabeth Street station, Roosevelt watched a police officer remove children from the line. In response to Roosevelt's inquiry, the officer noted that the first boy was the son of a real-estate dealer living nearby, said to be worth $75,000. The second boy was the son of an "expressman," a man employed receiving and delivering parcels, also reputed to own a considerable fortune. In a different precinct, Roosevelt watched as a "Hebrew woman" took away a ten-pound piece of ice. Not long after, however, the police in charge of the line recognized eight children, all belonging to that same woman. A policeman told Roosevelt that he believed they would try to sell the extra ice. All of this greatly offended the commissioner's sense of honesty and fair play. The ice was meant for the poor, and here were rich people intentionally trying to cheat their way into a piece of free ice—and using their children to do so. Another family was trying to make a profit on the free ice, and in every case this would deprive some needy, even desperate family. At the end of a ten-day heat wave, this was no mere case of harmless dishonesty but deceit that might have life-threatening consequences.

No wonder that it was this pattern of deception in the ice distribution that Roosevelt moved quickly to address. He gave out new orders to the police going on duty at 1:00 that afternoon. Each patrolman would be issued twenty slips of papers, or "orders," for free ice. The policeman would then give a slip of paper to the neediest people on their beats. No one would be served ice without a slip of paper. Roosevelt was very aware that this meant some people would leave the station houses that evening without ice. But for him it also meant a more orderly distribution system. "Order and Fair Play" might have been his motto, a guide for almost everything he did in his life and career.

This also applied to the "scientific" method of ice distribution Roosevelt developed. The night before, the police had cut the ice into greatly varying sizes. In some parts of the city people received only five pounds, while elsewhere people left the precinct houses with fifteen or twenty pounds. Roosevelt described his remedy for this: "All the ice delivered weighs in the neighborhood of 200 pounds to the cake. In order that all may be treated alike, I shall instruct the Chief to inform his Captains and commanding officers to have each cake of ice cut in twenty pieces or blocks. This, you see, will give to each about ten pounds."

On the one hand, it was slightly absurd that the president of the Board of Police Commissioners was issuing orders about the cutting of ice. On the other hand, such concern again reflected his obsession "that all may be treated alike." For Roosevelt, this should not be left to chance or to the whims of local precinct captains. Establishing a fair standard of distribution was the role of his authority and city government in general: to establish the framework of fair play that helped New York's most underprivileged and powerless get a fair shake, a "Square Deal."

The city appropriated a total of $5,000 to be used for the free distribution of ice, and as of Friday, August 14, had used only a fraction of the money—just as the heat wave ended. Still, from newspapermen to politicians, all agreed that the city had displayed unprecedented largesse in seeking to alleviate the suffering of the poor. One writer spoke of the "unrestrained joy of the tenement dwellers all over New York," especially the "women and children in the reeking East Side tenement-house district, where a stray breeze is a rare luxury." The *Tribune* offered a description of the "motley crowds" clamoring for ice similar to that of the *Times*: "They came long before the ice itself had reached the stations, and jostled and crowded about the steps, beating their tin pans to impatient tunes, and making of the neighborhood a veritable babel. The crowds were largely composed of children of Hebrew, Italian, and Greek nationalities, with startling variations in costumes and some contrast in the way of complexion, but all thoroughly voluble and for the most part unwashed." These "unwashed" multitudes of varying complexion "stretched half a block in length," and "piled three or four deep." The "combined banging of their pans, and the grind of shrill youthful voices would have given to a third-rate organ-grinder an attack of nervous prostration."

Roosevelt was not the only one to speak at the second mayor's meeting of department heads on August 14. Mayor Strong noted that he had received numerous complaints about the dead horses in the streets, many of which had been allowed to fester for several days. One such complaint had come from the offices of the Anchor Brewing Company, asserting that "in no small town or City . . . would a dead animal be allowed to decompose for four days as occurred under our office window last week, notwithstanding the fact that it was three times reported to the 'Board of Health.'"

Directing his pointed comments at Wilson of the Board of Health, the mayor repeated what newspapers, and Wilson himself, had been saying for days: that the horse carcasses were "a menace to the public health." Wilson replied that the heat had killed about 1,000 horses during the past week and that the offal contractor had simply not been able to remove them as fast as they died. Wilson estimated that about 180 horses still lay in the streets as of Thursday. While the contractor endeavored to remove them, the Health Department had been conducting a disinfecting campaign, "using as much bromine as it was safe to use to destroy the sickening odors." The mayor asked Captain Gibson of the Street Cleaning Department whether he could help the Health Department in the emergency. Gibson replied that he would try; he left the mayor's office to call the Street Cleaning Department's stables to order two teams with trucks to assist in the removal of dead horses. Wilson then announced that if any business-men would hire "truckmen" to remove dead horses from the streets, the Health Department would pay the bills.

The Commissioner of Public Works said that flushing the streets would continue in the tenement house districts. The poor children, he noted, received free "shower-baths" while the flushing was in progress, as the children played in the hoses' streams. Following the lead of the Street Cleaning Department, the Fire Department had recently volunteered to flush the streets in front of hospitals "and had cooled the hospital wards in the most gratifying manner."

While much of the official response to the heat wave had already taken place by the time of the mayor's meetings on August 13 and 14, the meetings show that a coordinated city response to the heat wave had been possible from the beginning. At both meetings steps had been taken and decisions made that required either mayoral-level decisions or communication among the department heads, which was fostered simply by meeting together in the same place. True, the meetings offered little new information that could not have been found in the city newspapers all week. The mayor's observations that he had received complaints about the dead horses, and that he considered them a health risk, were a bit obtuse, as New Yorkers had been complaining about this problem all week. Yet in affirming the actions already taken, such as flushing the streets and fostering coordination among city departments, the meetings showed that the city might have taken the lead in responding to the crisis right from the beginning.

How many lives might have been saved by distributing ice beginning on August 4? How much less foul might the air have been if the city attacked the problem of carting away dead horses a week earlier? How many New Yorkers might have found relief at night in the floating baths and city parks had the rules been changed earlier? No one would ever know. Instead, the department heads met on a day when the temperature inside the mayor's office was so pleasant, none of the men bothered to remove their jackets.

ON FRIDAY, AUGUST 14, the Bryan party visited Coney Island. Or to be more precise, William and Mary Bryan took the ferry to Coney Island, looked at the nation's amusement capital from the pier side, and then returned to Manhattan without ever having left the boat. It was an odd trip that probably had to do with the late hour of their visit to the island and the exhaustion of both the candidate and his wife. But it seemed to underscore Bryan's small-town and western disdain for all things big, eastern, and urban. "Mr. Bryan," the *Tribune* speculated, "may have wanted to take himself away from the city that had, even in boiling weather, frosted his choicest blossoms."

As Bryan's party of seven, including his host, William St. John, made their way down to the steamboat wharf on the Battery—close to where a dog was recently shot and clubbed to death by a policeman—their progress through the streets went unnoticed. No one waved; no one cheered. Either no one on the street recognized the Democratic candidate for president, or no one particularly cared, as New Yorkers went about their work that busy Friday. Even on the steamboat *Perseus*, the Bryans remained unrecognized by their fellow passengers. They did not depart from Manhattan until 4:30 PM, and the trip to Coney Island took over an hour. Once at the island, the Iron Pier afforded steamboat passengers a good view of Brighton Beach, especially as the land on each side of the pier curved gently into the water. Looking west the Bryans could see the Windsor, Bay View, Occidental, and West End Hotels, while to the east could be glimpsed the main Concourse, with its various colorful and noisy amusements. Beyond the Concourse the Bryans could probably see the massive Brighton Beach and Manhattan hotels. Apparently, just looking was enough for them. "Mr. Bryan either did not like the looks of the 'merry-go-rounds,'" one man commented, "or he was tired, or something else was the matter, for he did not leave the boat, but returned to the city with her."

On their return trip, the Bryans listened to a fellow passenger "very bitterly denouncing me," Bryan himself later remembered. "After he had exhausted language in expressing his contempt for me and my supporters, he was introduced. Mrs. Bryan and I tried to assure him that no harm had been done by his candid expression of opinion, but he was so deeply mortified he did not enjoy the remainder of the trip." It is doubtful that William and Mary enjoyed the remainder of their trip either, as the passenger's comments simply underscored the hostile reception New York had given them. With their departure set for the next morning, the violent denunciation of the man aboard the steamboat may well have been the last words the Bryans heard directly from an average New Yorker. Their boat, *Perseus*, was named for one of the heroes of Greek mythology, who was told to seek his destiny on the "island of golden apples to the west."

CONCLUSION:
A PHENOMENON

THEODORE ROOSEVELT, William Jennings Bryan, and the killer heat wave all departed New York City at around the same time. On Saturday, August 15, the Bryans took leave of their host's home en route for upstate New York. "Saturday morning we brought to a close our very pleasant sojourn with Mr. St. John and his mother," Bryan later wrote in his account of the 1896 campaign. These were his final words on the trip to New York. He made no further mention of the speech, the failed receptions, the criticism of the city press, or his frosty reception by New York Democrats.

There have been few instances in American history of a presidential candidate suffering such a reverse of fortune so quickly and so early in the campaign. On August 8 Bryan had started from his home in Lincoln, aboard a slow, eastbound train that allowed the candidate to stop and make dozens of speeches to thousands of people. He built anticipation for the most important speech of his career, more important even than the "Cross of Gold" speech that had won him the nomination in Chicago. With this single speech in Madison Square Garden, in the heart of "enemy's country," he had tried to win over skeptics and take the East by storm. No doubt he and his managers envisioned a repeat of the scene in the Chicago auditorium of only the month before: a spellbinding performance of the Boy Orator followed by a half-hour demonstration that would sweep aside all doubt surrounding the Great Commoner, the presidential nominee of both the Democrat and Populist parties. Only a week later, Bryan was slinking off to lick his wounds, forbidden by campaign managers even to continue his tour.

In their continuing autopsy of his New York visit, the newspapers noted one previous time when a politician had come to the city and shaped his own destiny and that of the country by way of a historic and well-received speech. On February 27, 1860, Abraham Lincoln addressed an audience at Cooper Union. Although he had been defeated two years before by Stephen Douglas in the Illinois race for the U.S. Senate, their debates had given Lincoln a national profile.

Lincoln went to New York in 1860 with handicaps equal to Bryan's in 1896. Both were seen as westerners with little to offer America's greatest metropolis. In 1896 Bryan's Nebraska had been a state for only thirty years, while in 1860, Lincoln's Illinois had been a state for only forty years. Lincoln and Bryan were both perceived as political ingénues. Lincoln had served one term in the House of Representatives, Bryan only two. By the time of their New York speeches, neither man was seen as being especially "presidential." Lincoln was a rough-hewn, gangly, small-town lawyer with a nasal twang New Yorkers found grating. Bryan was a self-righteous demagogue and small-town lawyer and editor, with a brash campaigning style that New Yorkers found off-putting. Both men came to the city with reputations as noted western orators (the *New York Times* called Lincoln "that noted political exhorter and prairie orator"). Both men sought to portray themselves as cool-headed moderates, avoiding rhetorical extremes and flowery language, while enunciating more rational and pedantic discourses. And, worried how the national press would report their speeches, both men resorted to reading from a prepared text.

The response that the city gave the two men could not have been more different, with historic consequences. Horace Greeley's *Tribune* called Lincoln "one of Nature's orators, using his rare powers solely and effectively to elucidate and to convince, though their inevitable effect is to delight and electrify as well." Two months later Lincoln received from the Illinois legislature his first endorsement for the presidency.

In contrast, days after his Garden speech, Bryan still had to defend himself over its failure and the resulting shift in his campaign schedule. Still, his New York supporters came to his defense. The young New York congressman William Sulzer visited Bryan on Friday, August 14, and left their meeting with a complacent smile. When asked whether Bryan had a fighting chance, Sulzer became excited. "A fighting chance!" he exclaimed. "He will sweep this country like a tidal wave!"

Democratic newspapers remained equally committed. Hearst's *Journal* kept up the drumbeat for Bryan in Friday's edition, comparing the Great Commoner to the Great Emancipator. "New York City then," the paper said of 1860, "bowed to chattel slavery, as it now bows to money slavery. Its motto was 'Cotton is King.' It was as subservient to Southern trade as it is now to European money lenders." Both Bryan and Lincoln, the paper noted, read their speeches "to avoid the unscrupulousness and mendacity of those who were instructed to misreport [them]." And both men had given orations "more statesmanlike and less 'catching' and inflammatory than their reputations had led their audiences to expect." The *Journal* even argued that Bryan's "victory" had been greater than Lincoln's because he faced "powerful and unscrupulous enemies." Bryan had faced "the entire Eastern press, backed up by the great trusts, syndicates, and combinations of capital of the United States." He had read his speech because "he knew that the purchasable newspapers of the East were prepared to twist his language and distort his ideas, to corrupt all sources of intelligence for their readers in so far as his mission was concerned." Bryan could easily have reached into his bag of rhetorical tricks to score a "mere personal triumph." Instead, he forced the opposition press to set forth the Democratic side of the argument for the good of the entire nation. "It was a great victory," the paper concluded in a lonely assessment, "and one that will long be remembered in the history of political warfare."

Like most New York observers, the *Evening Post* disagreed. In a blistering August 14 editorial, the paper that had been associated with reformers such as Carl Schurz and E. L. Godkin used the Garden speech as a means of mercilessly ridiculing the Democratic presidential candidate. The *Post* noted the "considerable anxiety" felt in some Republican quarters before the speech, as Bryan's opponents feared a great oratorical success like the one he had achieved in Chicago. "In place of vague fear," the paper said, "inextinguishable laughter has come. Mr. Bryan has broken his prestige, and broken it fatally, as it now appears." On the heels of his well-publicized and dramatic trip East, Bryan had either "to achieve the most brilliant success, or lose everything." In deviating from his strength—extemporaneous oratory—the *Post* likened Bryan to a comedian who tries his hand at heavy tragedy. Not only had he decided to depart from his role as fiery orator to become a cool statesman, but he had failed to inform his audience of this change. "The Madison Square Garden audience felt not only disappointed, but tricked," the paper said.

The *Post* also drew parallels to Lincoln, believing that the Nebraskan, in coming to New York, sought to achieve the same sort of influence on the East the Illinoisan had. Before February 1860, New Yorkers viewed Lincoln as a "rough-and-ready Western lawyer," while the Cooper Union speech showed him "the sinewy reasoner, the well-equipped thinker." The difference, the paper claimed, was the vulgar opinion of the East had been wrong about Lincoln but correct about Bryan. Lincoln did not have to change his character to win over New Yorkers. Bryan, however, "had to force a sea-change upon himself" and to "assume virtues he had not." But the greatest difference, the *Post* editorial concluded, lay in the fact that "Lincoln could appeal to the patriotic instinct and the sense of national honor, while his foolish young imitator has to argue for the cause of private dishonesty and public disgrace." This last was a dig at the Democratic silver platform more than Bryan himself, and it revealed that much of the criticism directed at the candidate really had more to do with the issue of the gold standard versus bimetallism. Yet the *Post* only echoed what virtually all the New York papers concluded about the speech. The *Journal* might claim Bryan's likeness to Lincoln, but few in the city would have accepted that comparison. Bryan was no Lincoln, and the Cooper Union speech, one of the greatest unknown speeches in American history, soared high above the Boy Orator's pedestrian effort.

Just as the Bryans did on August 14, Lincoln, too, had sat for a portrait while visiting New York. Lincoln visited the studio of Matthew Brady, destined within only a few years to become the greatest contemporary chronicler of the Civil War. Before his nomination for the presidency, before his controversial election without appearing on any Southern ballot, before Fort Sumter and four years of Civil War, and more than five years before his assassination, the Lincoln who visited New York in 1860 looked impossibly young. In his Brady photo, he is clean-shaven, with sunken, hooded eyes that give him a grave, unhappy look. The photo was taken just three weeks before William Jennings Bryan was born.

***

WITH BRYAN ALREADY on the ropes, the knockout punch was still to come. And the punch would come from within his own party. In a move calculated to shift attention away from Bryan completely, the Democratic Honest-Money League had arranged for William Bourke Cockran to be the keynote speaker at yet another rally to be held in Madison Square Garden on Tuesday night, less than a week after Bryan's speech there. In choosing a foil to Bryan, New York could not have found a better man than Cockran. If Bryan had only recently been labeled the Boy Orator of the Platte, Cockran had long been viewed as one of America's leading public speakers. Even across political lines, the admiring New York press was already assuming that where Bryan had failed, Cockran would succeed.

Cockran had gained an international reputation through his oratory that was rare for a man who never advanced beyond local New York politics. The record of people praising Cockran's speeches is almost endless. A British member of Parliament called Cockran "the most eloquent orator of his time among the English-speaking peoples, if not all nations." Theodore Roosevelt's presidential military aide and close companion, Archie Butt, once wrote, "One is fascinated by his power of oratory. Leonine always in his appearance, he looks like a lion ready to spring when he is speaking. His voice is like a low rumble of thunder, then has the sweetness of the lute in it. I had not heard him for years, but the moment he uttered his first sentence I felt that he had grown both in power and in sympathy." In 1910 Butt still served as aide to Roosevelt's successor, William Howard Taft. Riding home together after Cockran's speech, Taft turned to his aide and said, "Archie, you now see the difference between declamation and oratory. I believe Cockran is the greatest orator using the English language today."

Cockran also made a deep impression on the young William Jennings Bryan when they first met at the 1884 Democratic National Convention, when Bryan was only twenty-four. Although Cockran was only thirty, he had already achieved a prominent place in Tammany Hall and was but a few years from taking a seat in the House of Representatives.

At the convention, Cockran sat with Irish-Catholic Tammany delegates, led by boss John Kelly, all of whom were hostile to Grover Cleveland's nomination. Their opposition had led to rumors that Cleveland was anti-Catholic. Cockran rose to defend Tammany's position, decry the invocation of religion in the proceedings, and affirm the ultimate unity of the Democratic Party. Cockran called for calm and unity among the bitterly divided delegates:

> If my word of warning be heeded, you will find that every element of contest will be stilled; that although we may have been divided by the wild waves of factional tumult, as soon as the gavel of the chairman declares the nomination made we will become calm and placid as the bosom of the lake in summer. Though we may have been divided before we entered these halls, we are but the countless rivulets that go to make up a mighty stream, and which though

turbulent and violent while they are flowing in their separate courses, after they have passed the point of confluence, merge together and roll their united course to the sea in a majestic tide, all powerful in its strength and restless in its force.

Even the Cleveland supporters in the galleries joined the ovation that followed his speech. Cockran had scored a personal and political triumph that would lead the New Yorker to Congress.

Reading Cockran's 1884 speech, it might very well have been uttered by Bryan. There was the alliteration that both men employed at every turn. Bryan, too, favored the watery metaphors that Cockran used; in 1893 Bryan told the House of Representatives that Cleveland could not "measure the ocean's silent depths by the foam upon its waves." Both men used overt and unapologetically religious language to powerful effect. Indeed, Cockran's 1884 speech had a tremendous impact on Bryan. He had listened to Cockran in awe of his words and power over his listeners. In such oratory Bryan found something of the divine.

Cockran's speech was the making of Bryan the orator. True, Bryan had become a competent debater in college. As a young man he had listened to the speeches of Robert Ingersoll, Henry Ward Beecher, and Wendell Phillips, three of the greatest orators of their day. Still, the great model for Bryan's own political oratory, the father of the western Boy Orator, was none other than an Irish-born New Yorker, William Bourke Cockran. And Cockran was about to help destroy his own creation.

Even as they skewered Bryan after his speech, the New York press eagerly awaited Cockran's response. The *Post* claimed that Cockran should be grateful for the "manifest delivering of a Philistine into his hands" and gleefully anticipated "the sport which the lively Irish orator and pungent reasoner will make when he answers Bryan." The *Times* claimed that Cockran "has not a superior as a public debater and orator in this country. He has both logic and fire, and appeals to both the reason and the highest sentiment of his hearers."

Only two days after Bryan's speech the Gold Democrats had announced Cockran's own Madison Square Garden rally. It was a move calculated to draw attention and support away from the Democratic nominee for the presidency. It worked. News of the Cockran speech filled the papers and drew national attention. Demand for tickets was so great that the Gold Democrat organizers anticipated a full house. The New York Stock Exchange alone had requested 500 seats. Appeals for tickets were arriving from the neighboring states of Pennsylvania, New Jersey, and Connecticut. To make sure that average New Yorkers could hear the speech, only about 8,000 seats were reserved, while the rest would be available to the public. Recalling the spectacle of the police line surrounding the Garden for Bryan's speech and turning away the thousands who held no tickets, a Gold Democrat spokesman said that police would turn no one away from Cockran's speech, for which 4,000 more chairs would be placed in the auditorium. Few doubted that Cockran would pack every seat. "His speech will be something worth hearing," the *Times* said. "He will fill Madison Square Garden, not empty it." Even anticipation of Cockran's speech afforded New Yorkers further reasons to strike at Bryan.

COCKRAN WOULD ALSO be aided by the temperature, which was rapidly sinking to more temperate levels. Still, reminders of the heat wave remained, including piles of horse corpses that still littered the streets. In desperation, some New Yorkers had taken to lighting fires in the streets—not to dispose of the bodies but to keep the smell at bay. Such fires harkened back to the cholera epidemics of the nineteenth century and were motivated by the same fear of pestilence.

Pressed by Mayor Strong at the August 14 meeting of department heads, President Wilson of the Board of Health promised the mayor that all carcasses would be removed within the next twenty-four hours, as the contractor sought to remove the final fifty or so bodies. Stories abounded of people and businesses suffering as the result of rotting horses. On the previous Wednesday evening, August 12, a horse had died in front of Pierce and Company's grocery at Warren and Washington Streets (an intersection that no longer exists because of the West Side Highway built during the Great Depression). Despite requests to have the horse removed, by Friday morning the grocery employees were forced to stop work as a result of the horrible smell. The business closed at a large loss of income. Some wag had placed a sign on the body: "The Board of Health Will Meet Here at 2 P.M.; Mayor Strong is invited to attend."

The carcass problem was no joke, however. Thomas White, the contractor responsible for removal, had suffered losses among his men and horses during the heat wave. In attempting to remove the estimated 1,500 dead horses on the streets the previous week—nearly the number he removed during an entire *year*—White lost eleven horses and had six of his men prostrated. White had never seen anything strike down the horses of New York like the current heat wave. And he would know. For thirty years the White family had held the city contract for removing dead animals, which they took to their other family business on Barren Island: rendering plants that transformed the dead horses into fertilizer and glue. It was this business that was primarily served by the city contract to remove the horses.

The heat wave ensured a windfall of raw material for the Barren Island plants.

For most New York businesses the heat wave proved a disaster equal to, if not greater than, any hurricane or flood. Losses totaled in the millions of dollars. Retail dry goods stores, whose merchandise was immune to the effects of heat, lost a formidable proportion of their profits simply because of lack of customers. During the heat wave, shoppers stayed home. One store manager claimed that sales at his store during the heat wave decreased by half, and one-third of the store clerks had been given two weeks of enforced vacation. By one estimate, dry goods retailers in the city lost about $720,000 during the heat wave, not including lost wages.

The price of ice meant that storing fresh beef became so expensive that many of the large butchers refused to sell meat except early in the morning. Sales of beef by butchers dropped 70 percent, and many city abattoirs simply stopped work entirely. The estimated 850 retail butchers in the city lost an estimated $230,000 during the heat wave, while wholesale butchers lost another $400,000, both because of the general disposition to stop buying beef during a heat wave and because the retail butchers refused to close contracts made before the heat wave began. Hotels that normally made money through their restaurants also found a sharp drop in trade. During the heat wave hotel restaurants that might usually serve between 250 and 350 diners per night counted only a dozen or so customers.

Green grocers found it impossible to keep their food fresh, and the common custom of spraying the vegetables had no effect. Estimated losses among green grocers was 60 percent, while the market gardeners who brought their produce to the city could not find buyers. This sector accounted for another $100,000 in losses.

Almost every city trade suffered during the long heat wave. Candy manufacturers and retailers could not keep their wares from spoiling. Bicycle rentals, an enormous business in late-nineteenth-century American cities, calculated an estimated loss of over $100,000. Out-of-town visitors to the city's downtown wholesalers postponed their trips during the heat wave, causing a loss of as much as $8 million.

Not every business suffered. Charles Morse's great Consolidated Ice Company did a booming business during the heat wave. Morse's company had delivered 15,000 tons every day during the week, a Herculean task requiring seven hundred carts and more than 2,000 men working from early morning to late at night. Three men and twenty horses working for Morse died as a result. In comparison, all the smaller ice concerns combined sold only about 5,000 tons daily. In all this meant that approximately 200,000 tons of ice—the equivalent of about fourteen Brooklyn Bridges—had been delivered during the heat wave, solely within the confines of New York City. Hotels and hospitals consumed much of this supply, with hospitals using large amounts for treating cases of heat exhaustion.

The ice business was an exception to the economic disaster visited upon the city. New York was not alone in claiming great financial loss from the heat wave. Estimates in Chicago ran to $10 million, and a million and a half dollars was lost in Philadelphia. In St. Louis, residents compared the human and financial losses to the killer tornado that hit the city in May, killing as many as four hundred people and destroying millions of dollars in property. Such a comparison to a recent natural disaster that took an enormous toll in both lives and property reflected the view that the heat wave and tornado shared similar killer and destructive characteristics, despite the fact that the heat wave did not constitute a single "event" that left obvious property damage. While later Americans ignored heat waves as natural disasters because they did not kill with such drama and damage, those who experienced the 1896 heat wave evidently would have considered the tragic week comparable to killer earthquakes, floods, and hurricanes in the nation's history.

***

ALTHOUGH LESS THAN one week separated them, Bryan and Cockran's Madison Square Garden speeches contrasted sharply. For the Cockran speech there was no police cordon and no mad rush for seats. Top politicians from both parties attended the speech as one of the most noteworthy political events of the year. The New York press showered Cockran with the laurels it had withheld from Bryan. And the temperature that Tuesday evening, August 18, was one of the coolest of that August.

With the Cockran speech scheduled for Tuesday, Roosevelt remained in the city on Monday consulting with Acting Deputy Chief Moses Cortright concerning the police preparations. The next day Cortright would have under his command about four hundred policemen at the Garden. However, unlike the Bryan speech, no streets to the Garden would be blocked and no police line established. No police passes, such as the ones issued for the Bryan speech and subsequently ignored by the police, would be issued. Five different entrances would be used by ticket holders to avoid any crush, and any unoccupied seats would be available to the public. As many as 16,000 people were expected to attend, which would be a crowd greater than any before seen in that auditorium. Now that the heat wave had broken, the police did not bother to take the same precautions to deal with cases of heat prostration at Tuesday's Garden speech. No hospital was established in the basement, no stretcher bearers were to be placed among the crowd, and no flags with a red cross were to be waved in case of a prostration.

In the days before Bryan's speech, the heat itself had been the city's main topic of discussion. New Yorkers had scanned the daily death lists and studied the weather forecasts. Now both Bryan and the heat had departed. Cockran would give his speech on an evening when the day's high temperature would reach only 73 degrees, the coolest day the city had seen in almost three weeks.

Unlike Bryan's speech, every prominent New York politician attended the event. One early outburst of applause came when the Republican Mayor Strong appeared. Boss Platt was in attendance, as was Warner Miller. Former governor Flower attended and provided small American flags to the crowd, which were placed on each of the 15,000 seats. Abram Hewitt and E. L. Godkin, two former governors of Ohio, and New York congressmen Coombs and Fowler attended.

Theodore Roosevelt had not attended Bryan's speech. He had not even been in the city on that fateful Wednesday evening. On August 18, however, not only did Republican Roosevelt attend the speech of a Tammany Democrat, but he also brought his wife. When he entered the Garden he received loud cheers from the crowd and the honor of being the object of the old political chant: "What's the matter with Roosevelt?" someone shouted, to which the standard reply was, "Oh, he's all right." "Who's all right?" "Why, Teddy!" roared the crowd, as Roosevelt smiled at his reception. He may have also been smiling at the police arrangements for that evening. As the Garden's doors had been opened two hours early, there was no crush at the entrances, and no mad dash for seats. Before Bryan's speech, seats had filled in a matter of minutes as people sprinted through the doors. For tonight's speech all seats were filled an hour before Cockran even appeared onstage, as the band played "Hail to the Chief."

The auditorium was draped in red, white, and blue bunting. The boxes and galleries were adorned with American flags, while above the upper galleries hung flags with the seals of every state of the Union. The speaker's platform featured the national shield of the American eagle. Thousands of flags had been used for the decorations of the Garden, not including the 15,000 provided by Governor Flower. When the crowd waved them, the *Times* said, "they gave an effect that was as picturesque in appearance as it was patriotic in sentiment."

One of the most rousing moments of the evening came before Cockran even began to speak. He had just been greeted by a roaring ovation and had raised his hands to still the tumult. He waited until the noise had subsided, and when there were only a few scattered people clapping, he prepared to begin speaking. At that moment someone in the audience arose and, using one of the little flags as a baton, began singing "The Star-Spangled Banner." Before the first verse was completed, the entire audience of 15,000 had jumped to its feet to sing the remainder of the anthem, all the while waving their little flags. The *Sun* called the spontaneous scene as "perhaps the most thrilling and inspiring ever witnessed in New York," while the *Times* said "Few demonstrations such as greeted Mr. Cockran when he arose to speak have ever been seen in this city since war times—if, indeed, there were any then."

After the singing subsided, Cockran spoke without notes for a little over an hour, about half the time that Bryan had spent reading his speech. Incorporating mention of the anthem into the introduction to his speech, he improvised, "With the inspiring strains of the national song still ringing in our ears, who can doubt the issue of this campaign? That issue, stripped of all verbal disguise, is an issue of common honesty; an issue between an honest discharge and a dishonest repudiation of public and private obligations. It is a question of whether the powers of this government shall be used to protect honest industry or to tempt the citizen to dishonesty."

Cockran was blunt about the course of action for Democrats. "We must raise our hands against the nominee of our party, and we must do it to preserve the party itself." Throughout his speech he resorted to withering sarcasm that time and again drew laughter from the audience. Much of this was directed at Bryan himself. "We would look in vain through the speech delivered here one week ago to find a true statement of the issue involved in this canvass. (Laughter) Indeed, I believe it is doubtful if the candidate himself quite understands the nature of the faith which he professes. (Laughter) I say this not in criticism of his ability, but in justice to his morality. (Laughter)." Portraying Bryan as a clown may have been more effective than actually refuting the silver question. The New York papers had begun their portrayal of Bryan as an ignorant buffoon just after the candidate's Garden speech. Now Cockran completed the picture of Bryan as a well-meaning but terribly ill-informed simpleton.

He reached a crescendo as he took Bryan's famous speech from the Chicago Convention and turned it on its head. "To him we say, in the name of humanity, in the name of progress, 'You shall neither place a crown of thorns upon the brow of labor nor lay a scourge upon his back. (Applause) You shall not rob him of any one advantage which he has gained by long years of steady progress in the skill with which he exercises his craft and by efficient organization among those who work with him at the same bench. You shall not obscure the golden prospect of a further improvement in his condition by a further cheapening in the cost of living, as well as by a future appreciation of the dollar in which his wages are paid.' (Applause)." Cockran had masterfully turned Bryan's words against him, added the allusion to sound money through the "golden prospect" facing workers with a strong dollar, and in only an hour established Bryan as the enemy of the workingman.

It was a thrilling moment and the height of Cockran's oratorical career. While he would go on to speak to many large urban crowds in the weeks that followed, leading up to the election, never again would he speak to so large a crowd. Indeed, as Roosevelt would comment to his friend Lodge, few Americans not running for or holding political office would have been able to attract such a crowd. And Cockran was enormously successful in exactly the same place where Bryan had failed so miserably.

The speech caused an outpouring of praise from all quarters, as some even suggested it turned the tide of the election itself. Others echoed the *Sun* in seeing Cockran's effort as above partisan politics and serving the larger, national good. Just after the election a Philadelphia paper said, "Bourke Cockran's Madison Square Garden speech lifted the canvass to that moral plane where thousands of Democrats afterwards stood, and in it may be discovered the characteristic that carried the great orator beyond the environments of the political organization with which his first triumphs were associated." Republican boss Thomas Platt said, "It was the greatest speech I ever listened to. McKinley's election is now assured." Speaker of the House Thomas Reed wrote Cockran, "After your most noble effort last evening you are entitled to the highest honor the nation can bestow upon you." Roosevelt described the speech to his friend Henry Cabot Lodge as "a phenomenon." "It is extraordinary that a mere private citizen should be able to gather such an enormous crowd," he observed, "a crowd quite as large inside the Madison Square Garden and almost as large outside, as that which came to hear Bryan, the candidate for the Presidency. Cockran made a first class speech. I cannot but believe that the tide is beginning to flow against the free silverites."

From abroad, the twenty-one-year-old Winston Churchill offered congratulations on a speech the future prime minister called "not only a rhetorical triumph, but also a moral victory." Any change in currency policy, Churchill wrote, should be slow and cautious. "What Bryan is doing is like an inebriate regulating a chronometer with a crowbar."

Perhaps inevitably, hoping to enlist a promising candidate in their ranks, city Republicans made an offer to Cockran to run for Congress as a Republican from the Twelfth District. He declined. "While the Democratic organization remains a party to the Populist conspiracy against wages, I shall labor untiringly for its defeat," Cockran replied, "but I will not consent to profit by its overthrow." Cockran was even considered for a place in McKinley's cabinet, and Mark Hanna supported the idea of naming the New York Democrat as attorney general. Only when McKinley showed Hanna and others a statement from Cockran proclaiming, "I am a Democrat and unalterably opposed to the Republican Tariff policies," was the matter dropped.

The Cockran speech immediately invited contrasts with Bryan's. The *Nation* called the Cockran speech at the Garden "immense in every way," and said, "its effect upon the country as a contrast to the Bryan demonstration of the previous week must have been very great." The *Times* commented editorially in a column entitled, "The Boy Orator and the Man Orator." The paper noted the great improvement in the organization and the police arrangements of the Cockran meeting. Even the weather had been different. "The queer and picturesque element added to the Bryan meeting by the intense heat was absent last night," the paper observed, "the spectacle of a coatless crowd relieving itself by the waving of fans. But the management provided an efficient substitute for it last night by furnishing every seat with a little American flag, which produced an effect equally bizarre and more attractive."

The very replacement of 15,000 waving palm-leaf fans with 15,000 waving American flags provided a fitting symbol to the overall contrast between the two meetings. If Bryan's speech had sunk into a welter of heat, Cockran's had soared on a wave of patriotism. But in the end the speeches themselves provided the main contrasts. The *Times* said that Cockran's "affluent eloquence flowed on, interrupted only by applause as spontaneous as the applause for Bryan was perfunctory and managed, and by the hearty laughter which Bryan did not once elicit." In one week New Yorkers had had the chance to observe two of America's greatest public speakers address differing sides of the same issue and provide a dramatic start to the campaign season. For those who had gone to both Garden speeches, the *Times* believed "there must have been many who remembered with dim and remote wonder how they had suffered less than a week before in the place in which they were now delighted, and marveled at the vastness of the difference between an orator and a bore."

Gone were the headlines criticizing Roosevelt's police and the embarrassing stories of the arrest of a journalist. In his letter to Lodge, Roosevelt took credit for the better police measures. "This time I supervised the police arrangements myself," he wrote, noting that the chief of police had "run off to the country." Of course, a week earlier, Roosevelt had missed the Bryan meeting as he, too, had run off to the country, remaining in the cooler climes of Oyster Bay. "Everything went off without a hitch; there was very little legitimate ground for complaint even at the first meeting; it was chiefly reporters' grievances, as a number of their passes were not honored. This time I saw that they were all honored, and the police kept complete control of the crowd, having them thoroughly in hand; and yet they behaved with the utmost good nature. I determined that I would be able to testify as an eye witness to all that happened." Roosevelt repeated these observations to reporters. "It would be simple justice for the newspapers to state that the police could do no better than they have done tonight," he said. "This meeting is a bigger one than the Bryan meeting. I have seen no fault to find with the police. I have been at every point outside, and have nothing but praise for the police arrangements and the managements of the crowds." Roosevelt may have exaggerated his involvement in the police arrangements. In truth, his main contribution to that evening most likely was to serve as spokesman and booster for the police, especially after the criticism leveled against New York's Finest only the week before.

Having the Cockran meeting go off without a hitch was a boon for Roosevelt, allowing him to leave the city on a high note. He planned to take a three-week vacation in North Dakota, foreshadowing his leaving New York for good only a few months later. Just as his fight to uphold the Sunday saloon-closing law during the past two years had made any future career in the city virtually untenable, recent events had only confirmed his great desire to leave the city of his birth. The extreme heat, the criticism leveled against the police on the night of Bryan's speech, and his ongoing feud with Parker must have made the prospect of putting half the country between him and his problems extremely inviting.

In a rare display of weakness, Roosevelt told his friend Lodge, in a letter dated August 19, that he looked forward to his trip West. "I am very glad to go for I think the endless strain and worry had told on me a little." Despite the failure of Bryan's speech and the rousing success of Bourke Cockran's, he told Lodge he still worried that "the hatred of the East among many Westerners, and the crude ignorance of even elementary finance among such a multitude of well meaning, but puzzle-headed, voters, give cause for serious alarm throughout this campaign." A political animal even when he was hunting in North Dakota, Roosevelt looked forward to having a better understanding of western opinion: "I shall be able to speak more intelligently when I come back from the West."

His familiarity and even fame in parts of the West would eventually prove valuable to McKinley and the Republican National Committee, although not in 1896. By the 1900 election, however, Roosevelt's New York origins, his "western-ness," his reform credentials, and his heroism during the Spanish-American War all combined to make him the party's choice for vice president.

***

THE KILLER HEAT wave of August 4–13, 1896, claimed approximately 1,300 victims in New York and Brooklyn alone, making it the deadliest urban heat disaster in American history. The lingering effects of the heat continued to kill even after cooler temperatures arrived by the middle of the month. The heat wave probably claimed its last victim as late as August 21. Seven-month-old Fannie Hertzberg fell ill from the heat on August 13 and died on the twenty-first from what the doctor called "insolation," a full eight days after the heat wave's end. Under the "Occupation" section of the death certificate, the doctor wrote "Infant."

It was a common phenomenon among victims of heat exhaustion that few could remember when they had begun to feel sick. The early symptoms of heat exhaustion could easily be mistaken for normal discomfort, especially among laborers or the poor during an extended heat wave. Such symptoms include heavy sweating, paleness, weakness, tiredness, muscle cramping, and headaches, all of which a working person might regularly experience during a New York August.

During the 1896 heat wave, Frank McCoy gave a rare detailed description of what he had felt in the hours before he collapsed from the heat. "I was standing at the corner of Twenty-second Street and Third Avenue last Tuesday," he said. "My pulse had been high all day and I was more or less oppressed by the humidity. A great many deaths had occurred in the morning and on the day before, and I thought the best thing to do was to keep cool. I drank a great quantity of ice water and perspired freely. All the time, though, my tongue was getting very dry. I could not keep my mouth cool." Racing pulse was a classic early warning sign of heat exhaustion and the cause for many of the collapsed and overcome victims during the previous week. Drinking a large quantity of ice water was a good precaution, and sweating was a good sign that the body still had the means to cool itself off. Nevertheless, it is probable McCoy could neither sweat enough to cool down nor drink enough to replace the fluid lost by sweating. Feeling his tongue getting dry and unable to keep his "mouth cool" signified dehydration, a dangerous cause of hyperthermia.

A short while later, McCoy continued, "My head began to throb, and it seemed just as though it would burst. My tongue got heavier. A feeling of exhaustion gradually passed over my whole body, and I grew weaker and warmer." At this point McCoy was on the verge of collapse, already suffering from heat exhaustion. Although still conscious, he was clearly in a state of advanced dehydration, with his body temperature rising rapidly. "Suddenly I felt my skin cracking on my skull. I thought a thousand pounds had dropped right on the top of my head and then a wave of terrible heat swept over me, and I put my arm out to steady myself." At this point McCoy lost consciousness. "The next thing I knew I was here in the hospital, and they were taking me out of a cold bath. They put me in at 2:05 P.M., and took me out at 3:30. Since then I have been very weak and the shock has dulled my head a little." One and a half hours in an ice bath was a long time, indicating how elevated McCoy's temperature must have been when he succumbed. Although his temperature returned to normal, such a severe case of hyperthermia may have left McCoy with permanent damage to the heart or other organs. Three days after his collapse, McCoy was still not well enough to return home.

WITH A CARRIAGE waiting at the curb to take his party to the station, Bryan seized a last opportunity to speak to reporters. In a nice bit of diplomacy, he shook each reporter's hand warmly and gave him a campaign button with the candidate's picture. The reporters present were some of the men who had fiercely criticized and mocked him. They had portrayed the Madison Square Garden speech in the most negative manner, spreading word of its failure across the nation. They had lampooned the candidate throughout his New York stay, helping halt the momentum Bryan had built from the Chicago convention and his eastward train journey. Now he said he had been kindly treated by the reporters "personally," placing a small stress on the word. "The press of your city is against me, of course," he said, "but you boys have treated me very nicely."

Then Bryan gave his last speech before leaving New York:

> There are two things I want to say. One is that before I came here the New York papers frequently called me an anarchist. I do not believe any of them has called me an anarchist since I came. The

other thing is that they speak of me as the "Boy Orator." If I am elected no other young man in politics will be ridiculed for his youth. There are a great many boys in the country, and I am glad I am young.

I wanted very much to have the opportunity of seeing something of the people of New York. I wanted to meet them and shake hands with them, but my time here has been consumed entirely by campaign work. There was a great deal to be done, and little time for doing it, and I had to work. I hope, however, that I shall yet have an opportunity for seeing your people and talking to them face to face and as man to man.

It was an odd little speech. There was no mention of the Madison Square Garden meeting, although perhaps by that morning there was nothing more to say. Instead Bryan claimed a strange sort of victory in that no New Yorker continued to label him an anarchist—a pyrrhic victory, indeed, if this was the sole result of his New York trip. "I am glad I am young" seemed a trivial observation from the author of "Cross of Gold." Claiming that he had no opportunity to meet New Yorkers after a four-day stay in the city only underscored Bryan's isolation since arriving in the city. In America's largest metropolis, how could the Democratic presidential candidate have failed to come into contact with its citizens? Finally, characterizing New Yorkers as "your people" was little better than calling the city "enemy's territory." It was as if Bryan had stumbled on some alien culture, forcing him to communicate with hand gestures and pantomime.

No one bade farewell to the Bryans at the St. John home, and no one even greeted them at the New York Central Railroad Station, where they boarded the Croton local for their trip to Irvington. Aside from the Bryans, Sewall, and General John Brisben Walker, only John Cutright of Lincoln, Nebraska, accompanied the candidate as his secretary. Perhaps never in American history had presidential and vice presidential candidates traveled together with so small a retinue.

At the railroad station the New York Central offered Bryan the use of a special car. Just as he had after the Chicago convention, he declined the offer, saying he was much too poor to afford it, and he did not wish anything he could not pay for. The party paid the regular fare and sat together in the regular passenger car, beginning a journey out of the city that must have come as some relief to Bryan. It also began a two-week stay in upstate New York that afforded the candidate much-needed rest but also effectively removed him from the campaign only ten weeks before election day. Until early September, the normally verbose Boy Orator would remain virtually silent.

While the Bryans settled down for a long rest, the campaign did not stop. As the Democratic candidate sat looking at the Hudson River from the Walker veranda, the Republicans kicked off the Ohio campaign with enormous rallies in McKinley's home state. With special trains bringing people from all over the state, Senator John Sherman and former Ohio governor Joseph Foraker addressed thousands in Columbus, while McKinley stayed in Canton. Sherman—he of the Sherman Silver Purchase Act and the Sherman Anti-Trust Act—ripped into the Democratic monetary policy as "the doctrine of the Populist and the Anarchist." Sherman even stooped to "wave the bloody shirt" by noting that "570,000 Union soldiers, their widows and orphans," would be paid their pensions "with money of less purchasing power than gold coin." Sherman believed the free coinage of silver to be "a fraud and a robbery, and all the worse if committed by a great and free people."

By remaining in seclusion in Irvington, Bryan forfeited the field to the Republicans. In the days that followed, no Democrat stepped forward to rebut the Republican attacks. The failure of Bryan's Garden speech continued to have far-reaching ramifications, as the Democratic Party appeared to concede much of the country and the campaign to the Republicans.

This was good news for Theodore Roosevelt. Soon after the Cockran speech Roosevelt departed for North Dakota and remained there for the rest of August and early September. Hunting and camping in the "Bad Lands" had always restored Roosevelt's body and spirit after difficult periods in his life. In 1884 this had meant fleeing west after the deaths of his wife and his mother. In 1896 Roosevelt escaped over a year's worth of criticism concerning his saloon-closing crusade, the hostility of the press and his own party leaders, and, finally, the deadlock on the police commission caused by his feud with Parker. That August, of course, he also escaped the awful heat of the month that had caused so much work for his police and even contributed to officers' deaths.

Roosevelt had done more than just visit the police stations to supervise the distribution of ice. In a scene that recalled his trips with Jacob Riis into the tenement districts in the early 1880s, and his more recent midnight patrols as police commissioner, he set out to see what people actually did with the free ice. Commissioner Roosevelt visited a number of alleys and rear tenements along Mulberry Street, some of the poorest residences of the city's poorest street. He expressed being "agreeably surprised" by the way families used the ice. Roosevelt watched as fathers and mothers of large families cracked the ice into small pieces. Some pieces were then placed in a handkerchief or towel and tied around the foreheads and heads of sick infants.

While this took place, Roosevelt watched as some people made cooling drinks, while others simply held the chunks of ice in their hands, "from which they bit and chewed constantly." With some pride, Roosevelt noted that the city's distribution of free ice was the first time anything of the sort was ever attempted. True, the giveaway had not gone as smoothly as it might have, but this, Roosevelt said, was to due to the short time the police had from the time they received the order until it was put into practice. Roosevelt clearly doubted this would become standard practice for the city during heat waves. "It may never happen again," he said, "and if it does it will only be in such an emergency as this one."

Decades later, as he sat down to write his memoirs in 1913, Roosevelt remembered the terrible heat wave and the suffering it caused among the poor. He remembered the streets being flushed and his own contribution in suggesting and supervising the distribution of free ice in the Lower East Side. The fact that Roosevelt could recall such scenes in vivid detail, nearly two decades after they occurred, illustrated what a profound effect they had on him.

While history has forgotten Roosevelt's role during the heat wave, his actions foreshadowed his progressive presidency. His direct contact with the poor heightened his sense of noblesse oblige he had inherited from his father. Those in a position to help should help, and that included the government, if only during times of extreme emergency. Roosevelt was one of the few city officials even to suggest taking direct measures for relief of the poor. Moreover, he supervised those measures himself in order to ensure fair play. He also followed up on the ice giveaway and witnessed firsthand how families used the ice to cool their drinks or the brows of sick children. Finally, his actions were prompted by the ice trust represented by

Morse's Consolidated Ice Company. Here was a clear case of a trust fixing higher prices that had direct impact on the city's suffering poor. Giving away free ice helped bust this particular trust.

Late August found Roosevelt the urbanite heading west to hunt and camp and Bryan the westerner watching the boat traffic along the Hudson River. Their vacations left much time for recalling the historic week just finished. That single week in August 1896 witnessed a unique convergence of quintessentially American politics and personalities, with a great, urban natural disaster as the backdrop. In the blink of an eye Bryan had all but lost the presidential race by the time he finished his Madison Square Garden speech. Roosevelt himself had given up on New York politics and hoped instead for a post in a McKinley administration.

The heat wave shaped their careers and characters in unexpected ways. Perhaps Bryan might have given a rousing speech, if traveling to New York during a heat wave had not rendered him hoarse and exhausted. Maybe a New York crowd would have cheered his long speech, had the heat not driven them from their seats. For Roosevelt the heat wave marked another step along the path to a progressive presidency. He ordered city initiatives on behalf of the poor, personally supervised them to make sure all received fair treatment, and witnessed firsthand the suffering of the tenement dwellers.

Finally, the heat wave helped shape the history of America's greatest city. It ended a strike among the tailors of the Lower East Side, while forcing reluctant city officials to take positive measures to aid its suffering citizens. It also encouraged housing reform, as the tenements themselves indirectly caused hundreds of deaths.

The heat wave cut a swath of death through the immigrant laborers and their families, killing well over 1,000. While the smallest children suffered terribly, as they always did during the summers, in

the end it was those children's fathers who literally worked themselves to death in order to provide a living for their families. The average victim of the heat wave was a workingman, probably Irish,
living in the most impoverished and squalid of conditions. As he and
his brethren died, the philanthropists of the Progressive Era called
for reform on all levels: of working conditions and work hours, of
housing conditions, of sanitary conditions, of government conditions
that allowed corruption, and of economic conditions that had made
New Yorkers of August 1896 so susceptible to death and disease in
the first place. Such changes would take decades, but a natural disaster occurring during such an age of reform created a potent catalyst
for change.

EPILOGUE:
HOT TIME IN THE OLD TOWN

There'll be girls for ev'ry body in that good, good old town,
For dere's Miss Consola Davis an dere's Miss Gondolia Brown;
And dere's Miss Johanna Beasly she am dressed all in red,
I just hugged her and I kissed her and to me then she said
Please oh, please, Oh, do not let me fall,
You're all mine and I love you best of all,
And you must be my man, or I'll have no man at all,
There'll be a hot time in the old town tonight, my baby.

ROOSEVELT REMAINED IN North Dakota for the remainder of August and early September. Even while hunting and camping, the police commissioner continued to do good work for the party. While he was away, Roosevelt's article on the American vice presidency appeared in the journal *Review of Reviews*. While giving an overview of the history of the office, and pointing out the absurdity of Bryan running with two vice presidential nominees, one a Democrat and one a Populist, Roosevelt used the article to excoriate Bryan and Tom Watson. Roosevelt called Bryan a "sham and a compromise," as he represented a middle ground in the "Popocrat" coalition. Watson, however, Roosevelt viewed as truly destructive. "Mr. Watson would be a more startling, more attractive, and more dangerous figure," Roosevelt wrote, "for if he got the chance he would lash the nation with a whip of scorpions, while Mr. Bryan would be content with the torture of ordinary thongs." The article prompted Watson to write to Roosevelt directly, objecting to its "trenchant" tone. Roosevelt apparently did not reply, although he showed the "really very interesting letter" to his friend Lodge.

In North Dakota, as always, politics was never far from Roosevelt's mind. He talked politics with his cowboy friends, and during his return trip he stopped at the Republican headquarters in Chicago. On September 11, only one day after returning, Roosevelt gave a speech in New York attacking free silver and accusing the Democrats of menacing the Supreme Court and the Constitution. Within a week he and Lodge were campaigning throughout upstate New York, seeking to counter the influence of Bryan, who had just swung through the area on his way back to Lincoln. Roosevelt called the trip "very successful and pleasant." Mark Hanna apparently agreed, as he subsequently sent Roosevelt on a trip west through Illinois, Michigan, and Minnesota, which also copied Bryan's path through those states. Hanna saw Roosevelt, an easterner familiar to those in the West, as a perfect foil to Bryan's influence, foreshadowing Roosevelt's role as vice presidential candidate during the 1900 election.

After their campaign trip through New York state, Lodge and Roosevelt took a rather large detour to "drop in" on William McKinley in Canton. For Lodge, safe in his Senate seat for the next thirty years, this was perhaps little more than a courtesy call on the Republican Party leader and next president of the United States. It also served to soothe some bruised feelings, as both Lodge and Roosevelt had supported another candidate over McKinley's ascension to Speaker of the House in 1890 and had opposed McKinley's nomination in June. For Roosevelt, the visit, like his many visits to Hanna in New York and his speaking tours for the party, served a more important purpose: to permit him to leave his position as police commissioner and take up a new post in a McKinley administration.

Even with his service to the party that fall, securing Roosevelt a Washington post took some cajoling by his friends. The main obstacle appeared to be McKinley himself. He feared that Roosevelt was something of a hothead with an independent streak who might possess, in Lodge's own summary of McKinley's feelings, "preconceived plans which he would wish to drive through the moment he got in." Roosevelt had gotten a bad reputation. It had cost him the position of assistant secretary of state in 1884, had roused the animosity of Boss Platt and New York machine Republicans, and had almost pushed him out of his job as president of the Board of Police Commissioners. Acting as an independent reformer had helped Roosevelt as a New York assemblyman and secured him appointed posts in the small field of government oversight in Washington and New York City. It was not the strongest or broadest foundation for a higher political office, however.

After spending only three days at home in Lincoln, Bryan left for the longest of his campaign trips, this time leaving his wife at home. Mary was still a mother first, a candidate's wife second, and she insisted on staying at home as the children began a new term of school that fall. The candidate acknowledged his wife's value to him and to the campaign. "I had found her a great aid in my travels because she could assist in meeting the reception committees," he later wrote, "and thus give me more rest between stations. And then, too, she was able to insist upon more reasonable hours and greater freedom from interruption than I was able to do." Absent from Bryan's evaluation were his wife's charm, grace, and popularity on the campaign trail and the kind words reserved for her even by the most hostile presses of the East. If in 1896 Bryan revolutionized the American presidential campaign by barnstorming around the country, giving speeches in scores of towns to tens of thousands of citizens, Mary

Bryan revolutionized the role of the candidate's wife. She shook hands, gave receptions, and spoke to the press, all the while smiling as the umpteenth person of the day squeezed her bruised hand.

Bryan's autumn trip took him through the Upper South, through Missouri, Kentucky, Tennessee, and North Carolina, before arriving in Washington, DC. After a side trip to Baltimore, Bryan headed once again toward the Northeast, traveling to Wilmington, Philadelphia, and Brooklyn. At Yale University, constant catcalls and shouts of "McKinley" interrupted Bryan's speech. Bryan traveled to Boston and farther into New England before returning to New York City.

On September 29, Bryan stopped in Manhattan to give a speech in Tammany Hall, which was so packed with spectators and so poorly ventilated that the candidate almost collapsed. A later speech had to be canceled. Once again, New York had not treated the Nebraskan very well. In his short speech he made no mention of his previous visit to New York that sultry August. Before leaving, he visited the Bryan and Sewall Campaign Club, which, according to a July telegram, had been established with a membership of 635. Bryan claimed that this club "became a powerful influence in the campaign" under the direction of Congressman William Sulzer. Then where had its 635 members been in August when Bryan visited the city? Why had they not welcomed the Bryans when their boat ferried them across the Hudson from New Jersey or when they arrived at the home of William St. John? In later years the very value of such clubs was to facilitate mobilization of large crowds for campaign events. Either Sulzer and St. John had no communication concerning the August Bryan visit, or this simply reflected another display of political ignorance by St. John.

From New York Bryan made a 570-mile trip to West Virginia, before heading to the Dakotas, Minnesota, and Michigan, exactly the

states where Mark Hanna hoped Theodore Roosevelt would coun-
teract the Democratic candidate's influence. It worked, as on election
day Bryan lost the states where Roosevelt campaigned. A large
sweep through the Midwest completed the 18,000 miles Bryan traveled during the campaign. With the Northeast almost certainly lost
to McKinley, the Bryan campaign pinned its hopes on success in the
key states of Illinois, Ohio, Indiana, and Michigan. But the enormity
of Bryan's New York failure allowed Mark Hanna to firmly shift the
Republican focus to the midwestern battleground states. Of the eight
states he passed through on his 1,000-mile train journey from Lincoln to New York City, Bryan lost all except his home state. Almost
three months before Americans cast their votes, Bryan had lost the
election on August 12, the night of the Madison Square Garden
speech. Election night found the candidate in bed, as Mary brought
him the state-by-state results. By eleven o'clock the results were decisive. Bryan acknowledged his defeat and sent McKinley a congratulatory telegram.

Almost immediately Bryan began planning to secure the Democratic nomination in 1900. His strategy was twofold: give a series of
lectures throughout the country while publishing a memoir of the
1896 campaign. Both efforts were meant to keep positioning the silver question as a burning issue of the day. The sales of the campaign
memoir, *The First Battle*, would eventually hit 200,000. Unwilling to
compromise on bimetallism, Bryan refused to welcome back into the
party the Gold Democrats who had bolted in 1896. "The gold Democrats, if they come back to the Democratic party," Bryan stated,
"must come as silver men. There is no room for two Republican parties
in this country." In other words, the Gold Democrats were no more
than a wing of the Republican Party. Apparently there *was* room for
two *Democratic* parties, as Bryan rejected the reunion of the silver and

gold Democrats. Through 1897 Bryan succeeded in keeping himself and the silver issue in the public eye. He had no way of knowing that a "splendid little war" in the Caribbean would change the course of the 1900 election, his career, and the career of Theodore Roosevelt.

McKinley's election that November made Roosevelt's future no less uncertain. Roosevelt had served the party well and selflessly. The vast swath of middle and southern states predictably went to Bryan, all except for North Dakota, practically Roosevelt's second home. December brought even more doubt as the New York state legislature began proceedings to appoint a new U.S. Senator. A Republican legislature meant a Republican senator, and there were only two serious candidates: Joseph Choate, the old Roosevelt family friend and political adviser, and the boss of the Republican machine himself, Thomas Platt. Nicknamed "Easy Boss" because he was always pleasant and courteous (even when getting ready to stab you in the back), Platt was almost assured of a seat in the Senate. Would this constitute for Roosevelt yet another obstacle to a Washington post?

Showing again his political savvy and ability to compromise, Roosevelt requested a meeting with Platt and turned down requests to speak on Choate's behalf. Still, months went by without a word from the president-elect or his man Hanna. Inauguration Day came and went, and on the Police Board, Commissioner Frederick Grant now allied himself with Parker. With the main oversight body of the police force so publicly hamstrung, discipline in the ranks began to break down. Despite Roosevelt's efforts to build a professional force in the city of his birth, his feud with Parker almost destroyed what he had created.

Finally, in early April came word that Roosevelt had been named assistant secretary of the navy. Platt had apparently been convinced that Roosevelt would do less harm in Washington than in New York. Such reasoning would be repeated in 1900, when Governor Roosevelt was being considered for a spot on the ticket with McKinley. Just as he had with the New York police, as assistant secretary of the navy he endeavored to bring modernity and professionalism to the Navy Department. With the hypochondriac secretary frequently out of the office, Roosevelt was left in charge to make purchases and give orders. This included his famous order to Commodore George Dewey to ready the Pacific squadron to attack the Spanish Philippines in case of war.

When war came in April 1898, Roosevelt's friends urged him to stay on as assistant secretary. In a war in which naval battles were sure to figure prominently, they reasoned, what better way to serve your country—and what better path to advancement—could there be than a senior post in the Navy Department? Roosevelt disagreed. Perhaps haunted by the memory of his father's having paid for a replacement during the Civil War, and infused by Victorian ideas of manhood, sacrifice, and citizenship, he resigned and became lieutenant colonel of the First American Cavalry, later nicknamed "Roosevelt's Rough Riders." The regiment adopted the popular "Hot Time in the Old Town" as its song.

After a short spell of training in Texas, and a disorderly disembarkation in Florida, the Rough Riders gave up their horses—there was no room on the inadequate transports—and stepped ashore Cuba as infantrymen. Officers like Roosevelt, however, kept their horses, allowing Frederic Remington to later paint the iconic picture of Roosevelt on horseback, six-shooter in his hand, leading his men up the heights outside Santiago. It was the battle that won the war and the image that placed him in the New York governor's mansion in 1899 and the White House in 1901.

Just as Roosevelt's friends begged him to stay in office and avoid active service in 1898, Bryan's supporters made the same entreaties to the Boy Orator of the Platte. One Bryan biographer comments on such "unsolicited advice" in terms that equally apply to Roosevelt: "Bryan possessed a tough self-sufficiency in making decisions, and he was not one to anguish over them or to seek out the opinions of others." Just as Roosevelt had, Bryan offered his services to his country. Bryan, however, acted a bit late. With two Nebraska volunteer regiments already organized and shipped out, in May the Nebraska governor belatedly authorized the raising of a third regiment, with Bryan as colonel. Time was slipping away, however, as Roosevelt's Rough Riders had already arrived in their Texas training camp. Not until July 13 was Bryan officially inducted into the army as a colonel. The pivotal Battle of San Juan had been fought two weeks earlier, on July 1, with Roosevelt's regiment taking the heights above Santiago. On July 18, Bryan's regiment of volunteers departed Nebraska for the Florida coast. The day before, the Stars and Stripes had already been raised above Santiago as Spanish troops began their withdrawal from Cuba. By the time Bryan's train pulled into Jacksonville, Florida, on July 22, the war was over.

The Spanish-American War marked the moment when Bryan and Roosevelt began to battle each other directly. The war marked their divergence on an issue beyond the monetary supply. With the annexation of the Philippines, Puerto Rico, and Guam from Spain as part of the 1899 peace treaty, imperialism suddenly overtook silver as the key issue of the 1900 election. Bryan led the anti-imperialists, although with the American empire already a fait accompli, Bryan's opposition placed him in an awkward position. Not only did he appear out of touch with mainstream America, but he had actually supported the signing of the peace treaty when it came before the Senate in early 1899.

Roosevelt, on the other hand, had been consistent in his calling for an American empire, given the orders to Dewey to destroy the Spanish Pacific Fleet in the Philippines, and played a decisive role in driving the Spanish out of Cuba. In addition to the income from his best-selling memoir of the war, *The Rough Riders*, his reward was his election as New York governor and a place with McKinley on the Republican presidential ticket for 1900. Following Bryan's path across the country, Roosevelt often appeared on the speaker's dais flanked by the uniformed Rough Riders he had commanded during the war. The results of the 1900 election were more lopsided than those of 1896, with the McKinley-Roosevelt ticket even winning Bryan's home state of Nebraska. Roosevelt successfully sought reelection in 1904, using "Hot Time in the Old Town" as a campaign song.

Aside from the 1900 election, Bryan and Roosevelt came closest to outright opposition to one another in their differing stances regarding American involvement in the Great War. After deciding not to seek reelection in 1908, Roosevelt passed the mantle of the presidency to his friend William Howard Taft. But he soon became unhappy that Taft seemed to be cozying up to the conservative wing of the Republican Party and undoing Roosevelt's progressive legacy. Roosevelt challenged Taft for the party's nomination in 1912. Splitting the Republicans in this manner allowed Democrat Woodrow Wilson to be elected, with the pacifist William Jennings Bryan as his secretary of state.

With the outbreak of the European war in 1914, Roosevelt railed against the "Too Proud to Fight" philosophy of the Wilson administration and called instead for universal military training as part of an American "Preparedness" campaign. After the sinking of the British liner *Lusitania*, Wilson sent Germany an ultimatum to end its submarine attacks on civilians or risk war with the United States. In protest, Bryan resigned, a move characterized as treason by many Americans. With America's entrance into the war, Roosevelt, nearly sixty years old, volunteered to raise an entire division of Rough Riders to fight in France. Wilson declined the offer. Instead, Roosevelt sent all of his sons to fight in Europe. His youngest son, Quentin, died when his plane was shot down.

At the end of the war there was some speculation that Roosevelt might successfully run again for president in 1920, although even Republican friends like Henry Cabot Lodge never forgave him for splitting the party in 1912. The election was still far off when Roosevelt's heart stopped beating in January 1919.

Only eighteen months younger than Roosevelt, Bryan lived for another six years. Most Americans today perhaps still know him best for his role in the 1925 "Great Monkey Trial" in Tennessee. Dayton schoolteacher John Scopes, like Bryan a native of Salem, Illinois, was arrested for teaching evolution to his high school biology class, a violation of a recent state law banning the theory's teaching. The great Chicago lawyer Clarence Darrow agreed to defend Scopes, and Bryan agreed to lead the teacher's prosecution.

The trial took place during a wilting July heat wave that looked very much like that of August 1896: It covered much of the country, taking victims from St. Louis to New York City. During court proceedings, as Bryan attempted to recall his feats of oratory from earlier days, his face grew flushed. He continually waved a palm-leaf fan and took long swigs from a jug of ice water. Ten days into the trial Darrow called Bryan to the stand for a withering cross-examination, repeatedly getting Bryan to admit his belief in a literal reading of the

Bible. As Bryan's answers drew laughter from the great crowd assembled, Bryan jumped to his feet and accused Darrow of trying to slur the Bible. His hands shook, his shoulders slumped from exhaustion, and sweat poured down his face. The next day, July 21, the court ordered Scopes to pay a $100 fine. On July 26, the Sabbath, William Jennings Bryan failed to wake from a nap following his noonday dinner.

Dr. J. Thomas Kelly, who examined Bryan at regular intervals for over a decade prior to his death that July, attributed the Great Commoner's death in part to diabetes, but "with the immediate cause being the fatigue incident to the heat and his extraordinary exertions due to the Scopes Trial." As so many New York laborers had done during the 1896 heat wave, Bryan had worked himself to death.

When you hear dem a bells go ding, ling ling,
All join 'round
And sweetly you must sing, and when the verse am through,
In the chorus all join in,
There'll be a hot time in the old town tonight.

POSTSCRIPT

EVEN AFTER THE catastrophe of August 1896, heat waves continued to strike New York City, with severe spells taking many victims in 1899 and 1900. Lessons from the 1896 heat wave seemed limited and short-lived, however. Flushing the streets continued for several years. The city did not, however, adopt a policy of giving away free ice to the poor until 1919, over twenty years after Roosevelt had pioneered the scheme. During a 1905 heat wave, the city again opened its parks to sleepers. "The free public baths were kept open all night during the extraordinary torrid season of 1896," Commissioner Collis wrote in his annual report for the Department of Public Works, "and should be, under similar circumstances, in the future." This does not appear to have happened, and slowly the new indoor public baths replaced the floating baths of the city's rivers.

Today, heat remains the most deadly natural killer in the United States, on average killing more Americans than floods, earthquakes, tornados, and hurricanes combined. Cities and local authorities have developed a number of responses to heat-wave crises, including automatic "Heat-Wave Response" plans, cooling centers, and door-to-door checks on the elderly. Heat disasters still strike with horrific consequences. The Chicago heat wave of 1995 killed over 700 people. Moreover, the European heat wave of 2003 contributed to an estimated 52,000 deaths, 15,000 in France alone. While the 1896 New York heat wave and modern heat waves seem to have little in common, in reality they occur for similar reasons: heat sources in the city, pollution that traps the heat, asphalt and cement architecture that traps and reflects heat, and the lack of parks and shade. Even such modern entities that should mitigate heat-wave fatalities, such as the social safety net and air conditioners, regularly fail, as government officials do nothing or electric grids break down. According to the World Meteorological Organization, the number of heat-related fatalities could double in less than twenty years. Until governments, media, and average citizens understand that heat waves, while less dramatic, constitute as great or even greater a threat to human life than other kinds of natural disasters, people will continue to die from heat by the thousands.

ACKNOWLEDGMENTS

I WOULD LIKE TO thank the following for their support and hard work on my behalf: my Bilkent University research assistants, Dogus Ozdemir and Gulsah Senkol; Bilkent University for annual research grants; Bilkent University Library Director David Thornton for acquiring the Theodore Roosevelt Papers on microform; the helpful and efficient staffs of the Library of Congress Manuscript Reading Room, New York Public Library, New York Municipal Archives, and New York City Hall Library; Wallace Dailey, the exceptionally knowledgeable and helpful curator of the Theodore Roosevelt Collection, Harvard University; and my wife, Pelin, children, Alara and Arda, and my parents, Robert and Bette Jane, for all of their love and support.

APPENDIX A:
DEATH CERTIFICATES FILED,
AUGUST 4–17, 1895 AND 1896

	MANHATTAN		BROOKLYN	
	1895	**1896**	**1895**	**1896**
August 4	135	122	71	64
August 5	128	143	78	93
August 6	140	133	60	75
August 7	122	123	66	87
August 8	133	175	92	80
August 9	121	242	66	111
August 10	133	331	67	121
August 11	143	386	73	178
August 12	107	320	78	147
August 13	133	226	67	138
August 14	128	177	63	78
August 15	146	116	63	89
August 16	124	130	92	83
August 17	149	110	70	51
Totals:	**1,842**	**2,734**	**1,006**	**1,395**

Total excess deaths for Manhattan and Brooklyn, August 4–17, 1896: 1,281

Note: Two things seem of particular interest in these totals. (1) On August 4, and on August 6 in Manhattan only, the total deaths actually went *down* in 1896. During the same period in 1895, the weather was reported as "cool and delightful," meaning that the weather probably did not contribute to any extra deaths on those early August days that year. The totals seem simply to fall within the "normal" number of deaths that in Manhattan fluctuated between about 120 and 140 each day. (2) With the heat wave over, in Manhattan by August 17, the total number of deaths were under even the "normal" numbers. This was likely caused by the phenomenon of "harvesting": The heat wave contributed to the deaths of people who were soon to die anyway, leading to a slight dip in the number of deaths in the days just after a heat wave. I included these "low death" days to provide a more accurate reflection of the mortal effects of the heat wave, rather than giving seemingly exaggerated numbers.

APPENDIX B:
WHO DIED: MANHATTAN,
TUESDAY, AUGUST 11

AUGUST 11, 1896, was one of the deadliest days in New York City history. In Manhattan that Tuesday, more than two hundred people died from the heat. As the following numbers illustrate, the heat wave did not strike down New Yorkers indiscriminately. Although clerks, bankers, and brokers died, the heat wave took an inordinate toll among laborers. And although the heat had an enormous impact among the very old and very young, infants and the elderly did not compose a majority of the victims. The "average" victim was a work-ingman, an immigrant or son of immigrants, who lived in a tenement.

Total deaths (death certificates filed):[1] 386
Number identified as heat-related:[2] 217

Immigrant/Native/Other

Immigrant or child of immigrants[3]:	317
Native (white):	42
Native (nonwhite)[4]:	4
Unknown:	23

Class of Dwelling

Tenement:	267
Other:	57
Unknown:	62

Gender[5]

Male:	233
Female:	152

Occupation

Manual laborer:[6]	196
Other:[7]	171
Unknown:	19

Age

Over sixty:	51
Age one to sixty:	261
Infants under age one:	63
Age not given, but not listed as infant:	11

Profiles of Some of the August 11 Heat Victims

RICHARD CROKE, fifty-four, was just one of many Irish-born laborers who died during the heat wave. According to his doctor, he died in his tenement home of "sunstroke."

JOHN A. MAGEE, forty-seven, was born in England, worked as a lumberman, and lived in a tenement. He collapsed on the street that morning, and several passersby and a patrolman went to his aid. Before he lost consciousness, Magee gave the patrolman his name and residence, but when he arrived at Hudson Street Hospital, he was entered in the record as "Unknown." When Magee's brother saw John's name in the evening paper among the list of victims of heat prostration, he went to the hospital, only to be told that no one of that name had been admitted. After visits to several other hospitals and the city morgue, Magee's friends returned to Hudson and demanded entrance. There they found Magee unconscious on a cot. He was still listed as unidentified, although among his effects was a pocketbook containing letters and lumber bills that would have easily established his identity, including the name and telephone number of his employer. He died the same day of "insolation," with the contributing cause of death listed as "shock." The hospital superintendent told reporters they had simply been overwhelmed, having attended to over three hundred patients that day.

CLARENCE BRUSH was that rarity, a son of native-born New Yorkers. Better off than most families who suffered tragedy during the heat wave, eight-month-old Clarence lived in a flat and might have survived the heat wave had he not begun teething. The doctor attending him listed "heat exhaustion (teething)" as the direct cause of the infant's death.

MARGARET HARVEY, fifty-six, was born in Ireland and lived with her husband in a tenement. In addition to dying from "exhaustion," her doctor noted that she died of "hyperpyrexia due to heat." Probably the doctor sacrificed accuracy trying to be fancy, as hyperpyrexia occurs when the body's temperature is not just elevated but actually set at a higher temperature. Margaret most likely died of simple hyperthermia.

The experience of EDWARD HILDEBRANDT *after* he died illustrated the confusion in the coroner's office during the heat wave. Examining and processing hundreds of bodies inevitably led to mistakes. Both Manhattan coroners examined Hildebrandt, who was in his mid-thirties, lived in a tenement at East Ninety-Seventh, and died at Bellevue. But each coroner listed his age differently (one said thirty-four, the other thirty-six) and gave Hildebrandt different occupations (one said "carver," the other "fireman"). Both coroners agreed on the cause of death: "insolation."

JOHN SULLIVAN, sixty-five, was a widower from Ireland who at one time worked as a watchman. Like many elderly in the late nineteenth century without family or means of support, he ended his life destitute. John lived and died at the Home for the Aged of the Little Sisters of the Poor on Seventieth Street, a Catholic charitable order that cared for nearly five hundred men and women over sixty years old. He died from "asthemia."

EDWARD M. TEIN had been appointed a New York police officer less than a year earlier. Only thirty, married, and the son of native-born American parents, Edward died of "insolation," one of three policeman to die that day.

KATHERINE BRENNAN, sixty-six, a widow originally from Ireland, lived in a tenement. No occupation was listed, although the doctor noted she died of "Weakness of old age" exacerbated by "hot weather."

ALEXANDER RENHART, fifty-seven, was born in Germany, was married, and worked as a janitor in an office building on Beekman, where he also lived. He died of "excessive heat" and "heart failure."

EDWARD KEENAN, forty, was yet another Irish immigrant felled by heat. He worked as a plasterer and lived in a tenement. His doctor listed "coma" and "sunstroke" as causes of death but in a flourish of French also wrote "coup du soleil."

MARY BUSCHNER had arrived from Germany only five weeks before and had been fortunate to find work as a domestic. Evidently the work, in addition to life in a tenement, took its toll, as she died at only age seventeen of "cardiac failure" and "sunstroke."

LOUISA HOPKINS, fifty-seven, was a married housewife living in a tenement. One of three native-born black Americans to die in Manhattan that day, the attending doctor listed her color as "Ethiopia" and her death as caused by "asthemia" and "cerebral apoplexy due to heat."

ANNIE SULLIVAN was born in a tenement to native-born parents. Possibly because of the heat, her mother gave birth prematurely, and little Annie lived only seventeen hours. Most likely the same doctor who attended Annie's birth filled out her death certificate, listing her death as caused by "premature birth" and "exhaustion."

SISTER MARY of the Roman Catholic Marianites of the Holy Cross had come from Brittany, France, to work at the Asylum of St. Vincent de Paul on West Thirty-Ninth Street. The asylum was established, according to *King's Handbook of New York City*, "for the reception, care and religious and secular education of destitute and unprotected orphans of both sexes, preferably of French birth or parentage, over four years old." Only twenty-three years old, Sister Mary died of "syncope and coma from heat prostration."

ANNIE BOTCHKISS was born to Russian immigrants on August 6 in a rear tenement at 66 Market Street. She died after only five days of "collapse" and "insolation."

DIETRICH PRUSHEN, fifty-three, from Germany, died at Bellevue Hospital from "insolation."

PETER F. KAINE, thirty-three, a widower and the son of Irish immigrants, would have celebrated ten years on the New York police force at the end of the month. He died at home of "insolation" and "pulmonary aedema." At the time of his death the doctor noted that Peter's body temperature was 109 degrees.

Another police officer and son of Irish parents died at Roosevelt Hospital. Listed on his death certificate by the attending doctor as "JOHN W. GOOD-WIN," but by the New York police as "James Goodison," he was forty-two and died of "thermic fever."

JAMES P. DOANES, fifty-nine, from Ireland, died of "sunstroke." At the time of his death the doctor noted, "temperature in rectum 110 3/4 Fah."

JACQUES GILLES, forty-one, from France, worked as an artist and died of "insolation."

CATHERINE SOPHIA FREEMAN, twenty-six, was born in Germany, was married, and worked as a housekeeper. She had apparently just given birth, as the doctor listed as her cause of death "prostration from heat" and "lying in period." For women in the late nineteenth century, especially poor immigrants living in tenements, who were frequently unable to pay for a doctor, surviving the actual birth was only the first step toward recovering health and strength. The "lying-in period" after birth could be long and dangerous, both for the mother and for the newborn baby. At least one charity in the city dedicated itself to such cases. The New York Female Asylum for Lying-In Women was founded in 1827 to "provide free accommodation and medical attendance during confinement, to respectable indigent married women. It also gives the same aid to similar cases at their homes, and trains wet nurses for their profession." The training of wet nurses was of particular importance for the Freemans, now that Catherine had died and left the surviving Freeman baby without a source of milk. Doctors frequently listed "malnutrition" or even "bottle-fed" as causes of death on infants' death certificates.

ELLEN CARLIER, fifty-four, was born in Ireland. At the time of her death from sunstroke the doctor noted, "temperature in rectum 111 Fah."

Notes

1. Death certificates are a tricky archival source. While they supply an enormous amount of information, they were filled in by hand by doctors and coroners who were simply overwhelmed by the volume of heat-wave victims. Names were

frequently misspelled, and in at least once case, doctors filled in two certificates for one person. Moreover, duplicate copies of the same certificate were frequently transferred to microform. Any errors, while inadvertent, are completely the responsibility of the author.

2. As noted before, this refers to various ailments listed as the "direct" or "contributing" cause of death, including "exhaustion," "sunstroke," "asthemia," "thermic fever," and the very common "insolation."

3. At least one parent an immigrant.

4. These were three black Americans and one Chinese American.

5. One unknown, listed as "no name."

6. Often listed as "laborer" or simply "lab." Women's labor included "housework," "domestic," and "cook."

7. Often listed as "none" and including children. "Housewife" as opposed to "housework" is included in this category, as the doctor/coroner was attempting to make a distinction between the two.

BIBLIOGRAPHY

Note on Sources

By 1896, the era of an agricultural diarist like Thomas Jefferson noting detailed weather observations had passed. Housewife Elizabeth Merchant might have exclaimed, "Quite a hot day!" in her diary, and Theodore Roosevelt and Whitelaw Reid may have noted the extreme heat in a few of their letters. For the most part, however, New Yorkers of that August did not stop to take special note of the heat wave in their personal writings.

With the very nature of heat waves making them different from other great disasters, there are no specific manuscript collections, reports, books, articles, recollections, or memorials that address that tragic week. Press reports provided many dramatic stories from the heat wave but a very inaccurate record of deaths. As the daily lists of deaths and prostrations derived from police reports only, the newspapers did not record deaths that involved no call to the police. Instead, the death certificates from Manhattan and Brooklyn provide a detailed record of both the number of deaths and the victims themselves.

Each death certificate gives an enormous amount of information: name, date of death, age, color, martial status, occupation, place of birth, length of time in United States if foreign, mother's and father's names and birthplaces, place of death, "Class of dwelling: A tenement being a house occupied by more than two families," direct and indirect causes of death, duration of disease, and sanitary conditions. The death certificates offer intimate portraits of the heat wave's victims, many of them the poor, tenement-dwelling, immigrant laborers of the Lower East Side.

Archival and Manuscript Collections
Brooklyn Death Certificates, 1895–1896, New York Municipal Archives
William Jennings Bryan Papers, Library of Congress
William Bourke Cockran Papers, New York Public Library
Henry Cabot Lodge Papers, Massachusetts Historical Society
Henry Luce III Center for the Study of American Culture, New York Historical Society
Manhattan Death Certificates, 1895–1896, New York Municipal Archives
William McKinley Papers, Library of Congress
Elizabeth Merchant Diaries, New York Public Library
New York State Weather Bureau, Report for the Month of August 1896, State Commissioner of Agriculture, New York State Archives
Office of the Mayor, Subject Files, Mayor William Strong Administration, 1895–1897, New York Municipal Archives
Reid Family Papers, Library of Congress
Theodore Roosevelt Collection, Houghton Library, Harvard University
Theodore Roosevelt Papers, Library of Congress
Weather Bureau, Report of the Chief of the Weather Bureau, 1896, 1896–1897, U.S. Department of Agriculture, National Archives

Newspapers and Journals
Brooklyn Daily Eagle
Chicago Tribune
Harper's Weekly
The Nation
New York Evening Post
New York Herald
New York Journal
New York Sun
New York Times
New York Tribune
New York World
Washington Post

Books and Articles

Adelman, Melvin L. *A Sporting Time: New York City and the Rise of Modern Athletics, 1820–70*. Urbana: University of Illinois Press, 1986.

Alexander, DeAlva Stanwood. *Four Famous New Yorkers: The Political Careers of Cleveland, Platt, Hill and Roosevelt*. New York: Henry Holt, 1923.

Allen, Oliver E. *New York, New York: A History of the World's Most Exhilarating and Challenging City*. New York: Atheneum, 1990.

———. *The Tiger: The Rise and Fall of Tammany Hall*. Reading, MA: Addison-Wesley, 1993.

Allswang, John M. *Bosses, Machines, and Urban Voters: An American Symbiosis*, Port Washington, NY: Kennikat Press, 1997.

Auchincloss, Louis. *Theodore Roosevelt*. New York: Henry Holt, 2002.

Barnard, Harry. *Eagle Forgotten: The Life of John Peter Altgeld*. New York: Duell, Sloan and Pearce, 1938.

Barth, Gunther. *City People: The Rise of Modern City Culture in Nineteenth-Century America*. New York: Oxford University Press, 1980.

Batterberry, Michael, and Ariane Batterberry. *On the Town in New York: The Landmark History of Eating, Drinking, and Entertainments from the American Revolution to the Food Revolution*. 25th Anniversary Special Ed. New York: Routledge, 1999.

Bender, Thomas. *New York Intellect: A History of Intellectual Life in New York City, from 1750 to the Beginnings of Our Own Time*. Baltimore: Johns Hopkins University Press, 1987.

Binder, Frederick M., and David M. Reimers. *All the Nations Under Heaven: An Ethnic and Racial History of New York City*. New York: Columbia University Press, 1995.

Bishop, Joseph Bucklin, ed. *Theodore Roosevelt's Letters to His Children*. New York: Charles Scribner's Sons, 1919.

Black, Gilbert J., ed. *Theodore Roosevelt, 1858–1919: Chronology, Documents, Bibliographical Aids*. Dobbs Ferry, NY: Oceana Publications, 1969.

Blum, John Morton. *The Republican Roosevelt*. Cambridge, MA: Harvard University Press, 1954.

Bok, Edward. *The Americanization of Edward Bok: The Autobiography of a Dutch Boy Fifty Years After*. 1920. Reprint, Westport, CT: Greenwood Press, 1972.

Boyer, M. Christine. *Manhattan Manners: Architecture and Style, 1850–1900*. New York: Rizzoli International Publications, 1985.

Brands, H. W. *TR: The Last Romantic*. New York: Basic Books, 1997.

Brown, Everit, and Albert Strauss. *A Dictionary of American Politics*. New York: A. L. Burt, 1888.

Bryan, William Jennings. *The First Battle: The Story of the Campaign of 1896*. Chicago: W. B. Conkey, 1896.

———, and Mary Baird Bryan. *The Memoirs of William Jennings Bryan*. Philadelphia: United Publishers of America, 1925.

Bryce, James. *The American Commonwealth*. Vol. 1. 3rd ed. New York: Macmillan and Company, 1905.

Burrows, Edwin G., and Mike Wallace. *Gotham: A History of New York City to 1898*. New York: Oxford University Press, 1999.

Burton, David H. *Theodore Roosevelt*. New York: Twayne Publishers, 1972.

Campbell, Helen, Thomas W. Knox, and Thomas Byrnes. *Darkness and Daylight: or, Lights and Shadows of New York Life*. Hartford, CT: Hartford Publishing, 1896.

Cashman, Sean Dennis. *American in the Gilded Age: From the Death of Lincoln to the Rise of Theodore Roosevelt*. New York: New York University Press, 1984.

Cerillo, Augustus, Jr. "The Reform of Municipal Government in New York City." *New-York Historical Society Quarterly* 57, no. 1 (1973): 51–71.

Cherny, Robert W. *A Righteous Cause: The Life of William Jennings Bryan*. Boston: Little, Brown, 1985.

Chessman, G. Wallace. *Governor Theodore Roosevelt: The Albany Apprenticeship, 1898–1900*. Cambridge, MA: Harvard University Press, 1965.

———. *Theodore Roosevelt and the Politics of Power*. Boston: Little, Brown, 1969.

Christman, Henry M. *The Mind and Spirit of John Peter Altgeld: Selected Writings and Addresses*. Urbana: University of Illinois Press, 1960.

City of New York. *Report of the Department of Public Works, City of New York, 1896*. 1896.

———. *Report of the Department of Street Cleaning of the City of New York for 1895–1896–1897*. 1897.

———. *Report of the Police Department of the City of New York for the Year Ending December 31, 1896*. 1896.

Coletta, Paolo E. *William Jennings Bryan*. Vol. 1, *Political Evangelist, 1860–1908*. Lincoln: University of Nebraska Press, 1964.

Connable, Alfred, and Edward Silberfarb. *Tigers of Tammany Hall: Nine Men Who Ran New York*. New York: Holt, Rinehart and Winston, 1967.

Cooper, John Milton, Jr. *The Warrior and the Priest: Woodrow Wilson and Theodore Roosevelt*. Cambridge, MA: Harvard University Press, 1983.

Corry, John A. *A Rough Ride to Albany: Teddy Runs for Governor*. New York: John A. Corry, 2000.

Cowles, Anna Roosevelt. *Letters from Theodore Roosevelt to Anna Roosevelt Cowles, 1870–1918*. New York: Charles Scribner's Sons, 1924.

Croly, Herbert. *Marcus Alonzo Hanna: His Life and Work*. New York: Macmillan, 1912.

Czitrom, Daniel. "Underworlds and Underdogs: Big Tim Sullivan and Metropolitan Politics in New York, 1889–1913." *Journal of American History* 78, no. 2 (September 1991): 536–558.

Dalton, Kathleen. *Theodore Roosevelt: A Strenuous Life*. New York: Vintage Books, 2004.

DeForest, Robert, and Lawrence Veiller, eds. *The Tenement House Problem; Including the Report of the New York State Tenement House Commission of 1900, by Various Writers*. New York: Macmillan, 1903.

Dobson, John M. *Politics in the Gilded Age: A New Perspective on Reform*. New York: Praeger, 1972.

Durso, Joseph. *Madison Square Garden: 100 Years of History*. New York: Simon and Schuster, 1979.

Ellis, Edward Robb. *The Epic of New York City*. New York: Coward-McCann, 1966.

Erie, Stephen. *Rainbow's End: Irish-Americans and the Dilemmas of Urban Machine Politics, 1840–1985*. Berkeley: University of California Press, 1988.

Finegold, Kenneth. *Experts and Politicians: Reform Challenges to Machine Politics in New York, Cleveland, and Chicago*. Princeton, NJ: Princeton University Press, 1995.

Garney, Stephen. *Gramercy Park: An Illustrated History of a New York Neighborhood*. New York: Rutledge Books, 1984.

Garraty, John A. *Henry Cabot Lodge: A Biography*. New York: Alfred A. Knopf 1953.

Ginger, Ray. *Altgeld's America: The Lincoln Ideal Versus Changing Realities*. New York: Franklin Watts, 1958.

Glad, Paul W. *McKinley, Bryan, and the People*. 1964. Elephant Paperback Ed. Reprint, Chicago: I. R. Dee, 1991.

——. *The Trumpet Soundeth: William Jennings Bryan and His Democracy, 1896–1912*. Lincoln: University of Nebraska Press, 1960.

Gosnell, Harold F. *Boss Platt and His New York Machine*. Chicago: University of Chicago Press, 1924.

Griffith, Ernest. *A History of American City Government: The Conspicuous Failure, 1870–1900*. New York: Praeger, 1974.

Grondhal, Paul. *I Rose Like a Rocket: The Political Education of Theodore Roosevelt*. New York: Free Press, 2004.

Hagedorn, Hermann. *Roosevelt in the Bad Lands*. Boston: Houghton Mifflin, 1921.

Hammack, David C. *Power and Society: Greater New York at the Turn of the Century*. New York: Russell Sage Foundation, 1982.

Harbaugh, William Henry. *Power and Responsibility: The Life and Times of Theodore Roosevelt*. New York: Farrar, Straus and Cudahy, 1961.

Hoffman, Charles. *The Depression of the Nineties: An Economic History*. Westport, CT: Greenwood Publishing, 1970.

Hofstadter, Richard. *The Age of Reform: From Bryan to F.D.R.* New York: Vintage Books, 1955.

Hoogenboom, Ari. *Rutherford B. Hayes: Warrior and President*. Lawrence: University Press of Kansas, 1995.

Hurwitz, Howard Lawrence. *Theodore Roosevelt and Labor in New York State, 1880–1900*. New York: Columbia University Press, 1943.

Jackson, Kenneth T. *The Encyclopedia of New York City*. New Haven, CT: Yale University Press, 1995.

Janvier, Thomas. *In Old New York: A Classic History of New York City*. 1894. Reprint, New York: St. Martin's Press, 2000.

Jeffers, H. Paul. *Commissioner Roosevelt: The Story of Theodore Roosevelt and the New York City Police, 1895–1897*. New York: John Wiley and Sons, 1994.

Kazin, Michael. *A Godly Hero: The Life of William Jennings Bryan*. 2006. Reprint, New York: Anchor Books, 2007.

King, Moses, ed. *King's Handbook of New York City, 1892*. Boston: Moses King, 1892.

Kisseloff, Jeff. *You Must Remember This: An Oral History of Manhattan from the 1890s to World War II*. Baltimore: Johns Hopkins University Press, 1989.

Klinenberg, Eric. *Heat Wave: A Social Autopsy of Disaster in Chicago*. Chicago: University of Chicago Press, 2002.

Koenig, Louis W. *Bryan: A Political Biography of William Jennings Bryan.* New York: G. P. Putnam's Sons, 1971.

Kohn, Edward P. "Crossing the Rubicon: Theodore Roosevelt, Henry Cabot Lodge, and the 1884 Republican National Convention." *Journal of the Gilded Age and Progressive Era* 5, no. 1 (January 2006): 18–45.

———. "A Necessary Defeat: Theodore Roosevelt and the New York Mayoral Election of 1886." *New York History* (Spring 2006): 205–227.

———. "A Revolting State of Affairs: Theodore Roosevelt's Aldermanic Bill and the New York Assembly City Investigating Committee of 1884." *American Nineteenth Century History* 10, no. 1 (March 2009): 71–93.

———. "Scourge of Summer." *New York Archives* 8, no. 1 (Summer 2008): 8–11.

Kluger, Richard. *The Life and Death of the "New York Herald Tribune."* New York: Alfred A. Knopf, 1986.

Larson, Erik. *Isaac's Storm: A Man, A Time, and the Deadliest Hurricane in History.* New York: Vintage Books, 2000.

Leech, Margaret. *In the Days of McKinley.* New York: Harper and Brothers, 1959.

Lodge, Henry Cabot, ed. *Selections from the Correspondence of Theodore Roosevelt and Henry Cabot Lodge, 1884–1918.* Vol. 1. New York: Charles Scribner's Sons, 1925.

Lubove, Roy. *The Progressives and the Slums: Tenement House Reform in New York City, 1890–1917.* Pittsburgh: University of Pittsburgh Press, 1962.

Matlin, James C. "Roosevelt and the Elections of 1884 and 1888." *Mississippi Valley Historical Review* 4, no. 1 (June 1927): 25–38.

Mayer, Grace M. *Once Upon a City: New York from 1890 to 1910.* New York: Macmillan, 1958.

McClure, Alexander K., and Charles Morris. *The Authentic Life of William McKinley.* W. E. Scull, 1901.

McCullough, David. *Mornings on Horseback.* New York: Simon and Schuster, 1981.

McGurrin, James. *Bourke Cockran: A Free Lance in American Politics.* New York: Scribner's Sons, 1948.

McNickle, Chris. *To Be Mayor of New York: Ethnic Politics in the City.* New York: Columbia University Press, 1993.

Millard, Candace. *The River of Doubt: Theodore Roosevelt's Darkest Journey.* New York: Doubleday, 2005.

Miller, Nathan. *Theodore Roosevelt: A Life*. New York: Morrow, 1992.

Morison, Elting E., ed. *The Letters of Theodore Roosevelt*. Cambridge, MA: Harvard University Press, 1951.

Morris, Edmund. *The Rise of Theodore Roosevelt*. New York: Coward, Mc-Cann and Geoghegan, 1979.

———. *Theodore Rex*. New York: Random House, 2001.

Mowry, George E. *Theodore Roosevelt and the Progressive Movement*. New York: Hill and Wang, 1946.

Myers, Gustavus. *The History of Tammany Hall*. New York: Dover Publications, 1971.

New York State. *Report of the City Investigating Committee, 14 March 1884*. 1884.

———. *Special Committee Appointed to Investigate the Local Government of the City and County of New York: Hearings*. Vol. 1. 1884.

O'Donnell, Edward T. *Ship Ablaze: The Tragedy of the Steamboat* General Slocum. New York: Broadway Books, 2003.

Parkhurst, Charles H. *Our Fight with Tammany*. New York: Charles Scribner's Sons, 1895.

Patton, Clifford W. *The Battle for Municipal Reform: Mobilization and Attack, 1875–1900*. College Park, MD: McGrath Publishing, 1969.

Peskin, Allan. "Who Were the Stalwarts? Who Were Their Rivals? Republican Factions in the Gilded Age." *Political Science Quarterly* 99, no. 4 (Winter 1984–1985): 703–716.

Police Department Census of the City of New York Taken in April, 1895: By the Police Department and Compiled by the Health Department. 1896.

Pringle, Henry. *Theodore Roosevelt: A Biography*. Rev. ed. New York: Harcourt Brace, 1984.

Putnam, Carleton. *Theodore Roosevelt*. Vol. 1, *The Formative Years, 1858–1886*. New York: Charles Scribner's Sons, 1958.

Reeves, Thomas C. *Gentleman Boss: The Life of Chester Alan Arthur*. New York: Alfred A. Knopf, 1975.

Riis, Jacob. *How the Other Half Lives: Studies Among the Tenements of New York*. 1890. Reprint, New York: Penguin, 1997.

Riordan, William L. *Plunkitt of Tammany Hall: A Series of Very Plain Talks on Very Practical Politics*. Edited by Terrence J. McDonald. New York: Signet Classics, 1995.

Robinson, Corrine Roosevelt. *My Brother Theodore Roosevelt*. New York: Charles Scribner's Sons, 1921.

Roosevelt, Theodore. *Theodore Roosevelt: An Autobiography*. 1913. Reprint, New York: Da Capo Press, 1985.

———. *Theodore Roosevelt's Diaries of Boyhood and Youth*. New York: Charles Scribner's Sons, 1928.

———. *The Works of Theodore Roosevelt*. 20 volumes. National Edition. New York: Charles Scribner's Sons, 1926.

Rosen, Christine Meisner. *The Limits of Power: Great Fires and the Process of City Growth in America*. Cambridge: Cambridge University Press, 1986.

Ryan, Mary P. *Civic Wars: Democracy and Public Life in the American City During the Nineteenth Century*. Berkeley: University of California Press, 1997.

Schiesl, Martin J. *The Politics of Efficiency: Municipal Administration and Reform in America: 1880–1920*. Berkeley: University of California Press, 1977.

Schriftgiesser, Karl. *The Gentleman from Massachusetts: Henry Cabot Lodge*. Boston: Little, Brown, 1944.

Scull, William Ellis. *Great Leaders and National Issues of 1896*. Philadelphia: Non-Partisan Bureau of Political Information, 1896.

Skrupskelis, Ignas K., and Elizabeth M. Berkeley. *The Correspondence of William James*. Vol. 2, *William and Henry, 1885–1896*. Charlottesville: University Press of Virginia, 1993.

Smith, Carl. *Urban Disorder and the Shape of Belief: The Great Chicago Fire, the Haymarket Bomb, and the Model Town of Pullman*. Chicago: University of Chicago Press, 1995.

Smith, Joseph. *The Spanish-American War: Conflict in the Caribbean and the Pacific, 1895–1902*. New York: Longman Group, 1994.

Summers, Mark Wahlgren. *Rum, Romanism, and Rebellion: The Making of a President, 1884*. Chapel Hill: University of North Carolina Press, 2000.

Teaford, Jon C. "Finis for Tweed and Steffens: Rewriting the History of Urban Rule." *Reviews in American History* 10, no. 4 (December 1982): 133–149.

———. *The Unheralded Triumph: City Government in America, 1870–1900*. Baltimore: Johns Hopkins University Press, 1984.

Wagenknecht, Theodore. *The Seven Worlds of Theodore Roosevelt*. New York: Longmans, Green, 1958.

Werner, M. R. *Tammany Hall*. New York: Doubleday, Doran, 1928.

White, G. Edward. *The Eastern Establishment and the Western Experience: The West of Frederic Remington, Theodore Roosevelt, and Owen Wister*. 1968. Reprint, Austin: University of Texas Press, 1989.

White, Richard D., Jr. *Roosevelt the Reformer: Theodore Roosevelt as Civil Service Commissioner, 1889–1895*. Tuscaloosa: University of Alabama Press, 2003.

Wiebe, Robert H. *The Search for Order, 1877–1920*. New York: Hill and Wang, 1967.

INDEX